Doing Visual Research

Claudia Mitchell

Los Angeles | London | New Delhi
Singapore | Washington DC

SAGE Publications Ltd
I Oliver's Yard
55 City Road
London ECIY ISP

SAGE Publications Inc.
2455 Teller Road
Thousand Oaks, California 91320

SAGE Publications India Pvt Ltd
B1/1 1 Mohan Cooperative Industrial Area
Mathura Road, New Delhi 110 044
India

SAGE Publications Asia-Pacific Pte Ltd
3 Church Street
#10-04 Samsung Hub
Singapore 049483

Library of Congress Control Number: 2010936821

British Library Cataloguing in Publication data

A catalogue record for this book is available from the British Library

ISBN 978-1-4129-4582-0
ISBN 978-1-4129-4583-7

Typeset by C&M Digitals (P) Ltd, Chennai, India
Printed by TJ International Ltd, Padstow, Cornwall
Printed on paper from sustainable resources

Doing Visual Research

I dedicate *Doing Visual Research* to my dear partner, Ann Smith. Thank you for your inspiration and your imagination. I hope that you will find many pleasant surprises in this book.

Contents

Figures   ix
Preface   xi
Acknowledgements   xv

PART I   INTRODUCTION   1

1   Introduction: Getting the picture   3

2   On a pedagogy of ethics in visual research: Who's in the picture?   15

**PART II   VISUAL METHODS FOR SOCIAL CHANGE: TOOLS
            AND TECHNIQUES**   33

3   Not just an object: Working with things, objects and artefacts
    in visual research   35

4   Seeing for ourselves: A case for community-based photography   51

5   Community-based video-making   71

PART III   ON INTERPRETING AND USING IMAGES   95

6   Working with photo images: A textual reading on the presence
    of absence   97

7   Data collections and building a democratic archive: 'No more pictures
    without a context' (with Naydene de Lange)   116

8   Look and see: Images of image-making   135

9   What can a visual researcher do with a camera?   159

10 Changing the picture: How can images influence policy-making?   177

References   201
Index   213

Figures

2.1	Visual consent form	18
2.2	Consent form	26
3.1	T-shirts as artefacts	38
3.2	Wire car in context	40
3.3	Close-up of wire car	40
3.4	*Life Lines*	48
4.1	Participants working with their photographs	59
4.2	Poster-narrative as an analytical tool	60
4.3	Faculty lecturers presenting analysis of safety and security	62
4.4	Presenting PowerPoint on *Feeling safe and feeling not so safe*	62
4.5	Curatorial statement	63
5.1	The N-E-R (No Editing Required) workshop	74
5.2	Guidelines	76
5.3	Learning to operate the camera	77
5.4	Dance scene	80
6.1	Lost generation	102
6.2	Empty chairs in beauty parlour	104
6.3	School bus taking mourners to funeral	105
6.4	Empty desks	106
6.5	No children crossing	106
6.6	Staged suicide	107
6.7	Stigma	111
6.8	Hidden from view	111
7.1	Example of a data set in the digital archive	123
7.2	Example of a photograph with its metadata	123
7.3	Drawing of forest danger	127
7.4	Drawing of girl being propositioned by male	128
7.5	Drawing of unwanted pregnancy	129
7.6	Drawing of unwanted pregnancy: baby in toilet	130
8.1	Looking at looking: know yourself	137
8.2	Two boys looking	139
8.3	After hours	140
8.4	You can be raped in the bushes	143
8.5	The girl behind the camera	144

8.6	Girls taking pictures in a photovoice project	145
8.7	Group photo of girls with a video camera	146
8.8	Boy taking pictures of boys: 'feeling strong'	146
8.9	Taking a picture at the market	147
8.10	Reflecting on the video	147
8.11	Community video-makers viewing their video	149
8.12	Shadow of the photographer	152
8.13	Malia Obama as Photographer 1	156
8.14	Malia Obama as Photographer 2	157
10.1	Clothesline display of environmental issues at Ministry of Agriculture (Sierra Leone)	184
10.2	Clothesline display at school (Mozambique)	186
10.3	Use of chicken wire to mount exhibition (Montreal, Canada)	186
10.4	Handwritten captions	187
10.5	Individual poster-size exhibitions	188
10.6	The album project	190

Preface

Doing Visual Research offers researchers in the social sciences an innovative orientation to the ways in which visual tools such as photography, video, drawing and objects can be used as modes of inquiry, modes of representation and modes of dissemination in research related to social change. Funding agencies, community groups, educators, health care professionals, the general public and researchers themselves would like to see more academic research tackle pressing social concerns related to everyday life, and there are growing calls for 'research that matters', that makes a difference and that points more directly to policy implications. This book attempts to answer that call and as such is meant to be a resource for researchers investigating a wide range of critical issues related to poverty, gender, human rights, violence, education and health, across a variety of disciplinary areas, using such visual participatory tools as photography, video and drawing. Clearly, the field of visual studies is a dynamic one, particularly in the context of new technologies. Taken as a whole, the book addresses methodological, interpretive and ethical concerns that arise in the study of social issues, offering creative, practical ways to re-frame or explore them further. The book highlights visual participatory methodologies (sometimes referred to as VPM and sometimes termed participatory visual methodologies, PVM). This area, while a relatively new one within visual research and as part of qualitative studies, is a burgeoning one. It is an area that has led to new questions related to ethical considerations and to alternative tools for interpretation and representation.

Increasingly, social science departments and faculties are offering a more diverse range of qualitative research methods courses, with work related to the visual being a particularly rich area. Often, however, visual research is covered in only one or two chapters and must be supplemented by other authors and readings. The overall purpose of this book, then, is to provide both conceptual and practical 'takes' on working with visual tools and methods that are meant to be highly participatory in engaging communities themselves in research. Research designs that use the visual raise many new questions, including those that look at the blurring of boundaries related to research and intervention, for example. Is the work research or is it art, and how do we take account of the new technologies and challenges related to representation? The emergence of visual and arts-based research as a viable approach puts pressure on the traditional structures and expectations of the academy. Space, time and equipment requirements, for example, often make it difficult for researchers to present their work in the conventional venues and formats of research conferences. But there are other questions that interrogate even further the relationship between the researched and the researcher. Do we as researchers conduct ourselves differently when the participants of our studies are 'right there' – either in relation to the photos or videos they have produced? How can visual interventions be used to educate community groups and point to ways to empower and reform institutional practices? What ethical issues come to the fore in these action-oriented studies? How do we work with such concepts as 'confidentiality' and 'anonymity' within this kind of work?

While the study of visual cultures is a growing one, and while community-based research itself is seen to be significant, the 'doing' of this work, it seems, is often more implicit than explicit. Too often, the work is approached in a way that is unproblematized and in which images carry some extra truth value – particularly if they are produced by communities – or that they simply speak for themselves. They can, but they might offer even more when studied and interrogated with participants.

In writing this book – which comes out of many different collaborative projects, the bulk of them involving other colleagues in Canada and Southern Africa, with a variety of different communities, many of them in sub-Saharan Africa, where I have been working since the mid 1990s – I often struggled with coming to terms with the idea that no visual participatory project ever seems to end. Visual partici-patory studies that I had carried out five or six years ago or perhaps even longer, suddenly, as I was writing, compelled me to re-examine and re-interpret the work in the light of new understandings – either about the visual itself or about the phenomenon under study. Thus, I found myself writing about old data in new ways. One could regard this as one of the challenges of any kind of qualitative research, but perhaps exacerbated by the fact that the visual is forever in one's face. It is so easy to look again at a video, a drawing or a photograph and think something else. I prefer to think of this as one of the strengths of the 'doing' of visual research and why, as researchers working in the area of the visual, and particularly with communities, we need to be prepared for the iterative nature of doing visual research.

What I hope this book conveys is a sense of the richness of visual data, the democratic possibilities for engaging communities and the fact that the work is never completed (although contained by the need to finish a thesis or submit a manuscript). Perhaps the fact that this book is written in one voice (as opposed to an edited or co-authored book) may also contribute to a sense of this. Three books that greatly influenced me – Marcus Banks' *Visual Methods in Social Research*, Gillian Rose's *Visual Methodologies* and Sarah Pink's *Doing Visual Ethnography* – are each examples of 'one voice' books. Sarah Pink's extensive references to her own visual work with bull fighters in Spain, although far from my own interests, deep-ens an understanding of the full context of the work because of the 'one voice', and I have tried to give a similar sense of this in relation to visual participatory work with communities.

Finally, I hope that this book gives a sense of the creative possibilities in doing visual research – and overall, a sense of the 'why' of the visual. Some of my research colleagues and students laugh at me when I say 'make it up' when engaging in the interpretive process. By 'making it up', however, I don't mean pulling something out of thin air and without any back-up documentation on the questions under study. Rather, what I mean is that work with the visual creates a generative space for looking, and then looking anew (and with communities themselves). For researchers and research students new to the area of visual methodologies, this can be a liberating experience. And for colleagues who have been working in the area of visual research for much longer than I have, this book can be a reminder, I hope, of why we do what we do.

Acknowledgements

Doing Visual Research owes its existence to the contributions of many people, start-ing with all the youth, teachers, health-care workers, agricultural workers, parents and other community members in various parts of the world who have participated in the projects and studies I write about here.

I am grateful to the Social Sciences and Humanities Research Council of Canada (SSHRC) for its support of the study 'Seeing for Ourselves' and later the study 'What Difference Does This Make?' I would also like to acknowledge the National Research Foundation's support of our research team (led by Naydene de Lange) in two projects: 'Learning Together' and 'Every Voice Counts'.

This book comes out of collaborations with many colleagues and students, especially those at McGill University in Montreal, Canada, and the University of KwaZulu-Natal in Durban, South Africa. Collaboration, by its very nature, lends itself to a blurring of boundaries in knowledge production. This makes it extremely difficult, if not impossible, to acknowledge adequately the origins and various destinations of conference presentations and publications. I have attempted to deal with the difficulties through referencing, and also in the actual writing of each of the chapters, in which I try to contextualize the work as much as possible. Many of the ideas presented in the book first saw the light of day at several International Visual Studies Association (IVSA) conferences; at such con-ferences as the Education Association of South Africa (EASA) conference held in Durban in 2009, the First International Visual Methodologies Conference held at the University of Leeds in 2009, the Material and Visual Cultures of Childhood conference held at Goldsmith's College in 2006, the Consuming Childhood con-ference in Trondheim in 2007; and, of course, at the various symposia of the Centre for Visual Methodologies for Social Change. My thanks to the organizers of these events for giving me the opportunity to explore my ideas.

I am grateful to all the co-researchers who have worked on (and inspired) the various projects described in *Doing Visual Research* and who have made this work so exciting. What has given much of this work shape is my involvement with the Centre for Visual Methodologies for Social Change at the University of KwaZulu-Natal, and I am particularly indebted to my two colleagues, Naydene de Lange and Jean Stuart, co-directors of the Centre. With the 'up-for-it-ness' of Naydene de Lange, now the HIV and AIDS Education Research Chair at Nelson Mandela Metropolitan

University, it has been possible to carry out community-based work in South Africa, as well as in Rwanda and Ethiopia. Even at the risk of leaving anyone out, let me list (alphabetically) all the colleagues who have been part of the studies that led to the writing of this book: Thabisile Buthelezi, Naydene de Lange, Sarah Flicker, Myriam Gervais, June Larkin, Fikele Mazibuko, Relebohile Moletsane, Eun Park, Jacqueline Reid-Walsh, Jean Stuart, Myra Taylor, Linda Theron and Sandra Weber.

Over the course of writing this book, a number of people who used to be my doctoral students (and all of whom now have a PhD) have greatly influenced me in my own thinking about the visual: Susann Allnutt, Hourig Attarian, Pierre Doyon, Faisal Islam, Tony Kelly, John Pascarella, Jean Stuart, Ran Tao and Shannon Walsh. Thanks to each of them and also to Ingvild Kvale Sorenssen, Jennifer Thompson, Thuy Xi, Katie MacEntee, Kyung-Hwa Yang and Zainul SajanVirgi, who are currently working in the area of participatory visual research. I would like to acknowledge the work of the following former master's and doctoral students at the University of KwaZulu-Natal whose work through the Centre for Visual Methodologies for Social Change has been so central to the project of this book: Fumane Khanare, Thoko Mnisi, Maureen St. John Ward, Linda Van Laren and Thembinkosi Mbokazi.

I have also had the pleasure of working with several postdoctoral students whose interests and experiences with visual research have made important contributions to the development of this book: E.-J. Milne, Pontso Moorosi, Kathleen Pithouse and Monica Mak.

I would especially like to acknowledge several of my colleagues at McGill University, for their ongoing support and for the lovely conversations: Steve Jordan, JoAnn Levesque, Teresa Strong-Wilson and Susann Allnutt.

Many thanks to Lukas Labacher for his zealous and competent assistance in formatting the various chapters, checking references and working with the visual images, and to John Murray, Faisal Islam, Kyung-Hwa Yang and David Morton for jumping in to help just when help was most needed.

I am particularly grateful to John Murray, who so skilfully guided the final editing of this book. I have greatly appreciated his care and eye for detail.

To my family, as always, I appreciate all of your great ideas and willingness to entertain my obsessions with the visual: Rebecca, Sarah, Dorian, Jakob, Devon, Marcus and Zac.

And finally, I am grateful to Patrick Brindle of Sage for both his belief in the project and his patience.

PART I

Introduction

ONE

Introduction: Getting the picture

A few years ago Ardra Cole and Maura McIntyre, researchers at the Ontario Institute for Studies in Education in Canada, embarked upon a long-term study of adult caregivers caring for their elderly parents suffering from Alzheimer's disease. *Living and Dying with Dignity: The Alzheimer's Project* (Cole and McIntyre, 2006) focuses specifically on the fact that relatively little is known about the experiences of caregivers, particularly taking on the role of 'parent', and, critically, what kind of support they need to sustain themselves in their care of their parents – a care that cuts across legal issues, health care, emotional care and public education. In their work, Cole and McIntyre conducted many single face-to-face interviews with the caregivers, along with interviews of support groups, social workers and physicians. They translated their findings into an exhibition first shown in the foyer of the Canadian Broadcasting Corporation Headquarters in Toronto. This exhibition was comprised of a number of installations, one of which was titled *Life Lines* (2008) and was made up of a gigantic clothesline spread from one wall to another with undergarments and adult-sized diapers hanging from it. The website of the Centre for Arts Informed Research describes *Life Lines* as follows:

> *Description*: A free standing clothesline about 20 feet in length is held up by ropes and secured by concrete blocks at each end. Astro turf carpeting represents the grass below; a chair invites the viewer to sit and relax. The clothes on the line are blowing in the breeze. The undergarments are ordered from left to right according to the time in the life cycle at which they are worn. (*Life Lines*, 2008)

Another installation, *Still Life 1*, included a series of refrigerator doors, each with a different arrangement of fridge magnets holding a variety of artefacts: a school photo of a child (a grandchild), reminder notes about medication, and so on. In another of their exhibitions set up in Halifax there was a voice-activated tape recorder where viewers could sit and tell their own 'caring for' stories. Yet another installation, *Alzheimer's Still Life 2*, contained a series of visual images taken from family photograph albums of the two artist-researchers, both of whom themselves are adult caregivers who looked after their mothers suffering from Alzheimer's. As their curatorial statement expressed, the particular photos 'were chosen because they so clearly signify the mother–daughter connection over a life span and poignantly elucidate the role reversal that inevitably occurs when Alzheimer's interrupts, confuses, and redefines a relationship' (*Alzheimer's Still Life 1*, 2008).

Their work demonstrates some of the complexities related to what is actually meant by visual methodologies, showing, for example, the multiple forms of visual data: domestic photos taken from family albums and items taken from material culture (adult-sized diapers, fridge magnets). Their work also shows the multiple ways of working with the visual. Working with the visual is about both representation (transforming the interviews into visual representations through the use of material culture) and dissemination (creating a visual exhibition that drew the attention of the public as well as health care researchers and health care policy makers), but is also, as we see in the second level of interviews with the participants, a mode of inquiry (a type of data elicitation). But there are two other aspects of the visual that are also critical. One relates to epistemology and how it is that we come to know what we know (and how to account for subjectivity). Cole and McIntyre are inside their own experience as caregivers as much as they are studying the experiences of the hundreds of other caregivers who they have interviewed and met through their exhibitions. The other aspect relates to broader issues of engaging in social science inquiry in the first place and the question, 'What difference does this make anyway?' For Cole and McIntyre (2008), and for an increasing number of researchers engaged in social research, the idea of how data collection can in and of itself serve as an intervention and be potentially transformative is key. Given the impact of these installations, people with a personal connection to the topic are 'provoked' to tell their own stories (Knowles and Cole, 2008). And if visual data can mobilize individuals or communities to act, it may be possible to think of the idea of visual research and social action.

Participatory Visual Approaches

'Draw a scientist'; 'Take photographs of where you feel safe and not so safe'; 'Produce a video documentary on an issue "in your life"'; 'Find and work with seven or eight pictures from your family photographs that you can construct into a narrative about gender and identity'. Each of these prompts speaks to the range of tools that might be used to engage participants (children, teachers, out-of-school youth, women farmers, community health care workers) in visual research (drawings, simple point-and-shoot cameras, video cameras, family photographs) and suggests some of the types of emerging data: drawings, the photographic images and captions produced in the photovoice project, the video texts produced in a community video project, and the newly created album or visual text produced by the participants in an album project. In each case, there is the immediate visual text (or primary text as John Fiske, 1991, terms it) – the drawing, photo image, collage, photo-story, video documentary/video narrative, or album, and that can include captions and more extensive curatorial statements or interpretive writings that reflect what the participants have to say about the visual texts. In essence, participation does not have to be limited to 'take a picture' or 'draw a picture', though the level of participation will rest on time, the age and ability of the participants and even their willingness to be involved. A set of drawings or photos produced in isolation of their full participatory context (or follow-up) does not mean that they should therefore be discarded, particularly not in large-scale collections (Mitchell, 2005). Each of these examples can also include what Fiske (1991) terms 'production texts' – or how participants engaged in the process talk about their work, regardless of whether they are producing drawings, photo images, video narratives, or 'reconstructing' a set of photographs into new texts. Production texts are often elicited during follow-up interviews.

Each of the visual practices noted above and described in more detail throughout this book brings with it, of course, its own methods, traditions and procedures, ranging from approaches that are relatively 'low tech' and can be easily carried out without a lot of expensive equipment to those that require more expensive cameras; from those that are camera-based to those that provide for a focus on things and objects (including archival photographs); from those where participants are respondents to those that engage participants as producers; from work where researcher and participants collaborate to those where it is the researcher herself who is the producer and interpreter. The constant is some aspect of the visual as a mode of inquiry and representation, and as a mode of dissemination and engagement.

About *Doing Visual Research*

As the title suggests, this book focuses on the 'doing' of visual research. If the book had a subtitle, it would surely be something like 'Taking it personally'. The approaches that I take and the examples that I draw on come out of close to two decades of visual research, working primarily with photography, drawings, community video, collage, and more recently digital storytelling, with the focus on participatory research. The 'taking it personally' seems to me to have an obvious link to the nature of participatory visual research, in relation to both the researcher and the participants, and in relation to reflexivity as a critical feature of visual research.

There are, of course, many visual approaches, only some of which are addressed in the book, and many cross-cutting themes, including ethical concerns in the doing of visual research, the management of visual data and the ways in which doing visual research can contribute to policy change. Here, I offer examples that are mostly drawn from my own work and the work of the various research teams and graduate students I have had the privilege of collaborating with in a variety of contexts and geographic locations. Much of the work comes out of studies in sub-Saharan Africa, an area that as a function of history and circumstance is home to some of the most challenging health and social issues in the world but also some of the most generative work when it comes to the optimism for what *can* be done through the visual.

This book is made up of ten chapters organized into three main sections. In the first section, there are two chapters. In Chapter 1, 'Getting the picture', I simply try to provide something of a map of what constitutes visual research. Chapter 2 deals with ethical considerations in working with the visual. It may seem odd to offer a chapter on ethics at the very beginning of the book. Isn't that what one usually thinks of towards the end of a book, or something one includes after all else has been done in planning a project or research study? Ethical concerns, however, make up one of the three main sets of questions that I am repeatedly asked about in relation to doing visual research and, as such, seem like a good place to start. The other sets of concerns that underpin many of the subsequent chapters in this book relate to the questions, 'How to do this?' and 'What do I do with the data?'

Part II, 'Visual Methods for Social Change: Tools and Techniques', is made up of three chapters, each focusing on a specific method but located within a particular research area. The first chapter in this section, 'Not just an object', examines the uses of material culture in visual research. The issues of objects and things in visual research is one that is sometimes debated. However, the fact that even the tools and products of visual research (cameras, photographs, digital images) are objects and things suggests to me that they belong in a book on doing visual research.

The next chapter focuses on community-based photography and draws on an analysis of a number of photovoice projects with young people and adults in a variety of research settings and geographic locations. The third chapter (Chapter 5) in this section is on community video-making.

Part III, 'On Interpreting and Using Images', is meant to provide theoretical and practical approaches to working with visual data. Far from offering hard and fast rules for analysis, the various chapters in this section suggest a broad framework for what can be done with visual images. The section starts with 'Working with photo images: A textual reading on the presence of absence'. In this chapter, I offer what might be described as a situated reading of a set of photographs produced in one photovoice project in South Africa between 2004 and 2006. What I highlight here is the significance of developing a conceptual framework for analysis that complements method. The chapter uses the idea of loss – presence and absence – as an organizing framework for studying what's there and what's not there in the picture.

The next chapter, 'Data collections and building a democratic archive: "No more pictures without a context"', responds to the need for approaches to storing, managing and using visual data in ways that can be participatory. In so doing, it draws on recent work in the area of building digital archives and related studies on the use of technologies that make it possible to engage in participatory archiving with the actual 'producers' in community-based research. This makes it possible to add the dimension of participatory analysis to working with participatory visual studies.

The following chapter, 'Look and see: Images of image-making', is meant to draw attention to studying visually the producers themselves (and the process) in participatory and community-based research. What can we learn from 'looking at looking'? How do participants take pictures or work with video cameras, and how can a study of looking help to deepen an understanding of visual research?

Chapter 9, 'What can a visual researcher do with a camera?', builds on the work of visual anthropologist Jay Ruby and his essay in *Picturing Culture*, 'Researching with a camera: The anthropologist as picture taker' (Ruby, 2000b). In this chapter, I describe and analyse the idea of the composite video as an analytical tool (in its production), a tool of dissemination (in working with communities) and as a tool of inquiry (in generating new research questions with communities).

The book ends with a chapter titled 'Changing the picture: How can images influence policy-making?' There is probably no area within visual research, at least in the context of participatory research, that is more compelling than the area around the question of 'So what?' or 'What difference does this make?' (Mitchell, 2009c). The chapter provides examples of how the visual has been used in policy-making frameworks and, as such, offers some strategic possibilities for this work. Inevitably there is overlap between and among the various chapters. Many of the examples cited in relation to visual ethics have their root in photovoice work and work with participatory video. Consequently, a similar point will be argued in more than one place. For the reader this overlap will, I hope, help to emphasize certain points.

Critical Issues in *Doing Visual Research*

Working across genres of visual methodologies

One of the challenges of writing a book that sets out to provide something of a comprehensive look at some of the key aspects of doing visual research and which is segmented into chapters is that it might suggest a set of discrete approaches: this is photovoice, here is video, or this is what one does with drawings. In actual fact, much of this work cuts across genres. Drawings might be used as an entry point to working with video or photography, and, indeed, in one project with several of my colleagues in Rwanda, storyboarding (or using drawing in planning out a video) was the main activity with the participants, followed by the various groups performing their stories (Mitchell et al., in press). Thus, although 'video' was in the imagination of the participants from the beginning (what would this issue look like as a video?), the ways of enacting the issue came through the mode of drawing and performance.

Participatory engagement itself also varies, as a case study from Swaziland demonstrates. *The School Teacher* is a play written by two secondary-school teachers in a rural school in Swaziland as a way to highlight the situation of teachers (mostly male) who sexually harass and abuse students (mostly young women). As studies such as the Human Rights Watch *Scared at School* (HRW, 2001) study attest, the issue of teachers as perpetrators of violence is one of the various challenges of making schools safe. The play focuses on a male secondary-school teacher who singles out one of his students, Emma. In the drama, we see the teacher calling on Emma all the time, touching her face, handing out special favours and candy – all in front of the other students who are quite aware of his intentions. He regularly keeps Emma after class, invites her to his house and notes that it is really Emma who he loves and not his wife. His wife finds out that Emma has visited the house and points out to her husband the absurdity of this situation because in addition to everything else, they (the husband and wife) are both HIV positive. Meanwhile, Emma is in trouble with her parents when they discover that she has been at the teacher's house, and a visit from the teacher's wife further complicates the situation. In the final scene, which also involves the Principal, the full implications of the situation are realized with the teacher being fired.

The School Teacher is a good example of what Goldstein and others would describe as performed ethnography in that it draws on an emerging body of data on sexual violence in and around schools in Swaziland: sexual harassment of female students by teachers, non-monogamous relationships, power abuses, and so on. The term 'performed ethnography' as used by Tara Goldstein (2000) suggests ways that performance and drama can be used in a 'research as social change' framework, a feature which draws on the work of Clifford and Marcus (1986), who have proposed an agenda for ethnography that encourages more innovative, dialogic, reflexive and experimental writing, which can reflect a deeper self-consciousness of the workings of authority, power and the partialness of truth. In response, there has been both a literary and a performance turn in ethnography (Cole and McIntyre, 2004; Denzin, 1997; Goldstein, 2000; Gray, 2000; Gray and Sinding, 2002; Gray et al., 2000, 2001a, 2001b; Mitchell, 2004; Weber and Mitchell, 2004).

While the issues that are presented in the play are serious, the mode of delivery is melodramatic and uses greatly exaggerated physical movements. Although much of the play is spoken in Siswazi, it is not difficult to follow the storyline because so much of it relies on physical gestures. The play was originally staged outdoors and in front of a live audience made up of the entire student body of the school. Because of its melodramatic style and the familiarity of the various local characters in the play, it was received with hilarity and great applause. The actual comments of the actors afterwards were also very revealing in that they made it quite clear that schools should be safe places for all learners, and one could see how their enthusiasm from participating in the play was translating into commitment to doing something about the issues. The two teachers who were interviewed afterwards also spoke of how important it is for teachers to address these issues. Indeed, their work is a good example of the uses of performance as a tool for self-study through visual arts-based methodologies more generally (see Mitchell et al., 2009; Weber and Mitchell, 2004).

But *The School Teacher* did not stop there. Because I was working with a video-production team at the time that *The School Teacher* was staged (as part of a strategy of videotaping for UNICEF and the Ministry of Education's various youth-focused initiatives on sexual violence), it seemed useful to see if the live production could be converted into a video recording, with the idea that perhaps it would lend itself to a broader audience if it was available on video. At the same time, we recognized the limitations of video production. While live drama requires space, props, the availability of the actors and so on, it generally 'works' in relation to personal engagement. Producing engaging narrative on video is more challenging. In this case of video production, these limitations included the production quality itself (because the footage was all acquired in an outdoor space as opposed to a studio, where sound quality might have been more easily monitored) and, of course, the attention span of a television- or film-viewing audience as opposed to the attention of a live audience. We decided that the 45–50-minute span of the original drama production was too long as a video production. We also decided that because the mini-production of The School Teacher was to become part of a longer video documentary on youth speaking out against sexual violence, there was some necessity to signal that this segment of the documentary required a different stance in terms of viewing. For that reason, we produced the entire sequence of The School Teacher in black and white, using subtitles throughout to compensate at times for the quality of the sound (and also to make the production accessible to both English and Siswazi-speakers). The result is that the final production has the look of a print-text photo-story or photo-novella (see also Stuart, 2004).

At the same time, we experimented with various filmic conventions of filming a live production that would add something of the 'taking action' possibilities for future audiences. Drawing, for example, on the 1975 (Shikaneder and Bergman) film production of Mozart's The Magic Flute, we included shots of the audience from time to time 'artfully engaged' in viewing (laughing, applauding and so on) and a final line-up of the actors coming out on the stage one by one to take a bow. We also included shots of one or more of the film crew shooting from a different angle from time to time, so that we are reminded, as the audience, that we too are part of the production. At the end of the actual play but before the very end of the production, we switched back into full colour mode to include interviews with each of the characters and the teachers who wrote the play. How did 'the school teacher' himself, a young man in Grade 12, feel about the play and what messages did he want to get across? What did it mean for the Emma-character to play a sexually abused school girl? How does an 18-year-old play Emma's father, and how does taking on such a role contribute to a new understanding of the issues? And what difference did it make, we asked them, to see themselves on the big screen?

The point here is simply that the participatory aspects of participatory research can vary even within one project. The genres of the visual also vary. In this case, play-writing, performance, video production and the use of filmic conventions converge. Each component could be studied: final video production; the views of the actors playing the various roles; the producers (in this case the two teachers who wrote the play and the film crew); and, of course, the various audiences (the original live audience but then the various cinema audiences since the video can travel) – and there could also be the perspectives of the funders who had identified the issue of sexual violence in the first place.

About visual methodologies and technologies

I would be remiss if I did not say something about technology right at the outset. When I first started working in the area of film, as I describe in the last chapter of the book, my students and I worked with a cumbersome Super 8 camera that we had on loan for a short time each month, over the school year, from the National Film Board of Canada. Some of my most recent work with participatory video has involved a small Flip camera the size of a mobile phone, and the 'footage' can be immediately downloaded onto my computer for viewing. Close to a decade ago, when I first started doing work in the area of photovoice with communities, I worked entirely with disposable cameras or simple easy-load point-and-shoot cameras. In an urban setting, we were able to have the film processed at a one-hour or two-hour photo shop, and in a rural setting, we had to wait close to a week to see the prints.

Much of the recent work has been with digital cameras, where participants 'on the spot' create PowerPoint presentations and digital stories of their work and then as a group look at the images on a big screen. And up until recently my office was full of file cabinets full of prints and CDs and DVDs, as well as cardboard boxes full of drawings. And although increasingly these collections have been digitized, ways of working with digitized collections have still often been a challenge. Now, as I describe in Chapter 8, I have access to software that allows me to begin to study visual data related to a theme such as safety and security across three–four years. And even better, the participants in the rural community where our team works in South Africa can themselves access, code and work with the data. Even cost is a major consideration. A small Flip camera can cost a fifth of the price of a regular but modest camcorder. Moreover, many participants will already be steeped in the visual through their own use of mobile phones. As many recent news reports have pointed out, there are now eye-witnesses who have managed to capture visual data that would not have existed several decades ago. I mention all of these developments in visual research because they could be a little daunting in relation to what can be said about method, particularly in recognition of the fact that by the time this book is published, there will be other technologies that I haven't even thought of and indeed that might not currently exist.

However, beyond thinking about technology in a more general way, it is also important to note, as media expert Henry Jenkins (2006) indicates, that the approaches themselves often represent a type of convergence, particularly in the context of new technologies. A mobile phone, for example, can be a multimodal text in itself capable of producing still photographs and videos that are easily uploadable to Facebook or some other social networking space, which then becomes yet another visual text. For this reason, I focus on process and in particular highlight more the interpretive aspects related to the visual.

Interpretive processes and visual research

There is no quick and easy way to map out the interpretive processes involved in working with visual research, any more than there is a quick and easy way to map out the interpretive processes for working with any type of research data, although Jon Prosser (1998), Marcus Banks (2001), Gillian Rose (2001) and Sarah Pink (2007), among other researchers working in the area, offer useful suggestions and guidelines. Some considerations include the following:

1   At the heart of visual work is its facilitation of reflexivity in the research process, as theorists on seeing and looking such as John Berger (1972) and Susan Sontag (1977) have so eloquently discussed. Indeed, as Denzin (2003) and others have noted, situating one's self in the research texts – taking it personally – is critical to engaging in the interpretive process.

2   Close-reading strategies (drawn from literary studies, film studies and socio-semiotics, for example) are particularly appropriate to working with visual images. These strategies can be applied to working with a single photograph (see Moletsane and Mitchell, 2007), a video documentary text (see Mitchell et al., in press; Weber and Mitchell, 2007), or a cinematic text (Mitchell and Weber, 1999).

3   Visual images are particularly appropriate to working with drawing in that participants themselves are central to the interpretive process. In work with photovoice, for example, participants can be engaged in their own analytic procedures with the photos: Which ones are the most compelling? How are your photos the same or different from others in your group? What narrative do your photos evoke? (Similarly, with video productions as part of community video, participants can be engaged in a reflective process, which also becomes an analytic process: What did you like best about the video? What would you change if you could? Who should see this video?) The interpretive process does not have to be limited to the participants and the researcher. Communities themselves can decide what a text means. Because visual texts are very accessible, the possibilities for inviting other interpretations are key. The process of interpreting visual data can benefit from drawing on new technologies. Transana, for example, is a software application that is particularly appropriate to working with video data (Cohen, 2007). Digitizing and creating metadata schemes can be applied to working with photovoice data (see, for example, Park et al., 2007).

4   The process of working with the data can draw on a range of practices that may be applied to other types of transcripts and data sets, including content analysis and engaging in coding and developing thematic categories.

5   Archival photos (both public and private) bring their own materiality with them and may be read as objects or things. Where are they stored? Who looks after them? (See also Edwards and Hart, 2004; Rose, 2001.)

6   Visual data (especially photos produced by participants) is often subjected to more rigorous scrutiny by ethics boards than most other data because it is so

accessible. There are many different ways of working with the visual, and the choice of which type of visual approach should be guided by, among other things, the research questions, the feasibility of the study, the experience of the researcher and the acceptability to the community under study.

7   Working with the visual to create artistic texts (e.g., installations, photo albums, photo exhibitions, video narratives), as we saw in the case of Cole and McIntyre noted earlier, should be regarded as an interpretive process in and of itself. This point is a critical one in understanding the relationship between visual studies and arts-based research (Bagley and Cancienne, 2002; Barone, 2001; Denzin, 1997; Eisner, 1995; Knowles and Cole, 2008).

On the limitations and challenges of doing visual research

'By a more visual social science', writes Luc Pauwels, 'is meant a social science that not only looks into visual phenomenon but also tries to integrate visual approaches and techniques in its processes of research and communication' (Pauwels, 2006: 152). Lister and Wells (2001) stress the unprecedented importance of imaging and visual technologies in contemporary society and urge researchers to take account of those images in conducting their investigations. Over the last three decades, an increasing number of qualitative researchers have indeed taken up and refined visual approaches to enhance their understanding of the human condition. These uses encompass a wide range of visual forms, including films, videos, photographs, drawings, cartoons, graffiti, maps, diagrams, web graphics, signs and symbols. Although many of these scholars are located within visual sociology and anthropology, cultural studies, and film and photography, or media studies, a growing body of interdisciplinary scholarship is incorporating certain image-based techniques into its research methodology.

Research designs that use the visual raise many new questions and suggest new blurrings of boundaries: Is it research or is it art? Is it truth? Does the camera lie? Is it just a 'quick fix' on doing research? How do you overcome (or highlight) the subjective stance? The emergence of visual and arts-based research as a viable approach is putting pressure on the traditional structures and expectations of the academy. Space, time and equipment requirements, for example, often make it difficult for researchers to present their work in the conventional venues and formats of research conferences. But there are other questions that interrogate even further the relationship between the researched and the researcher. Do we as researchers conduct ourselves differently when the participants of our studies are 'right there' – either in relation to the photos or videos they have produced or in their performance pieces? How can visual interventions be used to educate community groups and point to ways to empower and reform institutional practices? What new ethical issues come to the fore in these action-oriented studies? How do we work with such concepts as 'confidentiality' and 'anonymity' within this kind of work (for example in research where stigma itself is a major issue)?

Clearly, some studies lend themselves to one type of visual data more than another (archival photos over video production, for example), and not *all* questions are best answered through the use of the visual. Using visual methods is not the only approach and not all audiences or recipients of research (funders, policy makers, review boards) are equally open to qualitative research generally or visual research specifically. At the same time, the preparation of new researchers in this area (postgraduate students, for example) relies on access to methodology textbooks and other course material that offers them full support for making informed choices about methods. It is incumbent on those who are teaching courses in research methodologies to ensure that students are exposed to a variety of approaches, and even if the students do not choose to work with the visual, they should be able to evaluate critically those studies that draw on visual methodologies in the same way that they can evaluate critically interview studies, case studies and so on. Concomittantly, it is critical that those of us whose research is grounded in visual methodologies ensure that we contribute to broader debates within and beyond our institutions about the kind of support that is needed, along with attention to critiques.

Changing the Picture?

'Why are there no white people in the film?'

'Why did you choose this talking head genre? Wouldn't it be more effective to create a storyline or a drama?'

'Where did you get the statistics about boys being at risk? Are those numbers true?'

'Could you help us do research?'

'Why can't we produce something like this right here in KwaZulu-Natal where the problems are even greater than in the Western Cape?'

The first three questions in this list may sound like the kinds of questions that would be raised by an external reviewer of a journal article, or the kinds of questions asked by a film critic. The last two questions, however, suggest a different relationship; they are questions that demonstrate a very specific purpose. These were questions posed to me at a Youth Day event in rural South Africa a few years ago by members of the audience, young people from the area, who had just viewed *Fire+Hope* (2004), a documentary that I produced (with Shannon Walsh as director) with young people in Khayelitsha, a township just outside Cape Town. *Fire+Hope* draws on a 14-month project on creative approaches to addressing HIV and AIDS and makes use of interviews with the participants, interspersed with statistics on the issues and performances by several well-known poets, such as the Common Man. As I stood on the stage and attempted to answer the questions posed to me, I think I would have preferred to have faced an external examiner or a film critic. They are tough questions because they raise an important point about research and social change. As has been noted by Burt and Code (1995), Gitlin (1994), Schratz and Walker (1995), Smith (1999) and many others, the issue of research accessibility is a critical topic within institutional practices. It becomes especially critical when the topics of the research are as vital a part of the social situation as health care, rural development or education, and where issues of power, control, regulation and access are ones that are central to policy development. Why are there no white people in a video addressing youth and HIV and AIDS in South Africa? Why is the situation of finding the solution to a social issue always the responsibility of those most affected?

Notwithstanding my struggle to provide appropriate answers when I was on the spot, what this event highlights is the 'migration' of the views of one group of young people (in this case from the Western Cape province of South Africa), as represented in *Fire+Hope,* to another group of young people in another part of South Africa (in rural KwaZulu-Natal) – through the visual. What this event also highlights is the dissemination of research findings about youth activism and HIV and AIDS to another group of young people who are attending a community pro- gramme on youth and HIV and AIDS on Youth Day. What started as research (a project studying youth activism and HIV and AIDS) and included a visual text (a 16-minute video documentary *Fire+Hope*) became an intervention (a screening and discussion at a Youth Day event) that yielded more research questions, both for the research team and the audience (who in turn also wanted to make their own video documentary). This example of engagement and transfer of knowledge suggests a type of social networking that while pre-dating Facebook and YouTube is no less striking for what it can inspire (see also Mitchell, 2006a).

Doing Visual Research, as a whole, is about changing the picture and the various approaches to social research that are meant to be in the service of community research, social action or social change – areas that are, of course, open to wide debate. Which communities? What constitutes social change? Is it necessarily positive? Who decides? What counts as sustainability? What are the risks in com- munities? Do we as researchers pay enough attention to the potential harm? At the risk of seeming to make exaggerated claims for visual methodologies, what this book sets out to do is lay bare some of the key elements of working with the visual as a set of methodologies and practices in social research. It is meant to address the possibilities for research at a time when questions of the social responsibility of the academic researcher (graduate students as new researchers and experienced researchers expanding their repertoire of being and doing) are critical. In so doing, it seeks to ensure that the term 'visual methodologies' is not simply reduced to one practice or tool and, at the same time, it seeks to ensure that the methodologies and practices of the visual are appreciated in their full complexity.

TWO

On a pedagogy of ethics in visual research: Who's in the picture?

Introduction

With the proliferation of digital images through Facebook and other social networking sites where it is so easy to upload images, it is hard to know where to start in mapping out the range of ethical issues when dealing with the visual. It is also a terrain that is quickly changing. However, the various organizations and professional bodies that have made addressing ethical issues a central part of their work (see, for example, the British Sociological Association's (2006) 'Visual Sociology Group's Statement of Ethical Practice' or the ESRC National Centre for Research Methods), the guidelines of the various Research Ethics Boards and a climate of human rights all call for ethical responsibility in working with images and have all within the last decade contributed to the development of this as a field. Indeed, increasingly the area of Visual Ethics can actually be regarded as a specialist area within Visual Methodologies as we can see in the work of Jon Prosser (2000, 2010), for example, but also as addressed in the work of Davidov (2004), Gross et al. (2003); Heath et al. (2007); Karlsson (2007), and Renold et al. (2008). The legal and moral components, protection and awareness of the vulnerability of children and young people, and new issues in dissemination as a result of social networking sites has made the area of ethics one that often seems like a minefield. And although 'doing least harm' and 'doing most good' must surely remain as the cornerstones of our work as researchers, these clearly are interpretative areas in and of themselves.

It is not possible to cover all the ethical issues associated with doing visual research in one chapter. What I try to do here is address the issues that pertain specifically to visual ethics in relation to community photography and community video. Obviously, there are many other issues relating to the ethical use of children's drawings or the use of family photographs, which the discussions here can also inform, and I direct the reader to a document produced by the National Centre for the Research Methods in the UK, *Visual Ethics: Ethical Issues in Visual Research* (Wiles et al., 2008).

Working with communities to address ethical dimensions strikes me as inseperable from pedagogy, with the idea that in community-based visual research the work is always about consciousness of community rights and responsibilities, and simultaneously about protection and advocacy. Because so much visual research involves those who often do not have a voice and who themselves are the producers and not just the objects or the consumers of research – that is the point – there is perhaps an even more compelling argument that says that the question of ethics is not one just for researchers in the usual sense of the word, but also for the participants who are themselves engaged in the process of community engagement. The pedagogy of visual ethics (a version of Media Ethics 101) is a central component of participatory visual research and one that rests on reflexivity, something that Jay Ruby and Norman Denzin have highlighted in visual research more generally. Indeed, one might argue that the cornerstone of community-based visual research is reflexivity – the reflexivity of the research team, but also the community and the production process: Which issues to focus on? Through photos? Through video? What to photograph? Which photos or video images to work with? What's missing? Not all of these questions of reflexivity pertain to ethical issues; some are more linked to aesthetics, personal expression and personal taste, and desired impact and as such reflect group processes. However, many of the issues are ones that do have something to do with ethics and, as social researchers, work with the visual offers a fascinating entry point to deepening an understanding of how communities operate. Pedagogy is not one-way. My research team and I were reminded of this in a photovoice project in Rwanda, where the group being trained in visual methodologies confronted us with the difficulties of obtaining informed consent from the people that they might be photographing in the market. While everyone seemed to understand the process and even helped in drawing up a very straightforward informed consent form that could be used with photo subjects who might not be literate, they suddenly informed us that it would be unlikely that anyone would agree to sign the forms because signing forms related to the visual was associated with having defaulted on a bank loan – and having your photo exhibited on a display board outside the bank. The solution was not to therefore abandon the forms but rather to add in a clause guaranteeing participants that their faces would not appear on a display board outside the bank. Ethical issues can also lead to creative thinking about 'alternatives'. As I describe in the second case study there are many images that are not of people or of obvious places that can help to symbolize an issue. And although this kind of creative thinking may disrupt more straightforward photo documentary, it does not necessarily subvert the meanings intended by the photographer.

In this chapter, I look at a number of case studies of ethical dilemmas or issues that either I have encountered firsthand or my various graduate students and colleagues have had to address. This section is far from being all-inclusive. Each research project has its own unique features, and it seems like the more projects I participate in or study, the more I see new issues to be addressed. Adding in the dimension of technology and the visual (digital cameras, the use of mobile phones, the potential for public postings, the use of restricted websites) simply contributes new layers of complexity to the already dynamic nature of doing research. The case studies that follow mostly pertain to work with children and young people or with adult populations who may have less access to the more mainstream avenues of speaking out because of social positioning. However, I also include reference to a study carried out by young people who 'study up' as an example of addressing other ethical issues around the notion of the under-studied and the over-studied in social research. This is also a point that Gitlin (1994) takes up and for that reason I include an example from South Africa where a group of young black youth from a township participated in a project on HIV and AIDS education that involved 'studying up' white youth from a private school.

Case Studies in Visual Research

Case study 1: How informed is informed consent?

One of the most basic considerations of informed consent is that consent is truly informed and that participants understand what they are consenting to. All forms of research have their own particularities and the visual is no exception. Once people have participated in a visual study, they are probably in a better position to decide whether their consent is informed, but in the early stages and at the time when it is necessary to get consent in the first place, the situation may be more difficult. What would it mean to exhibit photos – in a public venue, for example – if one has never taken a photo? How might participants think about producing a video and the various ways of making it public (including through YouTube and other social networking sites) if the process is new to them? While, as many researchers such as David Buckingham (2008) are now pointing out, a strong participatory culture is changing the notion of production and who is a producer, there are still many grey areas in what it means to give consent. There are, of course, many ways of giving out information about a project, but one that is worth considering is the use of a visual consent document. Jennifer Thompson, in preparing for her field work using photovoice with an intergenerational group in Sierra Leone looking at environmental issues, decided to produce an ethics 'letter' that is itself visual in nature. Her concern was that most people do not know what they are agreeing to. Using the visual letter gave her an opportunity to walk the participants through all stages of

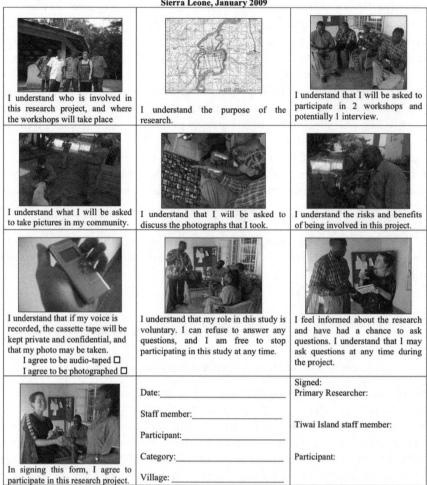

Photo-Voice Project – How We See This Place
Sierra Leone, January 2009

I understand who is involved in this research project, and where the workshops will take place	I understand the purpose of the research.	I understand that I will be asked to participate in 2 workshops and potentially 1 interview.
I understand what I will be asked to take pictures in my community.	I understand that I will be asked to discuss the photographs that I took.	I understand the risks and benefits of being involved in this project.

I understand that if my voice is recorded, the cassette tape will be kept private and confidential, and that my photo may be taken.
    I agree to be audio-taped ☐
    I agree to be photographed ☐
	I understand that my role in this study is voluntary. I can refuse to answer any questions, and I am free to stop participating in this study at any time.	I feel informed about the research and have had a chance to ask questions. I understand that I may ask questions at any time during the project.

In signing this form, I agree to participate in this research project.	Date:_____ Staff member:_____ Participant:_____ Category:_____ Village: _____	Signed: Primary Researcher: Tiwai Island staff member: Participant:

Figure 2.1   Visual consent form

Source: Thompson (2009) in collaboration with the Environmental Foundation for Africa

the process and to give them an opportunity to raise questions that could be informed by the visual. She commented after the fact that the process was by no means straightforward and that the participants had many questions about what would happen during the study. Her assessment of this, however, was that, rather than the usual nods that are often elicited upon explaining ethical issues and informed consent, the participants were really engaging with the issues and so they had many questions.

In other projects, the researcher has produced a short Q&A about the project, which addresses in an audience-appropriate way key aspects of use of the visual in place of the more conventional letter of explanation (see box below).

What you will learn in this study

The XXXX Study is an opportunity for you to share with us your ideas and thoughts on the steps you feel would support you in acquiring a higher quality of life. We are also interested in understanding how we can further develop your capacity so that you are able to improve the quality of life. Finally, we also look forward to understanding from you how systems and institutions can enable you to acquire a higher quality of life.

What is the point of being in this study?

If you join this study, you will get a chance to:

- Work on photography. The photography will be about identifying how the education, health and economic sectors can better serve your needs. It will also be about understanding what it means to be a girl and understanding the unique challenges that you have in your life in comparison to boys, particularly as it relates to building capacity that will enable you to access a better quality of life. The photography will also be about the impact of HIV and AIDS on your life as a girl. It will also be about other community issues you feel are important.
- Think of new ways for girls to get involved in developing knowledge and skills needed to begin the process of having a better quality of life. It will be about having a safe space to talk about issues that are important to you and to consider the ways together that these issues that you have raised can be addressed.
- Present your ideas as part of the group to members of the school, community, church, as well as other decision makers like not-for-profit organizations, government and donors.
- Take action on issues that you and the group believe are important.

What will happen in the study?

First, you will be in a workshop. Here is what you will do in the workshop:

- Learn how to use a camera and take photos.
- Learn about capacity building.
- Talk about the challenges you face as a girl in developing your capacity.
- Talk about the ideas you have for solving the challenges you have identified.
- Work in small groups to translate your ideas into photography.
- Meet in small groups to talk about your work with the other people in the study.
- If you want, you can write about your work and say what it means to you.
- If you want, you can also write about your experience in participating in the workshops.

On the last day of the workshop, you will present your work to the other people in the study. You will also present your work at two photo exhibitions to be held within the community and in the city. The photo exhibition in the city may be attended by decision makers like not-for-profit organizations, government and donors.

(Continued)

(Continued)

Could anything bad happen from being in the study?

I hope not, but there are a few risks. I am taking all the steps I can to keep these risks down:

- There is a risk that you may get upset or confused by something that comes up in the group discussions. You may find it hard to talk about issues like HIV, issues related to poverty, challenges you may be facing in your life.
- People might get angry with you if you take their picture without getting permission.
- Even though we will all promise to respect each other's privacy, there is a chance someone could break her promise and talk about you outside the group.

What are the good things that could come out of it for me?

- You will get training on how to use a camera. You will learn about how photos can be used to create social change.
- You will learn a lot about capacity building and how you can make yourself more aware and stronger.
- You will also learn about the role and impact of HIV/AIDS in relation to developing your capacity.
- You will get a chance to talk about issues that concern you.
- You will get a chance to talk about the ideas you have that may solve the challenges you face.
- At the end of the study, you may feel like you have grown a lot. For instance, you may feel that:
  - you can have more direction and control in your life
  - you are a better leader
  - you can think through issues better.

How will you protect my privacy?

- Each person who joins the study will promise not to discuss the things said in the workshop outside the group. You do not have to say anything in the group that you don't want to, for any reason.
- The photos that you take for the study will belong to you. I may ask you to let me publish your photos to show the results of the study. I will only use your photos with your written permission. I will talk with you about which photos I can use. You can decide if you want your name on your photos or not. You will sign a form telling me which photos I can use.
- If you do not want your name used in the study, I will change your name on our records so that you cannot be identified. I will store the study records safely at my home, in a place that only I and/or my assistant(s) will have access to. We will not share any of your personal information without your permission.

Will the sessions be audio-taped?

- In order for me to understand and record your ideas accurately, all sessions will be audio-taped.
- If you do not wish the session to be audio-taped, notes will be taken.

Case study 2: No faces

As I note in Chapters 4 and 5, photography or video projects do not always involve human subjects, and working with more symbolic subjects may help to address certain ethical issues. I do not think we should regard the taking of photos of objects (or a part of the body other than the face) as necessarily 'second best' (or just as a way to get around ethical issues) but rather, as Stephen Riggins (1994) and others working in object studies might regard it, working at a more symbolic or abstract level. One community health care worker in a rural setting in South Africa when addressing challenges and solutions to gender and HIV and AIDS, for example, took pictures of a set of hairdryers in a beauty salon and comments that she took this photograph because of what's missing. As she notes, there should be beautiful young women in the beauty salon having their hair done. Instead, they are sick and at home or they are no longer alive (see Chapter 7). The photo is a poignant one and I often use it to illustrate various genres of photos (and to highlight that taking pictures of people is not the only approach).

Where community photographers will be taking photos of people, we can still consider ways that do not make the identity of the photo subject so apparent: a set of hands or feet, a photo image taken from the back, a photo at a great distance. Arguably, not all of these photos provide equal anonymity, especially in school settings and rural areas where there may be a great deal of familiarity with individuals, their clothing, knapsacks and shoes. Indeed, even a photo that displays photo subjects from the knees down may still render the person identifiable.

To further a Media Ethics 101 approach, I now regularly use a PowerPoint presentation called 'No faces' that is made up of images that may be acceptable – but which may still require discussion among the group: the photo of the hairdryers noted above, a set of hands, a from-the-knees-down photo of a group of school girls, a crowd scene at a distance, a group of five young women with their back to the photographer, a picture of barbed wire and chain linked fence with an empty school ground in the background, and an image of an AIDS campaign T-shirt. With a group of new photographers, I will go through this presentation, and we will discuss the various issues associated with each photo (and why it would be acceptable or unacceptable) in their context. The answers will vary from one community to another. And while the whole process may only take 30 minutes or so, it contributes to the question, 'Is this okay?'

Case study 3: What about providing anonymity for places?

As Karlsson (2007) and Prosser (2007) argue, photos without people but that are very clearly of recognizable places (a public place such as a school or church, a store or other commercial enterprise, or someone's house) may also be problematic. One empty school ground does not look the same as another, and some identifying feature may be of concern. Clark (2008) writes the following in his discussion of anonymity for spaces:

> There were a number of reasons why we considered anonymizing place in our visual data. One is to protect the identities of the fieldsite and individuals (participants or others) who live there. While it may, in theory, be relatively straightforward to disguise place in text through the use of pseudonyms or limiting the amount of geographical context, it is almost impossible to adequately anonymize place in visual data; those familiar with the places will continue to recognize them. Partly due to our aim to disseminate results of the research, we did not aim to achieve complete anonymity of place, but rather decide in which contexts to use images of place, among which audience, and the purposes for which we are presenting a photography of place. Despite our best efforts, we did not entirely resolve the challenges of anonymizing place. In some instances a failure to anonymize place can also unwittingly reveal the identities of individual participants as well. For example, the use of a quotation positioned alongside a particular photograph (in this case, of a patch of waste-ground in my research site) during a seminar paper I gave was sufficient to enable one member of the audience who was familiar with the research site to identify the participant who gave the quotation, even though I believed I had anonymized both participant and name of the fieldsite and ensured that there was seemingly, no identifying feature of the photograph. (2008: n.p.)

Interestingly, however, in our efforts to 'do most good' and not just to do 'least harm', anonymizing may erode some of the benefits of research. We consider this in visual work involving several schools in South Africa. For example, one school that is making great strides to address social issues deserves to be recognized and applauded for its efforts. And another, which continues to struggle despite its efforts, may actually attract local donor support if its situation were more publicly recognized.

Case study 4: Do you mind if I take your picture?

'Do you mind if I take your picture?' asks 12-year-old Laura. She is part of a photovoice project in her school, focusing on safe and unsafe spaces. She wants to know something about how her seventh-grade peers see school safety. But she doesn't just ask. She also carries with her a consent form for her photo subjects to sign. In the end, she might not even use the particular photo she is taking in a follow-up exhibition, or as a research team it may not be one of the images we use (even if Laura does obtain permission), but at the time that she is taking the photo, she is fully complying with some type of Media Ethics 101 protocol. Indeed, building a Media Ethics 101 is critical, and below is sample wording that we regularly include in an ethics application.

> Participants will get appropriate training on getting proper permission before taking someone's photograph. Participants will be trained to inform individuals being photographed about the use of the photographs and the risk of being visually identified. Potential subjects will be asked to sign photo consent forms (see below) before being photographed. All participants will carry these forms with them. We will also discuss privacy and the ways that privacy can also be respected by taking pictures in such a way that the identity of the people in the photograph is not clear, for example by taking pictures from far away, by blurring out faces after the picture is developed, or only taking one part of the body (e.g., hands or feet).

Consent for Taking My Picture

I consent to be photographed as part of the XXX Study.

I know that means my picture might be published to show the results of the study. For instance, my picture might be used:

- in a dissertation
- in book chapters
- on a website
- in journals
- at a conference presentation
- at photo exhibitions to be held with community, school, church, not for profit, donors, government, academic, civil society groups, etc.
- at meetings with community, school, church, not for profit, donors, government, academic, civil society groups, etc.
- be provided to media for publishing.

Print name   Sign here   Date

Where there is a clear need to take a photo of a person (or a group) and where the image is such that they are recognizable, it is important to inculcate a culture of informed consent among the participants and at the same time satisfy our own institutions that require this. Making a case for providing media training for community photographers may seem very straightforward, and once they have received some idea of how to go about asking permission to take a photograph and working with a special consent form, that may be the end of the issue. It could, however, be just the beginning. One of the cornerstones of ethical research, as we know, is to do least harm.

However, it is important to consider what community photographers are actually asking when they take on such issues as 'challenges and solutions to addressing HIV and AIDS' or something like 'feeling safe and not so safe'. One school principal with whom I worked in an informal settlement in South Africa was keen to use photovoice with a group of sixth-grade learners, many of whom were regularly missing school on Fridays (Mitchell et al., 2006a). As I describe in more detail in Chapter 10, the outcome of the project was very positive. However, as we learned after the project was finished, there were hidden risks in the study. Significant to this discussion of ethics is the fact that the principal was aware that it was not necessarily safe for the learners to be approaching the adults in the market who were employing children, and so he accompanied the children as they carried out their investigative journalism. At one point, he even explained to the children the dangers that journalists might experience. The images that the children took of their informal settlement depict poverty, unemployment and alcoholism, including adults drinking in a shebeen (local bar). In follow-up publications where we describe the study, we have partly masked the people shown, but it is possible that the people would still be recognizable.

As Bagnoli (2008) highlights, the various approaches to removing all identifiers of photos or drawings, and the use of pixelating techniques or blurring images, may call into question the overall aesthetics of the images. Indeed, she points out that the young producers of the works she describes questioned the need to do this. Clearly, they felt that their work had lost something.

One of the questions that is always asked on an ethics form relates to potential risks and in this case there were risks because those running the market had obviously little to gain by being cooperative. They were going to be losing their Friday employees, who worked for very little money, an issue that was also of concern to Mizen (2005) in his study of children's photos of their 'light work' in the UK. Ultimately, however, if one also considers the question of whether the gains outweigh the risks, in this project, the images produced by the children became part of an exhibition presented to local stakeholders. The outcome was that the feeding scheme, which only ran from Monday to Friday, was extended over the weekend so that there was no longer a reason for children to be working in the market on Fridays (and, of course, no reason to miss school).

Case study 5: Who owns the images?

One of the first times I was ever involved in a photovoice project – one using simple point-and-shoot cameras and where my colleagues and I went off and had the pictures developed – we made two huge errors. First of all, we made only one set of prints, which we took to a follow-up workshop with the community photographers. Second of all, we left the package of negatives in the envelope of prints. We distributed the envelopes to the appropriate producers and from there proceeded to engage them in a number of follow-up activities. These ranged from having people select what they considered their 'best' photo on the particular topic we were exploring to using chart paper where the photographers might display their preliminary analysis of their work. When it came time to gather up all the materials from the workshop, we realized that aside from the photos that were taped or glued on to the chart paper, there were almost no others around. Where did they go? Understandably, the people who took the photographs in the first place regarded the photos as theirs and took them home. The only real data we were left with could be found on the chart paper. The experience was an important one for raising a critical question around ownership and the idea that the participants were not just there to collect data for our team. This should not have been a surprise to us. The work of Elizabeth Edwards (2002), Gillian Rose (2001) and others who have studied the materiality of photos shows clearly that ownership is important, regardless of whether one is talking about family photographs that have a long-term history (who owns the family album?) or whether, in the case of photovoice, one is talking about more recently produced images. And notwithstanding the fact that the images are representational objects that reflect the work of the producer, they are also, as we have seen in the many exhibits that result from this work, artistic pieces. Obviously, although making reprints is usually quite straightforward, the experience was a dramatic one for reminding our team to first of all make at least two copies, and if there is a case of working with negatives, to make sure that they do not get mixed up with the rest of the photos. A rule-of-thumb, then, is to make sure that participants have copies of their own photographs.

Another issue relates to getting permission to use the images. There are several different ways that the idea of permission to use the photos might be lived out. Some participants will say that it is okay to analyse photos but not to exhibit them in any public way (including a book, dissertation or photo exhibit). They themselves may not feel comfortable with the idea of exposure, or they may fear some sort of reprisal. Others will give permission to use some or all of the photos. It is critical to ask, and it is critical to respect the wishes of the producer. The form reproduced below is one that has been used in quite a number of projects and is one which respects the rights of the photographer-documentarian-artist.

I agree that the XXX study can use the photo(s) I have taken. You can only use the photo(s) I have listed below. You can use it in any way that helps to educate people about this study and its message. For instance, you can put it in a dissertation; in book chapters; on a website; in journals; use it at a conference presentation; use it at photo exhibitions to be held with community, school, church, not for profit, donors, government, academic, civil society groups, etc.; use it at meetings with community, school, church, not for profit, donors, government, academic, civil society groups, etc.

(Continued)

At least one school staff person was involved with the study and I have looked at my photos very carefully. We both feel that there is nothing that might cause me or anyone I know harm or embarrassment.

These are the photos you can publish:

1) _____
      Title   Description

2) _____
      Title   Description

3) _____
      Title   Description

4) _____
      Title   Description

5) _____
      Title   Description

Check one:

Please give me credit with my full name at all times.   ☐
Never give my name when you show this art.   ☐
Please use my 'pen name' to credit me.   ☐ My pen name is: _____

Print name   **Sign here**   **Date**

Figure 2.2 Consent form

Case study 6: A matter of judgement

In the cases previously noted, the focus is on ensuring consent when it is appropriate to include a photo or visual image as data. But what about cases that are not ethically appropriate? Drawing on the work of Lee (1993) and others, how does one inculcate a culture of sensitivity? Jean Stuart (2004, 2007), in her work with pre-service teachers, invited them to use a range of media forms to explore issues of HIV and AIDS in their lives. One medium that the teachers chose to work with was photography. What she describes in the following pages are some of the ethical issues that arose in her work with the students in relation to the use of visual images. However, while Stuart argues that visual images can be problematic, she draws attention to the ways in which the politics of the visual, and especially the ethical concerns, helped her raise many of the sensitivities surrounding the issues but which are often hidden from view. Stuart (2007) writes:

> Dealing with the ethical dilemmas in photography proved to be vital. We were all confronted with and forced to see HIV and AIDS in the social context, as attempts to capture photographs were met by fears of being associated with the stigma and discrimination that can result in unhappy or even life-threatening situations. Pre-service teachers needed to be supported as they grappled with ways of dealing with the fact that photography captures recognizable copies of people. Looking at

examples of ways around ethical dilemmas related to photography's tendency to create an illusion of, or represent, reality proved useful and helpful in that it modeled solutions to ethical dilemmas. Being on the receiving end of the fears related to being identified as HIV positive however, also offered pre-service teachers an opportunity to experience the depth and consequences of social stigma. (2007: 230)

She then goes on to include some of the comments of the pre-service teachers as evidence of a range of ethical issues:

The difficulty I faced when doing this assignment was that my friends refused to be in the photographs as that would mean that they had to pretend to have AIDS (the thought of that seemed to horrify them!!!).

It is difficult to go up to a person and ask them questions related to HIV/AIDS because they will presume you are saying they are HIV positive.

It is not easy to get people to photograph or video-tape because people fear being stigmatised.

Some of the people whom I intended to photograph refused, as they didn't want to be identified as HIV/AIDS victims. (2007: 230–231)

More than anything, though, the pre-service teachers begin to realize some of the power differentials:

An implication for teachers is that the choice of photography as a medium introduces particular problems because of society's attitudes to the HIV and AIDS affected, and teachers need to be aware and offer guidance here, but I suggest that precisely because it creates this problem, there is a strong reason for using photography. Doing so leads to embodied experience of rejection for producers and a deeper understanding of the effects of social stigma. The ethical dilemmas forced a realization of the power of the stigma related to AIDS and this realization is capable of promoting more compassionate and sensitive engagement. (2007: 231)

As Stuart goes on to point out, it is precisely the dilemmas and problems created by the use of photographs that becomes a pedagogy in itself. While the pre-service teachers began to see some of the tensions, Stuart herself as the researcher also began to see many of the issues around stigma more clearly. This was particularly the case when the teachers needed guidance and support around negotiating access to some of the sites where they wanted to take pictures. For example, one group wanted to take photos at an antenatal clinic. However, this clinic is visited by patients who could become victims of discrimination if they found themselves associated with the virus. As Stuart observes, the difficulties of accessing this clinic caused some of the teachers to think of other sites:

In group discussion about how to deal with gaining access, one of the pre-service teachers suggested that taking photographs of young children in a rural school far from the campus may be a route around this difficulty. (2007: 232)

However, as she concludes, 'This suggestion accentuates the need to ensure that anyone working with this medium has a thorough understanding of the need for ethical integrity' (2007: 232).

Daniela Sime (2008) looks at another dimension of content, specifically in relation to the work of child photographers and some of the tensions related to the consent of the parents or caregivers once they see what the children are photographing. Sime offers the case of engaging young people living in poverty (and studying poverty) in participatory research. Notwithstanding the fact that the young people themselves may not see their socio-economic situation the same way that middle-class university-educated researchers do – an ethical issue in itself – parents may at first agree to have their child participate but then may wish to withdraw consent once they see how their privacy at home is being disrupted by the camera. As Sime observes:

> … a number of children took photographs of spaces in the home that may have offended the other family members through the intrusion of their privacy. Such examples include a mother sleeping, a young brother in underwear, the family bathroom or the contents of the fridge. … As sensitive representations are more likely to appear in photographs taken in the home, it is reasonable to assume that families should have the right to exclude certain photographs if they find the content inappropriate or to accept their use for research purposes, but prohibit their use in any dissemination activities. (2008: 71)

In a situation in a study that I conducted with a graduate student with 11- and 12-year-old girls who took pictures of 'feeling safe' and 'feeling not so safe', we were struck by the complexities of working with a photograph taken by an 11-year-old of a pair of slippers. Her caption was 'I am scared when my stepfather hits me with his slippers [sic]'. On the one hand, had the picture (with or without the name of the photographer) been included in the local photo exhibition it would have exposed the behaviour of her stepfather, and if viewed by the stepfather could potentially put the girl in a vulnerable position in her home. On the other hand, the photo raises the possibility that the girl may need protection, in which case, the project could serve a different purpose if the school counsellor is involved.

Case study 7: Who isn't in the picture? And the ethics and politics of studying up

A critical issue surrounding HIV and AIDS in South Africa relates to the way in which the pandemic is seen to be primarily an issue of black South Africans. White South Africans often say that it has nothing to do with them. And yet, a competing and compelling discourse is one that says that 'everyone is infected or affected', and the idea of one racial group absenting itself from the issues is a problem in itself. The face of AIDS in the media is seen to be black, and at the same time not that much is known about how young people growing up white even see the issues. Over and above everything else, there is the issue of over-studied and under-studied populations. And while one could argue that this goes far beyond the politics and ethics of doing visual research, the issue of visual representation is nonetheless a critical one. Shannon Walsh (2007), in her work with a group of black youth living in a Khayelitsha township, was confronted with their questions: 'What about white people?' 'Why are there so many videos and so much media coverage of us talking about HIV and AIDS and why not white people?' Walsh delves deeper:

> One of the project participants, Thabo, explained his desire to increase his knowledge (about HIV and AIDS and discrimination) in a discussion session:
>
> 'What would I do if I could make a project? I wouldn't want to duplicate the issues but to uncover more of the deeper underlying issues, so we came up with Facing the Truth (FATT) – to try and seek the truth about why young people are vulnerable to AIDS. There is racism for sure. Why are black people always the faces we see as HIV positive? It is rare to find white people (in the pictures). What is the real situation in Constantia? I've heard there is no clinic there. Why is that? Are they more protected from the virus than we are here in Khayelitsha? Why are poor people and black people always the face we see of AIDS? I want to propose to do research and find out answers to these questions. … The young people are not thinking about the future. There needs to be a "brand new strategy" … we had a new strategy, but now we need a "brand new strategy".'

She writes about how a group of five black youth (both male and female) from Khayelitsha decided to interview boys at a private school not so far away. As she notes, the Khayelitsha youth were outside Rondebosch Boys' School with notepads, a tripod, microphone, boom and a video camera:

> Teachers and students passing by glance curiously in their direction. What could this group of young people be doing *here*? The predominantly white private school stands like a stone castle against the wind, its wide halls resounding with music, arts and science. Just beyond the film crew, the closely groomed rugby field looms in the sun. Two young white boys, neatly clad in their school uniforms and knee socks, anxiously wait for the next question to be asked. The black female interviewer, 16 years old and a resident of the township of Khayelitsha asks, 'Do you think AIDS is affecting black people more than white people? Why or why not?'

> Boy 2: *I think it is affecting more of the black community …*
> Boy 1: *Unfortunately.*
> Boy 2: *Unfortunately … because, uh …*
> Boy 1: *That we know of …*
> Boy 2: *That we know of, because that's what we've been taught unfortunately. Because at this school, during the apartheid era, uh, um, we were educated on the results of having unsafe sex and education didn't reach as far as Crossroads and District Six, so they, no fault of their own, but they had no idea of the consequences of unsafe sex so it spread like wild fire. Or, that's what we know, it spread like wild fire [Boy 1 looking very pensive, deep in thought] and unfortunately it is a predominant threat in the black community today.*

Walsh goes on to note:

> The FATT project, in its assertion of using video as a means of investigating power, revealed the continuing hesitancy of the majority of researchers to take up a study of elites in any substantial way. The FATT group were so curious about what white kids were thinking about AIDS, and in the relative void of information available to them, they decided to take up the investigation themselves.
>
>   Part of the reason 'studying up' or 'researching up' is rarely done is in part due to how much more difficult it is than researching a less powerful social group. Simple issues like gaining entry, being given time and being respected and legitimized as a researcher are all often called in question when researching 'up' the social ladder.

Walsh concludes that the project shows some of the ways in which video ethnography can be a tool for collaboration and disruption:

> Involving research participants from Khayelitsha as 'knowers' and creative agents allowed for the possibility of an engaged pedagogy. Beyond engaged pedagogy, shifting power dynamics within the research space can function as a valid political intervention. Understanding and positioning participants as instigators and producers of knowledge can dislodge power dynamics in a given social context. (Adapted from Walsh, 2007: 241–55)

Case study 8: Doing least harm and exploitation

A criticism of participatory research and interventions, particularly those involving children, is that they may be regarded as their own form of exploitation, especially when adults recognize that it is impossible to achieve any sort of insider status or insider insight without the assistance of children. Here, one might think of projects such as Zana Briski and Ross Kaufman's *Born into Brothels* (2004) based on Kids With Cameras work, which has been criticized as exploitative, deceptive and potentially harmful to the children. How can we ensure that research with marginalized populations does not further marginalize them, or worse, endanger their lives, by putting them in a more vulnerable position than they might have been as a result of our participatory research? The idea of 'doing less harm' (and by corollary 'doing more good') is a critical one in working with children and young people (see also Moletsane et al., 2008). In her analysis of studies on gender-based violence in and around schools where girls in focus groups and in one-on-one interviews were asked to comment on the behaviour of male teachers, Fiona Leach (2006) addresses the question: What right do researchers have to uncover these sorts of situations and then inevitably 'walk away' from them? As she observes, it is one thing for the research team to help communities to document cases of gender-based violence, and to identify ways of negotiating consensual sex, but how does the research team help to protect the participants? How does the research team ensure the often-promised anonymity and autonomy of the participants in cases where such participants are minors and female and are under the guardianship of the very teachers (and other adults) guilty of abusing them? What happens when the perpetrators of such violence are other children (e.g., boys) possibly also participating in the very interventions?

In particular, when considered within the context of participatory research, other ethical considerations emerge. First, how do researchers understand and guard against the dangers inherent in interventions that involve children, in particular girls, in using cameras in and around schools and/or asking questions about sensitive issues, such as gender-based violence, AIDS and other issues, and thus breaking some of the gendered and culturally based taboos set to regulate their behaviour in these communities? How do they address the implications inherent in interventions that assist girls to challenge the notion that they can never say 'no' to sexual advances from adult males, but also from their male counterparts? Would adult researchers accompanying them during their picture-taking or informing them about the dangers of visual work suffice (see, for example, Mitchell et al., 2006a)? Would teaching researchers to request informed consent from their subjects be enough? Second, as Leach (2006) asks, are participatory research methodologies and interventions inherently exploitative and what can researchers do to guard against this? What happens, for example, to the producers (the boys or girls) when the video has been made? In what ways do the children themselves benefit? How do the researchers mediate the fallout that possibly occurs when the adult perpetrators of the violence depicted in such productions have seen them and object to the content? In these contexts, it becomes imperative that researchers and others using these methodologies take all possible precautions to ensure that no harm or the least harm befalls the participants and that their participation benefits them in the end.

Case study 9: But it's fiction

Unlike direct conventional interviews, the distance and anonymity provided by visual data, particularly staged images of controversial and taboo subjects such as gender-based violence (including rape and incest), HIV and AIDS, and HIV-related stigma, are key to opening up dialogue and for safely disrupting the commonly held views and attitudes towards the disease and those who are infected or affected by the virus. Other approaches that could provide such distance and a sense of safety for young people to participate meaningfully in research and interventions aimed at addressing the negative impacts of violence and AIDS might include drawings, films, theatre and music. However, as we illustrate in the analysis of *Rape* in Chapter 5, the fact that the scenes in the production are staged is not always a guarantee that our research does least harm to the participants. Instead, such interventions, unless carefully mediated, can cause further harm, for example, by reinforcing negative stereotypes about individuals and groups (e.g., boys as violent and as prone to carrying out rape) and about the very issues they target for change (e.g., gender-based violence as inevitable) (Moletsane et al.,

2008). The issue of staging, often used in photovoice projects and video-making projects, may help to counter some ethical issues where the participants are also the photo subjects. The image in Chapter 6 (Figure 6.6) of the boys who stage a hanging to represent the despair related to stigma in the community seems to all who participated clearly one that is not real. And the very dramatic and horrific rape scene described in Chapter 5 is clearly staged. Both the quality of the filming in this case and the overall production indicate that the scenes are constructed. Notwithstanding the possible trauma to the participants, however, how do we ensure that audiences see this work as fictional? As Stuart (2007) found, being photographed in a play on HIV and AIDS may be seen as being synonymous with being infected. In the video production *Our Photos, Our Videos, Our Stories,* which includes some of these staged images, we added a disclaimer at the beginning of the video that makes it clear that the images are all fictional representations. And in curatorial statements that we have developed to accompany exhibitions, our research team has begun to include statements that indicate the staged component of the work, particularly in the context of HIV and AIDS.

Conclusion

This chapter may convince the reticent researcher that visual research is not for her (or him), and that it would be much easier to simply interview participants, or ask them to write something, or send out a survey. I have placed this chapter towards the beginning of *Doing Visual Research* as a way to ensure that the ethical issues are front and centre. At the same time, as I hope that the remaining chapters will demonstrate, much of the community-based work described here is not simply about our own research. The engagement process is a critical one, as is the idea of democratizing the research space so that communities also participate in identifying, representing, analysing and interpreting the issues, and even engaging in disseminating findings. As Jenkins (2006) has explored in his discussion of an emerging participatory culture context for citizen engagement, much of the work that I describe in this book as 'research' is already happening within social movements. A few years ago, Sandra Weber and I published a chapter called 'Imaging, keyboarding and posting identities' (Weber and Mitchell, 2007) where we looked at a convergence media involving young people using mobile phones, blogs, PowerPoint technology, digital cameras and video cameras to represent their lives to the rest of the world. As visual researchers, we are in a good position to influence these practices and the study of this work through approaches that seize on the idea of Media Ethics 101 within a digital futures pedagogy.

PART II

Visual Methods for Social Change:
Tools and Techniques

THREE

Not just an object: Working with things, objects and artefacts in visual research

Introduction

Stephen Riggins offers a compelling argument for studying objects in social research. He notes:

> Postmodern social theory conveys an image of society as being in constant flux. Featherstone (1992: 27) refers to '... the rapid flow of signs and images that saturate the fabric of everyday life in contemporary society'. This perspective has been constructed by concentrating primarily on studies of public life: the street life of metropolitan cities, tourism, consumer culture, popular entertainment, such as fairs and carnivals, and the informational overload of the mass media. However, American [or in any other country] homes are not department stores with continually changing exhibits. Domestic artefacts appear to give personal identity a stability it would otherwise lack, and a refuge from the unstable, fragile flux of public life. (Riggins, 1994: 141)

As researchers, we may ignore the meanings in things and objects in our research sites, and yet, as Sherry Turkle (2007: 6) points out, 'We live our lives in the middle of things.' As seen in the work of scholars from such diverse backgrounds as media and technology (Turkle, 2007), science (Daston, 2007), anthropology (Brown, 1998, 2004; Miller, 1998) and the interdisciplinary area of object studies (Candlin and Guins, 2009), the analysis of material objects offers the possibility of theorizing abstract concepts in a grounded manner and, in so doing, expanding the possibilities of what counts as evidence in research. What counts as evidence in social research has often relied on the analysis of responses in interviews, focus groups, documents and surveys. This chapter seeks to add the study of material culture (things, objects and artefacts) to what counts as evidence or texts for analysis in social research. In drawing on a variety of approaches and tools, ranging from socio-semiotics, memory work and working with photographs to such arts-based approaches as installation and performance, the chapter situates the study of material culture within what I describe elsewhere as a *new materialism* in social research (Mitchell, 2010).

In this chapter, I highlight the rich (and mostly untapped) possibilities for work with things, objects and artefacts as visual culture in social research. In our various field sites – schools, hospitals, communities, for example – and in our research questions (related to schooling, health care, gender, identity and poverty reduction), we indeed live 'our lives in the middle of things', as Turkle (2007: 7) says, including physical spaces and the artefacts of a particular institution. In the case of schools, for example, these artefacts, which might have both personal and collective meanings, can include chalk, student desks, the teacher's desk, wall charts, the teacher's day-book or record book, the bell (see Mitchell and Weber, 1999) and items of clothing such as school uniforms and gym suits (Weber, 2004). They are the social accessories of institutions and everyday life that are imbued with history and with meanings. Then there are the social accessories that seem to go beyond everyday life, or that suggest an everyday life that must be contested. Sarah Nuttall, for example, in the chapter 'Girl bodies' (2009), investigates accounts of two devices – a type of chastity belt and an anti-rape condom – both designed (and publicized through local media and the Internet) to protect the bodies of girl babies in South Africa from rape. She focuses on these devices as a response to the horrific rape of nine-month-old Baby Tshepang, one of 21,000 reported rapes that took place in South Africa in 2001. (Baby Tshepang, not her real name, was raped and sodomized. Six men were initially charged but only one man has been prosecuted.) For example, Nuttall looks at the anti-rape condom as it is described in the marketing survey:

> [It] is shaped almost like a tampon, this tampon, however, is hollow inside. The inner wall of the tampon is lined with small hooks. ... When an unwanted man inserts his penis into the girl the inner sheath, which is armed and wired, attaches itself to the penis. ... There is no way that the man can get it off. As the penis becomes flaccid, the device shrinks with it. To get it off, he must stretch the skin, which is so painful that it must be done in a hospital. Thus the 'suspected rapist' can be identified and caught. (2009: 139)

Nuttall uses her analysis of these somewhat bizarre dress items to examine public trust and the situation of gender-based violence in South Africa, especially in relation to apartheid/post-apartheid masculinities.

But how do we get at the meanings of these everyday (and not so everyday) objects, and how might their meanings enrich our research? In exploring this question, the chapter is divided into three main sections. The first section, 'Objects as representational agents of change', serves to frame a consideration of objects in the context of social research. In the second section, 'Objects-in-inquiry, Part 1: Not just a wire car', the focus is on socio-semiotics as a reading strategy in working with objects and things. In this section, I use Stephen Riggins' categories of denotation and connotation to read the meanings of a child's wire car, an object that might be read as a type of accessory in the lives of boys in traditional, mostly rural settings in many parts of Africa. In the third section, 'Objects-in-inquiry, Part 2: Not just a dress', I look at the ways in which socio-semiotics can serve as a means of doing research in relation to the study of dress as material culture within visual studies. Here, I draw on work with the visual through family albums, memory work, installation and performance.

Objects as Representational Agents of Change

Are objects merely conversation starters or part of building rapport, or are they used as tools to gain entry into the interview process? Or can they also be texts of visual research in and of themselves? Social texts – objects and things – are texts of materiality. They can be seen, touched, sometimes tasted and heard, and, as Sarah Pink (2004) reminds us in her study of household objects, even sometimes smelled. It is not surprising that two books published on things in 2007, Glenn and Hayes' *Taking Things Seriously* and Sherry Turkle's (2007) *Evocative Objects: Things We Think With*, include photographic images of each of the things along with the descriptions. Objects are meant to be seen – and photographed as Marina Warner (2004) argues in the introduction to *Things: A Spectrum of Photography, 1850–2001*. 'Photographers', she writes, 'have a special relation to the mystery of "thingness", for a photograph so often reaches out to possess and stay the moment when the thing was there, in the here-and-now that was happening when I was there or you were with a camera or another means of making an image' (2004: 10). Christian Boltanski, in his MoMA exhibition *My Favourite Things*, writes about the act of photographing the objects that children from a school in Chicago brought as 'the single favourite object of his or her lifetime' (quoted in Mitchell and Reid-Walsh, 2002: 81). Boltanski wanted to ensure that objects received identical treatment, that they were shot at the same scale and angle under uniform lighting. As noted elsewhere, '... there is a democratization of the relationship between the camera and the object with the result that no one (of 264 objects) stands out from the rest' (Mitchell and Reid-Walsh, 2002: 81).

Objects, we found (Mitchell et al., 2005b), played a central role in the images produced in community-based photovoice projects. In fact, as described in our work elsewhere, the deliberate photographing of objects and places (as opposed to people) often raises possibilities for working with the symbolic (and in ways that are also less ethically fraught in relation to issues surrounding informed consent). As noted in Chapters 1 and 6, a community health worker-as-photographer in rural South Africa, for example, chooses to photograph hairdryers in a beauty salon as her image of 'challenges in addressing HIV and AIDS' (Mitchell et al., 2005a). When she is interviewed about the photograph, she explains, 'In this beauty salon you would expect to find beautiful young women. Instead the chairs under the hair dryers are all empty. The beautiful young women are sick and disfigured, or they are dead' (Mitchell, 2009a). Items of clothing also appear in some of these images. When one of the teachers is asked to suggest solutions in addressing HIV and AIDS, for example, she takes a picture of several T-shirts that carry messages related to community campaigns.

Figure 3.1 T-shirts as artefacts

Further, it is important to acknowledge that the 'tools' of visual research – Super 8 movie cameras, Kodak Brownie instamatics, camcorders or Flip cameras – are also objects, each with their own object biography. We are reminded of this in video artist Sadie Benning's account of receiving a Fisher-Price Pixelvision video camera for Christmas from her father when she was 15. Commenting on her disappointment, she notes: 'I thought, "This is a piece of … [expletive]." It's black and white. It's for kids. He'd told me I was getting this big surprise. I was expecting a camcorder …' (cited in Paley, 1995: 69). In actual fact, having this $89.95 piece of equipment was the beginning of her career in video. Susann Allnutt's (2009) description of the Brownie camera that she received from one of the neighbour women at a summer cottage when she was 7 or 8 also draws attention to the object itself. She states: 'I believe this was the first camera our family owned. My memory is that I didn't get to keep it and it became the family camera. I remember what it looked like though, and how it felt, the smell of the black plastic' (Allnutt, 2009: 36).

Objects-in-Inquiry, Part 1: Not Just a Wire Car

Step into the living room, study, office, or den of just about any engaged, imaginative, passionate individual and you'll gravitate toward an item that, although it may not appear particularly valuable, is reverentially displayed as though it were a precious and irreplaceable artefact. Inquire about the object's provenance and you'll be treated to a lively anecdote about how it came into your host's possession. Keep digging, and you might crack the code of what the thing means. Just as we are collectors of things, things are collectors of meaning. (Glenn and Hayes, 2007: 1)

The significance of Joshua Glenn's observation in his introduction to *Taking Things Seriously* struck me one very cold and snowy New Year's Day in Montreal. My gas furnace had gone off during the night – a terrifying event in mid-winter when it is minus 40 degrees Celsius. The fact that it was a public holiday made it almost impossible to find any furnace repair company willing to send someone to come out and look at what the problem might be. Still, the public gas utility company did have a set of emergency personnel on call, and late in the morning on New Year's Day along came a pair of workers who not only made sure the furnace was running properly but also even cleaned some parts of it. As they were leaving, one of them spotted a wire car in a somewhat dilapidated state sitting on a shelf in my living room. I had purchased the wire car in Rwanda a few months earlier but unfortunately it had not travelled well. The main stick used for steering it had broken off in transit, and the whole body of the wire car had been squashed into a rather odd shape after having gone through the baggage mechanisms of Air Canada. Nonetheless, it was still recognizably a toy wire car, the kind that are customarily made and played with by young boys in many parts of sub-Saharan Africa – and an example of the kind of local art that is sold to visitors like me. The repairman looked quizzically, and I said 'Rwanda', and without being asked explicitly except by my expression, he replied 'Angola'. And so began the coded conversation.

What was I doing in Rwanda? How long had he been in Canada? What type of work do I do? Did he make these wire cars as a boy? Where in Rwanda did I get this wire car? Angola – oil and a new prosperity? I wanted to apologize for the state of the wire car and explain how it got like that, but really, in that instance, it did not matter. It was seen as a wire car, not a dilapidated wire car. The entire conversation about the wire car lasted no more than about two or three minutes. I was aware that there might be more customers in need of service on this public holiday, and in such extreme cold, and if not, the pair surely wanted to get home to continue the New Year's Day celebration. Nevertheless, the conversation serves as a reminder to the truth of Lorraine Daston's (2007) observations in *Things that Talk: Object Lessons from Art and Science*:

Imagine a world without things. It would be not so much an empty world as a blurry, frictionless one: No sharp outlines would separate one part of the uniform plenum from another; there would be no resistance against which to stub a toe or test a theory or struggle stalwartly. Nor would there be anything to describe, or to explain, remark on, interpret, or complain about – just a kind of porridgy oneness. Without things, we would stop talking. (Daston, 2007: 9)

The repair person and I would have carried on some version of a conversation no matter what. I was extremely grateful that he had made a service call

Figure 3.2 Wire car in context

Figure 3.3 Close-up of wire car

on this public holiday – and even though I had actually managed to re-ignite the pilot light on my furnace by myself just seconds before he arrived, I was more than pleased to have him check it out. It was New Year's Day, so there was the phatic communion about the New Year. And of course, both being Canadians, and with a great deal of snow currently falling, we would have had a lot to say about the weather. But the wire car took us to completely different places. He was no longer the service provider, and I was no longer just the client.

Socio-semiotics and the social-ness of things

What can a wire car from Rwanda in my living room in Montreal mean? Stephen Riggins (1994), as a socio-semiotician, would look at both the denotative and connotative meaning of the wire car, and even its position in my living room. Using his parents' living room he systematically photographs each object in it (starting at the doorway into the living room, and ending up back at that door): the wall hangings, photographs, lamps, television set, easy chairs, books in the book case and so on. For each object, there is its denotative meaning (the first television set exhibited in the 1940s; the purchase of the particular television set in the living room), and then there is its connotative meaning (the stories of that particular television set). Riggins uses the term *referencing* to describe 'all of the content that is about the history, aesthetics, or customary use of the objects' (1994: 109). He claims that this information is often 'brief and superficial'. It is also often taken for granted – as, for example, by the fact that refrigerators or washing machines are often coded as gendered objects – or their history is forgotten or simply not known. Do we remember a time, for example, before television and, hence, the invention of the television? As described elsewhere (Mitchell and Reid-Walsh, 2002), John Hartley (1999) looks at the links between the invention of the television set and the widespread access to refrigerators. As he points out, not only did the invention and mass distribution of the refrigerator lessen the amount of time people (women) had to spend purchasing and preparing food, but the television show also became sponsored by ads for food preparation, food clean up and food elimination.

To explore connotative meaning, Riggins (1994) uses the term *mapping* to describe the ways in which objects serve as entry points for the telling of stories about the self. By mapping, he means the ways in which 'the self uses the displayed objects (gift, heirlooms, photographs, etc.) as a way of plotting its social network, representing its cosmology and ideology, and projecting its history onto the world's map, its spatial spread so to speak' (1994: 109). Riggins goes on to write that the taking of the photographs is central to the process of visual ethnography:

> Many of the subtleties of domestic artefacts will elude the researcher unless it is possible to closely examine photographs. Consequently each room must be thoroughly photographed. Unlike the practice followed by the professional photographers employed by decorating and architectural magazines of removing all ephemeral traces left by users and inhabitants in order to avoid dating the photographs, ethnographers should make an effort to include the permanent as well as the ephemeral. Both are relevant to the research. (1994: 110)

He then offers an approach to the written account. Again, he emphasizes the importance of being systematic rather than impressionistic:

> One might want to begin the written account of a room with the first object visitors are likely to notice upon entering (something directly opposite the door or some other highlighted space) and from that point proceed systematically

around the room. The same procedure should be applied to the contents of cabinets or shelves. Begin with the object farthest to the right or left and proceed down the shelf. (1994: 110)

Denotative meaning

For the toy car, the denotative meaning would focus on the ways in which such artefacts are made out of scrap wire in various parts of Africa, and mostly by boys. The denotative meaning might include socio-cultural studies of children's toys in Africa. The gendering of the toy becomes further explored by the fact that one of the storylines for the *Sara Stories* (a social marketing series developed by UNICEF to promote girls' education and tested out in sub-Saharan Africa a few years ago) deals with a girl who makes a wire car on her own. In the community focus groups that I participated in, a criticism offered was that the story is not possible. A girl called Sara, they said, would not make her own wire car. And still, within the denotative, a website on wire cars in Africa, along with links to wire art more generally, says this about the wire car:

> Children in Africa don't have money to buy toys so they make their own playthings. One of the forms is to make a car from discarded wire. The kids call this kind of toy 'galimoto' (a Chichewan word that means almost real). The car has wheels that rotate, and a fully functional steering wheel. This is operated by 'remote control' – a stick extending from waist high to the car's front wheels. (www.junglephotos.com/africa/afpeople/afplay/boyscar.shtml, accessed 8 November 2009)

At the same time, the denotative reading might also link to the meaning of children's play in parts of sub-Saharan Africa in the context of HIV and AIDS and the widespread conditions that have led to orphaning, children heading up households, and so on. Anthropologist Patty Henderson (2003), for example, has written that the AIDS pandemic may force us to reconceptualize childhood:

> Prevalent notions of the authority of adulthood may be reshaped by the fact that very young people will be the majority of the survivors in places where the AIDS pandemic results in widespread deaths of productive men and women. It will often devolve on youths to devise ways of contributing forms of sociability, responsibility and the protection of younger children. (Henderson, 2003: 8)

In this context, will boys still make wire cars, or will the wire car be entirely something for tourists to purchase at craft markets? And what do girls play with? Do girls even get to play? Perhaps in the case of boys, it depends on whether the wire car's history is being told by an aid worker, by a tourist or by a scholar of African culture.

Connotative meaning

What personal stories does the wire car carry? When I bought it in a craft market in Rwanda, I thought it would be fun to give to my grandson, Jakob. He is intrigued by 'going to Africa'. And even though the wire car is now not really suitable for a child, defying all standards of child safety (it has a sharp stick and is more or less dysfunctional), he remains interested in it. Now that the car has been noticed by the repair person, it has additional significance, simply by virtue of the conversation that took place between us. What should be clear, however, is that each person's connotative reading of the wire car will be something else. The repairman – I wish I knew his name – may have a long story to tell about making a wire car in Angola as a boy. Perhaps he went home on New Year's Day and commented to his family on seeing a remnant of Africa, or maybe it was just an item of nostalgia, associated with Angola but not necessarily in his own life-history.

Objects-in-Inquiry, Part 2: Not Just a Dress

The application of Riggins' work to the reading of the wire car above suggests that the object under investigation is more than just a wire car. Riggins' analysis could of course be applied to many different contexts – from children's play (Mitchell, 2010) through to the workplace. In this section, I consider the particular case of dress, drawing on the denotative aspects of an item of clothing (the history of wedding dresses, hot-pants, neckties, or academic robes). This is a rich area for exploration as the body of work by Taylor (2002) and Küchler and Miller (2005) and the many dress publications by Berg Publishers attest. But the actual stories – the connotative meanings – that are evoked by the items of clothing, or what Sandra Weber and I describe elsewhere as *dress stories* (Weber and Mitchell, 2004), belong to an area that is less well developed in the area of dress research although, as Taylor (2002) highlights, there is a close relationship between oral history and the study of dress. Quoting Majorie Shostak, she writes, 'No more elegant tool exists to describe the human condition than the personal narrative' (Taylor, 2002: 242). In this section, then, I consider some of the ways in which visual and other arts-based methodologies might be applied to personal and social meanings and engaging in social research.

Working with family albums

As noted in the discussion of Riggins' parents' living room, and then in the analysis of the wire car, the visual is a very important component of this work. One can take pictures, as I did of the wire car, or we might use family albums. Family albums are full of history and dress stories. In a fascinating study on the use of family albums as historic record, Ran Tao combines the denotative and the connotative in reflecting on the personal and political history of China (Tao, 2005). In using eight photographs of her friend Yu's mother, Ying, who was born in 1944, Tao traces significant historical movements in China, as she writes:

> Ying is my friend Yu's mother who has been experiencing great movements and changes in contemporary China. Her journey of self-discovery and social understanding spans from a girl of a mid-class family in old China, a student learning knowledge at a school of new China, a discriminated but optimistic youth, to an independent career woman and a retired teacher now. Her photographs tell us a visual story (through dress) that shows how an ordinary, routine self is intricately connected with wider social issues and social relationships. (Tao, 2005: 1)

In the essay, she traces Ying's life, starting with the 1940s where she is depicted wearing Qipao, a traditional Chinese female dress. Then she shows her in the 1950s when the People's Liberation Army freed the 'suppressed, including peasants, working class and women from the suppresser. ... Ying, with other boys and girls, was studying in a secondary school, openly and proudly. She was dressed in white uniform and wearing a red scarf called Honglingjin, which represented a part of New China's five star red flag' (2005: 3). During the Cultural Revolution (1966–76), we see Ying in a Mao jacket. 'Ying, as a child of middle-class family, could not escape the terrible political storm. Her father was put into prison and then sent to some reform-through-labour farms ... Ying always felt self abased and shamed among her classmates and then isolated herself from them' (2005: 4). In the 1980s – the spring of China – we see Ying dressed in a plain shirt and simple hairstyle. As Tao writes, this demonstrates 'people's life and characters then, simple, austere but sincere and honest' (2005: 6). In the 1990s, when there is more prosperity in China, we see a picture of Ying with her daughter Yu; as a young woman, Yu is wearing a beautiful sweater that her mother would never have dreamed of when she was in her 20s. Finally, we see Ying in the twenty-first century on the occasion of her 63rd birthday. She is dressed in more Western attire, but there is another photo from the same era, which suggests access to a more contemporary Chinese-influenced dress. As Tao concludes, 'Images in her family photographs greatly enhance our understanding of the human condition and existence of human agency with its wider backgrounds' (2005: 10).

Memory work

Memory work through 'deliberate remembering', as Annette Kuhn (1996) writes, can serve as a useful way of engaging in personal and social narrative as well. One way of using memory to study dress is through Patricia Hampl's (1996) work on first draft and second draft memory writing. In this approach to memory, which also draws on the work on collective memory of Frigga Haug (1999) and June Crawford et al.

(1992), the point is to move from unselfconsciously mediated remembering (free recall-first draft memory) to working back in a systematic way that interrogates memory (second draft memory). In various memory-work projects, the focus has been on the act of deliberate remembering – as opposed to solely accidental remembering – with the idea that working with the past can serve as a useful feminist tool for contesting (and sometimes recovering) the past. Thus, when Jacqueline Reid-Walsh and I (2002) were studying the 'afterlife' of children's popular culture for our book *Researching Children's Popular Culture*, we each decided to engage in deliberate remembering around cowgirl play, which included dressing up as a cowgirl. The denotative aspect of our work was around the popularity of cowboy play in the 1940s and 1950s, and then the significance of cowboy play in more contemporary nostalgia, as explored in the *Toy Story* films, *Toy Story* (1995) and *Toy Story 2* (1999), through the characters of Woody the Cowboy in both films and Jessie the Cowgirl in *Toy Story 2*. Drawing on published accounts of women's memories, including bell hooks' (1994) story of a missing photograph of herself in a cowgirl suit, we wrote first- and second-draft memories of growing up in the 1950s and early 1960s, highlighting some of the dress-related features of these memories. Jacqueline Reid-Walsh writes:

> Talking with my parents, during the summer of 1999, of this period of my childhood, I am reminded of my girlhood suit. I vainly look for old photographs. In my mind I am able to imagine myself again complete with red braids. The photographs, it seems, have either become submerged because of my parents' many moves, or more likely are somewhere in my small apartment locker. I asked them about the cowgirl suit. All I remember is the fringe on the vest, the holsters, with guns, and the hat. But apparently, I had boots and a skirt as well. My parents related how we went to Frontier Land, and my father told how one of the lead actors of the television series – he played Bat Masteron, I think – came and enacted a shoot-out on the streets of Dodge. (Mitchell and Reid-Walsh, 2002: 63–4)

She later goes back to a second draft of this memory; in this account she interrogates the details and images and looks for gaps. She writes:

> … it soon became apparent that I had mis-remembered the events and elided different periods from my childhood together. … My parents were able to correct me about numerous specifics, for instance the actor who came to Frontier Land was Hugh O'Brien who played Wyatt Earp, the other television shows [that I couldn't remember] that were westerns were Roy Rogers, Hopalong Cassidy, Have Gun Will Travel, and my cowgirl suit was specifically a Dale Evans outfit which was pale blue. Most significantly, as the differences between shows such as Roy Rogers and Wyatt Earp indicate … a collapsing of time has occurred in my memory. I was a little girl in the early grades of primary school when I liked the singing cowboy and his partner Dale Evans, and older when I liked the drama series, Wyatt Earp. The trip to Frontier Land was at a later stage in middle school. … [W]hat is the significance of the mis-remembering and the elision of the two periods?. … Perhaps in a Gilligan-inspired move

I am attempting to move back in my own life to a period before the shutter of adolescence was erected, to connect with the earlier 'child' and discover who she was. (2002: 64–5)

Dress in this account of remembering/mis-remembering is a central organizing feature and it offers a way of linking the personal to theories of identity.

Then, in *Not Just Any Dress*, Sandra Weber and I (Weber and Mitchell, 2004) include dress stories, many of them based on memory work, from 30 authors, on everything from a little girl Polly Flinders dress through to school uniforms, burial dresses, maternity outfits and prom dresses, and even the story of a dress that the author was wearing on 11 September 2001 in New York City. Ardra Cole writes a moving essay called 'The Christmas Doll' that harkens back to her childhood, but then also brings memory forward to a much later time of caring for her mother. In the essay, Cole recounts the memory of the stories her mother told her of her special dolls received every Christmas. As she writes, 'My mother loved to tell doll stories – of the long hours she and her best friend spent playing with their dolls, dressing and undressing and dressing them again, changing their outfits to suit the many and varied occasions they imagined' (Weber and Mitchell, 2004: 118). Cole goes on to talk about how much her mother loved to dress her up:

Every occasion or event demanded a new outfit. Wardrobe was as much a part of the ritual and tradition associated with special occasions, as were each occasion's social, cultural, or religious customs. Donning a new nightgown preceded the hanging of the Christmas stocking; Christmas dinner could not be eaten in anything but a new dress; a birthday girl couldn't start a new year in last year's attire. ... (Weber and Mitchell, 2004: 119)

The poignancy of the essay is revealed in a shift of time and place to when Cole is an adult going to see her mother one Christmas, only the family home no longer exists, and her mother's new home is a nursing home where she is living because she can no longer live alone. Cole writes about sizing up her mother's condition and realizing that, no matter what she needs in order to carry out that Christmas doll tradition, a dress is 'not just a dress'.

With no time to change her clothes, I could at least dress up what she was already wearing. Rifling through her dresser drawer I found the beads and matching earrings I had bought her for last Easter. I fastened her necklace and clipped her earrings in place. The Christmas corsage I had bought for her lay unforgotten in her lap. I picked it up, pressed it under her nose and pinned it close to her left shoulder so she could smell the carnations – her favourite flowers – if her head happened to move in that direction. ... As I wheeled her through the doorway, I glanced back at the colourfully wrapped parcels on her bedside table. I would help her open them later: the cozy flannelette nightie that she would wear to bed tonight and a new dress for Christmas day... (Weber and Mitchell, 2004: 143)

This account of dressing her mother takes us back to the description of Ardra's childhood at the beginning of the essay, and we see the Christmas doll in a new light.

Installations

Another way in which dress and material culture can be explored is through installation. As Delahunt (2007) defines installation, it 'is art made for a specific space exploiting certain qualities of that space' (cited in Cole and McIntyre, 2008: 289). Marcel Duchamp is regarded as the first artist to use everyday objects to create works of installation art (Cole and McIntyre, 2008). T-shirts in Figure 3.1 might be regarded as an installation. In artfully arranging the T-shirts on a desk in the classroom as objects, the teacher-photographer makes sure that we pay attention to the messages. There is no wearer to distract us.

Described briefly in Chapter 1, one of the most poignant installations I have ever seen is titled *Life Lines* and was created by Ardra Cole and Maura McIntyre as part of *The Alzheimer Project* (Cole and McIntyre, 2006).

> The venue: a public building located in the downtown core of Toronto, Ontario, Canada's largest city, and home to three million people. The building, the central broadcast centre for the country's national public radio, is open to the public 24 hours a day and has a high volume of pedestrian traffic. (You are one of over 30,000 people who pass by the exhibit during its month-long stay; one of hundreds, perhaps thousands, more who 'view' the text during its stay in cyberspace.) The exhibit occupies most of an expansive space that serves as one of the main throughfare [*sic*] corridors. The busyness of the area is tempered by its size and, despite the steady flow of people through the space, it has an ambience of quiet reverence. Entering from the street through a set of double glass doors, you are immediately struck by the presence of a free-standing clothesline. You pause to take stock of what is around you.
>
> A large plexiglass sign on one of the long walls grabs your attention: 'The Alzheimer's Project.' You return your gaze to the clothesline and slowly walk its length. You trace the line of laundry from a baby's diaper to lace garter belt to multi-hooked brassiere to adult diaper. The overwashed, white, female undergarments mark the shift in personal power and changing nature of dependence across a life span. You are tempted to move closer to the adorable baby's undershirt to see if it smells like powder; you giggle to yourself as you imagine slipping away to try on the padded push-up bra; you groan as you recognize the full-size nylon panties with the elastic waistband slightly stretched; and you pause in silence in front of the adult size diaper hanging heavily at the end of the life line. (http://ccfi.educ.ubc.ca/publication/insights/v09n01/articles/cole.html, accessed 11 November 2009)

The vastness of the installation is part of the point of the work; the clothesline (life line) stretches across the huge expanse of the CBC building like a clothesline in someone's huge backyard or in the wide open spaces of a rural area.

Figure 3.4 *Life Lines*

Performing dress

Performance as an arts-based methodology has been used by a number of research-ers, particularly in the context of the body. Ross Gray, for example, in his work with women with breast cancer, has used performance as both a mode of inquiry with women but also as a mode of dissemination for reaching physicians in relation to more sensitive and appropriate delivery of health services (see Gray and Sinding, 2002). Inspired by the work of Gray and others (Gray et al., 2000), Sandra Weber and I embarked a few years ago on a series of dress-body performances, carefully crafting a sequence of wardrobe moments and then performing them at various conferences and live performance venues. Once we even rented a small theatre to stage a two-act dress performance *Accessorizing Death*. As I describe in the essay 'Was it something I wore?' (Mitchell, 2004), these performances clearly place the performer in a type of embodied space. When I performed one of these vignettes, called *Was it Something I Wore*, I narrated an episode of sexual harassment that I experienced while I was supervising a group of student teachers in a Montreal high school. The harasser was one of the male teachers. When I performed this scenario (and really this is so for most of these scenarios), the audience was mostly made up of female educators:

> I sense the nods around me that pick up on many of the collective (and cumulative) tensions of our lives as women. The scenario is part of a collec-tion of short vignettes called *Wardrobe Moments*, all based on autobiographical clothing episodes in my life: the role of the little black turtleneck in distancing myself from being 'just a teacher', my love/hate relationship with suits, the politics of dressing for interviews and so on. When I perform these scenes on

stage, I also include slide projections of photographs from my picture album. There is one of me, for example, looking very self-satisfied as a first-year teacher in my horn-rimmed glasses and artsy black turtleneck. The caption reads 'I am a writer, perhaps, and not "just a teacher"'. Then there's another of me dressed for success in the 1980s-version gray flannel suit, and another of me in my not-quite-suit denim ensemble but with matching top and bottom. The centrepiece of these wardrobe moments, for me, at least, is *Was it Something I Wore?* – the only scenario for which there is no photograph, and hence, no visual evidence [of sexual harassment]. There is only my testimony, and maybe that's the real point in trying to understand sexual harassment. (Mitchell, 2004: 85)

It is hard to put into words what I felt as I performed this piece. Perhaps I would manipulate my audience to a certain extent because the scenarios that came before – *Little Black Turtleneck* and *Does It Suit You?* – are humorous and a little light, even though they carry a deeper message. When I would start into *Was it Something I Wore?*, I would almost feel as though I should issue a warning: 'This is no laughing matter.' But it really wasn't necessary. It was almost as though the minute I started into the performance of *Was it Something I Wore?*, every woman in the room knew what was coming; and, while this episode was not the beginning of my work as an activist-academic, it is one of the dress stories or wardrobe moments that I keep front-and-centre in working with dress and with material culture.

Conclusion

Ian Hodder (1998), as an archaeologist, refers to the interpretive potential of working with the mute evidence of artefacts and written documents:

> Such evidence, unlike the spoken word, endures physically and thus can be separated across space and time from its author, producer or user. Material traces thus often have to be interpreted without the benefit of indigenous commentary. (1998: 155)

Hodder goes on to point out that too often the spoken word is privileged over the written and artefactual, even when we know the limitations of the various actors. As he notes: '… actors often seem curiously inarticulate about the reasons they dress in particular ways, choose particular pottery designs, or discard dung in particular locations' (1998: 155). Informants in a study may even say something quite different in an interview when asked the same question a day later. While the point here is not to discredit qualitative studies that rely primarily on interviews and focus groups, it is worth considering the interpretive possibilities of objects, documents and things: the wire car, a cowgirl outfit, uniforms as prescribed dress and so on. In so doing, we can situate the thing or object within broader societal questions.

Elsewhere, I have written about the idea of a new materialism in childhood studies as read through the study of children's play objects (Mitchell, 2010). As Edwards and Hart observe, 'Materiality can be said ... to have a positivistic character, in that it is concerned with real physical objects in a world that is physically apprehendable not only through vision but through embodied relations of smell, taste, touch and hearing' (2004: 3). As real physical objects, artefacts carry with them social and historical narratives that have seldom been investigated in posing and studying research questions related to health, education and social development. At the same time, they have the potential to evoke and carry with them autobiographical narratives. In this respect, work related to auto-ethnography, autobiography and narrative inquiry can be enriched through the inclusion of texts of material culture, as I have argued in this chapter. Located within textual approaches to research, under the umbrella of qualitative research and visual studies, the study of material culture in the social sciences is relatively new. It is not without precedent, however, and it can productively draw on work in anthropology, archaeology, environmental studies, art history, communication and dress studies, to name some of the academic areas about which the study of material culture is already underway. What is critical about social research is its potential to raise (and answer) new and ongoing questions, its potential to offer new evidence related to social accessories, and its ability to complement other qualitative methods (photo elicitation, memory work, autobiographical interviews). In such contexts, a dress is much more than just a dress, and an object is not just an object.

FOUR

Seeing for ourselves: A case for community-based photography

Introduction

There is probably no area of visual participatory research that has received more attention in the last decade than the use of simple point-and-shoot cameras (from disposable cameras and simple load cameras to digital cameras and mobile phones) by community photographers. The terms to describe this work vary from the 'shooting back' projects of James Hubbard (1994) involving native American youth and those of Wong involving children of the Nairobi slums to native image-making techniques (Wagner, 1979, cited in Packard, 2008), photo elicitation projects, the creative storytelling and photography work of Mary Brinton Lykes (1997, 1999, 2001a, 2001b) with women in war-torn Guatemela, photovoice (the term coined and patented by Caroline Wang and her colleagues to describe a type of grassroots policy-making where populations whose voices are often absent from policy are given simple cameras to express their point of view on a particular issue), and the photography work of Wendy Ewald (1985, 1992, 1996; Ewald and Lightfoot, 2001) with children of Appalachia, northern Canada, India and the townships of South Africa. These projects focus on groups of people who do not normally get to speak: the homeless (Hubbard, 1994), rural Chinese women (Wang, 1999), dialysis patients (Allen and Hutchison, 2009), girls on the street in Rwanda (Umurungi et al., 2008), school children identifying issues of safety and security in Swaziland (Mitchell, 2009b), children in informal settlements in South Africa (Mitchell et al., 2006b) and college students in China in relation to sexuality (Tao and Mitchell, 2010), to name only some of the geographic areas, focus populations and thematic areas covered. Rather than trying to map out this vast literature on the various projects – which arguably could be the subject of a whole book – what I set out to do in this chapter is to offer something that has a *how-to* component to it, drawing primarily from the various photovoice projects that I have been involved in over the last decade, and then a section that attempts to probe some of the conceptual areas that seem to be important in planning and interpreting findings. I think it is important to avoid any sort of orthodoxy in this work, and to avoid making sweeping statements that suggest that there is only one right way to do this type of research. Because many of the ethical issues are covered in Chapter 2, and the interpretive issues in Chapter 6, in this chapter, I will focus more on the doing.

Community-Based Photography: Is There a 'How-to'?

Throughout this chapter, I alternate between the term *community-based photography* and Caroline Wang's (1999) term *photovoice* to describe the work. Within a qualitative research context, this work is regarded as a radical departure from more conventional forms of data-collecting, such as focus groups, questionnaires and interviews, incorporating both the possibilities for visualizing what is at stake (through the eyes of community photographers) and shifting the boundaries of knowledge (through the eyes of insiders). Within a research context, this work also expands our understanding of the visual, particularly in relation to first-time photographers: what does it mean to see? As Packard (2008) argues, however, this area of qualitative research requires a critical lens. Not all visual work necessarily alters the unequal relationship between researcher and researched, and not all work using this methodology is necessarily more illuminating in relation to the issues under study than other visual approaches (participatory video or drawing), or other qualitative approaches (narrative life histories or even more conventional interviews). Packard offers as an example his work with a group of homeless participants, highlighting some of the limitations of how it might have been empowering for the participants.

Since 2002, I have worked on more than a dozen community-based photography projects, and have supervised many more involving master's and doctoral students in their field work. This work has varied from studies carried out under the auspices of organizations such as UNICEF and CIDA, to those pursued through the channels of university research. The work has been drawn from a variety of geographic locations (Sierra Leone, Swaziland, South Africa, Ethiopia, Rwanda, Trinidad and Tobago, China, and Canada), with various populations (children in informal settlements, university students at McGill, students and faculty in an agricultural faculty, teachers, community health care workers, primary and secondary school students, pre-school children and child care workers), and addressing such issues as poverty, safety and security, HIV and AIDS, stigma, economic empowerment, environmental issues and sexuality.

Even within the limits of this data set, there have been many variations on 'doing photovoice'. In one project that I conducted with 11- and 12-year-old children in Swaziland, *Feeling safe and feeling not so safe*, the entire process of getting started and taking pictures involved sessions that lasted 45 minutes, followed up later that same day with a one-hour session out on the barren school grounds, where the children sat in small groups looking at their envelopes of pictures. In another project, the introductory component took place over several weeks, involving teachers and health care workers; this still continues six years later with various other participatory visual engagements (drawings, collage, participatory video). The types of cameras available and the use of technology (disposable cameras, simple point-and-shoot cameras, digital cameras, different models of mobile phones), the varying group size, the circumstances under which the project can take place (including time available and number of sessions), and the age and experience of the participants all influence the outcome of the work. In our edited book titled *Putting People in the Picture* on working with the visual (mostly within South Africa) and in which many of the chapters address some aspect of community-based photovoice projects, my colleagues and I (De Lange et al., 2007) not only note the range of issues, settings and participants – 11- and 12-year-olds photographing informal settlements, ninth-grade students in a rural community looking at stigma in the context of HIV and AIDS, women teachers looking at sexual violence, victims of a polluted urban landscape commenting on their health – but also acknowledge the range of issues identified by the researchers themselves (ethics, technologies in working with data, and interpreting the data).

What is difficult to ascertain from a single article or a chapter about a photovoice project is the full process itself: what was done when, by whom, to whom, under what circumstances, for what reason, and with what consequences? Here, I map out a general set of practices that the research teams with whom I have worked with have found helpful. Broadly speaking, the practices of doing photovoice can be divided into (1) before taking pictures, (2) taking pictures, (3) after taking the picture, and an optional (4) making photos public. The practices I highlight are ones that I think evoke the richest possibilities for not only seeing through the eyes of participants but also taking the resulting visual products as far as possible towards social change; this last point is described in more detail in the last chapter of the book.

Before Taking Pictures

The time devoted to getting started depends on the context – whether you are working with a group that you have a long-term relationship with, such as a group of students or a community group, or whether you are just meeting them for the first time as a researcher, and even how many sessions you will be able to have with the group. Regardless of the context, we have found that it is important that there is some time allotted to getting to know the participants and understanding their relationship to the issues under investigation. In one of the first photovoice projects that we conducted in rural South Africa, involving 25 teachers and community health care workers, the focus was on *learning together* (the *Learning Together* Project was an NRF-funded study in South Africa).

In order to identify challenges and solutions to addressing HIV and AIDS, we decided to start with a drawing activity: teachers drew community health care workers and community health care workers drew teachers. Their drawings provided an entry point to come together in mixed groups, and to establish a type of common ground (De Lange et al., in press). Drawings have their own advantages and disadvantages. However, in this case, they were helpful for establishing the use of the visual (seeing for ourselves) in a group that was not familiar with using cameras, for ensuring group participation (in an environment where there had been few opportunities to participate in interactive ways), for setting an agenda within the group (as opposed to from the outside), and from the beginning, for showing (rather than telling) that it was the groups themselves that would be the interpreters of the data that came out of the project. In the end, through the use of drawings, small groups made up of teachers and community health care workers engaged in a process of interpreting what their images might mean. It was also enjoyable – and even though there may be, among some adult groups, a hesitation to draw, in this case, the group was clearly keen to return to the activity.

Preparing to take pictures 1

A crash course in camera work and learning some photo angles probably best describes the next stage. Packard (2008) makes the observation that, with widespread access to cameras in the general public, there is probably less of a need for the researcher to take on a teacher role. This may be true in Western contexts, and may also be true of well-educated participants in Ethiopia or South Africa who will have their own digital cameras. It is less likely, however, to be the case with rural populations in Africa, and may also vary in relation to the age of participants (the very young and the very old may not have had access to cameras). At a minimum, this session has to address the basics of operating the cameras and making sure that participants understand such basics as operating the flash. In the *Learning Together* group of close to 25 participants, there were at least five of the members of our research team available to offer assistance. The segment of the crash course on camera angles, photo subjects and other aspects of composition may not always be possible, and some would argue unnecessary (and, in fact, inappropriate because it may influence participants to take only certain types of pictures). However, we have found it useful to bring along copies of a few pictures representing different angles (a close-up, a distance shot, a shot of looking up and where the photographer is positioned on the floor, a shot of looking down and where the photographer is above the photo subject) and photos of different subjects (posed and staged images of people, landscapes, objects and parts of the body). For some, the idea of taking pictures of objects and things as opposed to taking pictures of people may be quite new. In essence, this component of the session is about looking. We have never been quite certain whether this part of the process actually makes much difference to the overall quality of images produced, especially with first-time photographers, other than that it opens up possibilities. Participants have mentioned in follow-up interviews that they valued learning new skills during these crash-course sessions.

Where possible, this session on learning about camera use should also offer participants an opportunity to take pictures. In the *Learning Together* project, we had mixed groups of community health care workers and teachers working together to take pictures of *Feeling strong and feeling not so strong*. It is a prompt that is low risk, fun to work on in groups (of adults or children), and ensures that everyone has a chance to use the camera as well as help to direct photo shots. We try to avoid using a prompt that is going to be used in the overall project. In the case of the *Learning Together* project, our focus was on recognizing challenges and solutions to addressing HIV and AIDS in the community, so *Feeling strong and feeling not so strong* as a prompt was sufficiently removed from the main focus. This component of the session doesn't have to last more than 30–40 minutes – and, ideally, is followed up by a debriefing session where participants have a chance to give their impressions, talk about what they found easy or difficult about the activity and, in the case of working with digital cameras, have a chance to look back over the images taken. If the pictures have to be developed, then the beginning of the next session can be devoted to having groups look at their *Feeling strong and feeling not so strong* photos – and can even involve participants engaging in a first stage of analysis around a few key questions: Which photo(s) are the most visually interesting? Which ones best show feeling strong or feeling not so strong? Are there any observations about gender or class? If possible, each small group should give a short presentation to the whole group. If working with digital cameras, then, of course having an LCD projector is ideal. If working with the physicality of photographs (with its own advantages), then groups can use poster board or flip-chart paper to present their findings.

Preparing to take pictures 2

The issue of prompts for the photovoice project needs to be considered carefully. Obviously, because the focus of each project differs, it is difficult to be prescriptive. In our work, we have tended to use something open-ended but that is also quite specific: *Feeling strong and feeling not so strong*; *Feeling safe and feeling not so safe*; *Challenges and solutions to addressing HIV and AIDS*; *Challenges and solutions to addressing stigma*; and *Challenges and solutions to women's economic empowerment*. One of the most open-ended prompts our team has used is *Issues in my life* or *A day in my life*.

A prompt can also be framed within a broader analysis of a topic; for example, in the TIG Xpress project involving young people in Toronto, Canada, and rural KwaZulu-Natal, South Africa, the focus was on the structural features of HIV and AIDS (Larkin et al., 2007): each group participated in a workshop that highlighted the connections between HIV and AIDS and global inequities. In working through a chart of the micro and macro determinants of HIV risk, the youth could see that individual behaviour such as unsafe sex, drug use and the presence of sexually transmitted infections (STIs) is only part of the larger picture. Social factors, including gender violence, racism, immigration, poverty, war and other forms of conflict and inequity, also play a crucial role.

The presentation was followed by a discussion – and in the case of the young people in South Africa, the session included what might be regarded as a media literacy activity. The participants working in pairs or trios looked at enlargements of some of the images (minus captions) produced by the group in Toronto, talked about how they thought the images linked to the structural features of HIV and AIDS, and what they thought would be appropriate captions. Only then did they go off to take their own photos (Larkin et al., 2007).

Informed consent

The preparing-to-take-pictures component of the project also feeds into a discussion of ethical issues: what can you photograph other than faces (and why)? This can be a thorny issue, but one that, like the discussion of camera angles, also contributes to building the skills of those working with the visual in relation to media ethics and informed consent. If a group is going to be taking photographs in public (as opposed to, say, the somewhat protected environment of a workshop setting), it is important to try to raise some consciousness about the rights of others to not be photographed. Even in school settings, where subjects who are not part of the project are likely to be filmed, this is critical. A simple consent form can be produced ahead of time that photo subjects could be asked to sign. As I highlight in Chapter 2, informed consent is far from easy to negotiate, and when the topic of study is about HIV and AIDS, where there is often already a great deal of associated stigma, it is even more important to incorporate some form of informed consent into the project. In the pre-photo-taking stage, I like to show images of objects (or a landscape, or a part of a body, such as a hand or a leg) as possible subjects for exploring the issue at hand. Not only does this help to address the concern around informed consent and human subjects, but it also moves even very young photographers into exploring the issues in more symbolic ways.

Taking Pictures

Many of the projects in which I have been involved are organized as small group projects so that the photographers do not work alone. This is particularly the case when the photo-taking sessions occur during a workshop as opposed to participants taking the cameras away to use on their own. There are several advantages to photographers working in small groups of three or four with cost being a key one. This means that if there is a class or community group of

25 people or so, there is only a need for seven or eight cameras. However, cost is not the only consideration. The social constructions made available by the group process are also critical. I have been fascinated, for example, in going back over the group photos of three girls in Swaziland who depicted rape in the bushes (see Figure 8.4). One girl is on top of the other, and a third is taking the picture. What kind of negotiation goes on before the shutter is pressed down? How do these girls come up with the idea for staging this photograph? How do they decide who is going to be the one raped, the rapist, or the photographer of the rape?

In another dramatic photograph that I explore further in Chapter 6, a group of boys exploring issues of stigma stage a hanging. One boy is hanging, and there is no one else in sight. But there are four members of the team – the photographer, the subject and two others on the sideline who are assisting and directing, that is, carrying the school desk outside, positioning the subject and so on, and we are left to wonder about what is being said among the three boys. What kinds of discussions take place throughout the picture-taking process, and how is it decided that X will be the one to hang? Notwithstanding the discussions that, of necessity, take place, and to which we as researchers may not be privy unless we equip the participants with a tape recorder, or conduct an after-the-fact interview, the decision to ask groups rather than single participants to take photos may also contribute to richer follow-up discussions.

A special case for group work can also be made if there are any issues of safety and security occurring within the population of participants. As described in Chapter 2, a school principal with whom we worked in South Africa went into an informal settlement where his students lived, and they worked as a whole group to capture issues of poverty, unemployment and environmental issues – all the scenes that the children regarded as contributing to why so many of them worked in the market on Fridays instead of going to school. He also accompanied them into the market itself, and noted that some of the hawkers were angry at being photographed. The presence of the principal and the group itself ensured the safety of the young photographers (see also Mitchell et al., 2006a).

The main disadvantage of group work is related less to group dynamics and more to location. Taking photographs as part of a workshop may preclude shots in more natural environments unless the issue is, for example, school-based, or unless the workshop site is nearby to other habitation. In a photovoice workshop that we carried out with graduate students and faculty at the University of KwaZulu-Natal, participants were contained on campus, and in another project with a group of women principals on a leadership course, the participants carried out the initial picture taking in an empty school on a Saturday, when classes were not going on. In both cases that I describe in the following pages, photographers adapted to the picture-taking process by using staged shots. In the TIG Xpress project involving a group of 20 young people, the group took pictures in the village where the workshop was held. Thus, although the work was carried out in groups, the community setting was natural. The *Learning Together* project involved both group photos at the workshop site (in preparing for the *Feeling strong and feeling not so strong* activities) and individual photos of challenges and solutions in addressing HIV and AIDS in the community.

After Taking Pictures: Community-Based Interpretations

What to do with the photographs? As Annette Kuhn writes, this is not necessarily a straightforward process:

> Photographs are evidence, after all. Not that they are to be taken at face value, necessarily, nor that they mirror the real not even that a photograph offers any self-evident relationship between itself and what it shows. Simply that a photograph can be material for interpretation. ... In order to show what it is evidence of a photograph must always point you away from itself. (Kuhn, 1996: 474)

Working with the photographers and their pictures is of course at the heart of the research, and includes the first moment when participants have a chance to look at their photographs, continuing through to them actually working with the photographs, and of course to the discussions and perspectives on the photos among the research team. At the most basic level, there must be time for participants to just look at their pictures in a free flowing way. As Barbara Harris (2002) notes in her study of people picking up their pictures at a photo shop in a mall, this part of the process is critical. In one of our projects with school children, where we had photographed every aspect of the process, we actually went back over the photographs of photographers looking, noting the intensity of the gaze by children who were otherwise somewhat uninterested in school (Pithouse and Mitchell, 2007).

Nonetheless, there needs to be some time (and context) for photographers to sift, sort and comment on the photographs. Where possible, it is good to organize some sort of walk about, where participants get to walk around and look at everyone's photographs. When we have worked with pictures that had to be developed, we enlarged a few, along with some regular-sized prints, and put them up on the wall for people to look at when they arrived for the workshop. In the case of working with digital photos that can be printed out, we, as a research team, have often chosen some photos simply at random, and hung them on the wall. This part of the process precedes working with any individual photos.

Then, in working with individual photos, the process might involve individuals or groups offering captions or choosing the photographs that best represent the issues. In the *Learning Together* project, teachers and community health care

Figure 4.1   Participants working with their photographs

workers came back to working in mixed groups so that they could compare and contrast each other's photos, and were asked: What do the pictures of teachers and health care workers have in common? How do they differ? Is there one photograph out of the work of the various group members that stands out? In group work, we have always built in time for groups to actually present their analysis to the whole group and to the research team.

In a workshop session, participants used flip-chart paper to organize their findings as photo-narratives or poster-narratives. I see this work as drawing on the analytical skills of the photographers themselves. What do the participants see as important in the images? What points would they like to convey through their images? The question of captioning is an interesting one, as Chaplin (2006) and others have discussed in the literature: to caption or not to caption? Du Toit (2006) regards the process of caption writing an important part of the process, and within her work offers some guidance on what constitutes a caption. Specifically, how the words of the participants are used in the process may vary, but what is critical is that the photographers have a chance to talk about their images or the process of taking the pictures. This should not be a forced process and, in my experience, this has been one of the richest parts of the work, particularly in group work. For example, I have seen groups in heated debate when choosing eight to ten photographs that represent the topic under investigation. Groups may also work on choosing a title; interestingly, genres will, and often do, vary. Some of the poster-narratives become a type of storytelling (see De Lange et al., 2006). In other work groups, the participants will follow a more factual analytic; for

Figure 4.2   Poster-narrative as an analytic tool

example, one indicated that 'these photos speak to poverty in relation to women; and these photos speak to some of the solutions'. At the level of greatest intensity, I have seen a group of community photographers engage in an in-depth analysis of the gendered face of poverty in Rwanda, using the poster-narrative as the vehicle for communication of their analysis to the rest of the group.

Another approach to participatory analysis, as Larkin and colleagues (2007) highlight, is the SHOWED model, used as part of a photovoice project in Toronto with urban youth:

> *What do we **S**ee or how do we name this problem?*
> *What is really **H**appening?*
> *How does the story relate to **O**ur lives?*
> ***W**hy does this problem or strength exist? What are the root causes?*
> *How might we become **E**mpowered now that we better understand the problem?*
> *What can we **D**o about it?*

In Larkin et al. (2007: 37–8), we include a staged image of a woman whose face we cannot see. The community photographer has given the title *Immigrant Woman* to the picture. Below, I include an excerpt from the SHOWED analysis:

- *What do we **S**ee and how do we name this problem?*
  The picture shows an immigrant woman from a developing or underdeveloped country. Surrounded by famous corporate brands, the picture

attempts to place the weak and vulnerable position of the woman in a larger economic and political context. She is positioned in a suitcase that moves her around the globe, despite her will, and only for the profit of multinational corporations. Being put beside famous corporate commodities signals the commodification of her labour and her individuality.

- *What is really _Happening_?*
  This woman has been made vulnerable to HIV and AIDS by unjust global economic forces that destroy local jobs, create unsafe and exploitive working conditions for women workers in developing countries, and induce many of them to immigrate and seek refuge in foreign (often developed) countries despite their will not to leave their home countries. The problem here is unfair patterns of economic development that create mass poverty, which leads to the spread of HIV and AIDS and other socio-economic disasters.

- *How does the story relate to _Our_ lives?*
  We, in developed countries, are the main consumers of products that are made cheaply in developing countries at the expense of women's health and economic social security. We are the beneficiaries of this unjust state of global affairs; so we cannot ignorantly assume that AIDS is the problem of only the developing and underdeveloped countries, and that it has no relation to our consumption patterns and privileged lifestyles. (Larkin et al., 2007: 37)

If, as previously noted, the participants have been using digital cameras, there are several possibilities for them to present their images to the audiences. One is to print out pictures right there on the spot, something that we have done in a number of projects. In a project in Rwanda, for example, group members coming back from their photo shoot in a market simply went over to the small portable printer and printed out the images. In other cases where we have used digital cameras, participants downloaded their images onto a laptop, and then selected a series of their images to be presented to the whole group through an LCD projector. In work with more sophisticated audiences, the group has presented an actual PowerPoint presentation, complete with title and 10 to 15 images with captions.

One of the advantages of presenting the photo images in the form of PowerPoint slides relates to being able to project the images on a big screen. The whole group can look at the images together and discuss the images, while individuals can point out the significance of their interpretations. Figure 4.3, taken by a group of faculty lecturers from an Ethiopian university, shows an image of potential gender-based violence just outside the gates of the university. While everyone in the room was familiar with the situation, being able to look at the image during the discussion was very important. Re-discovering it made the situation real, not just for one individual, and not only when the event initially happened. It allowed the event to be re-discovered and shared by others who also had found themselves in the same situation, which made it impossible for any one group member to ignore or subvert it.

Figure 4.3   Faculty lecturers presenting analysis of safety and security

Figure 4.4   Presenting PowerPoint on *Feeling safe and feeling not so safe*

Making Photos Public

I offer this section not as an absolute requirement of a photovoice project but one that, in my view, extends the life and reach of photovoice and, in the language of development, might be regarded as *value added*. While I extensively discuss the practicalities of display in Chapter 10, here I want to highlight more the place of *making public* in the process itself. What do participants make of the work of the group as a whole? Of their own work? How can the project lead to planning and the politics of representation? Where do we go from here? This is probably the component of the work that is most critical in relation to changing methods/changing worlds. Who, in the eyes of the photographers, should see these photos? How and where should they be presented? Are there any photographs that should not be exhibited, particularly in the context of confidentiality? This last point is important because it is only after the pictures have been taken that the photographers can have a full realization of protecting photo subjects. In the *Learning Together* project, the participating schools and the community health clinic all had different ideas about how best to show their photographs. For example, the community health care workers were quite happy to have a permanent exhibition at the entrance of the clinic.

Figure 4.5   Curatorial statement

Many people in the village, along with international visitors, visit the clinic, and would see the exhibition. One of the schools noted that there was no place in the school to exhibit the pictures and, even if there were, few people from the community would see the photos. Any public display would have to take place in the village itself. Beyond where and in what format (both issues taken up in Chapter 10), an important part of the post-picture-taking process is the design of the exhibition (which pictures and why, in relation to a particular audience) and decision-making related to a title and the production of a curatorial statement. The curatorial statement is very simply a statement by the photographers themselves, about the exhibition and what it is meant to convey to audiences. Obviously, the statements can vary in length, but experience indicates that a text of 150–200 words is a good length. Along with the title, a list of the photographers and any acknowledgements serves to *make a statement* about the collection (see box below). While there may be differences of opinion about who writes the curatorial statement, where possible it should come from the photographers themselves. It should be their exhibition.

Through Our Eyes: The Fight against HIV and AIDS

World-wide approximately 5000 young people between the ages of 15 and 25 become infected with HIV every day. (UNAIDS, 2008)

The photographs in this exhibition were all taken by learners in the Vulindlela district of KwaZulu-Natal, South Africa, as part of the 'Learning Together: Participatory methods for an integrated approach to addressing HIV and AIDS in rural KwaZulu-Natal' project. This collection, from a photo-voice project with Grade 8 and 9 learners in one of the schools participating in the project, tries to identify, understand, and interpret incidents related to stigma and discrimination against people living with and affected by HIV and AIDS. This is a critical issue in an area where young people are particularly at risk. The stigma of AIDS may mean that young people do not access voluntary counseling and testing (VCT) services. Stigma then becomes a death sentence.

The learners used inexpensive 'point and shoot' cameras. 'On location' at school and by 'staging' their own pictures, they explored the pivotal question: 'What is stigmatisation like in your community?' They were then asked to write about their photographs. Some wrote in isiZulu while others chose to write in English.

The photographs in the collection, numbering more than 140, serve in their sepia expressiveness as poignant narratives of the everyday experiences of young people in many rural areas of South Africa, and their concerns about the present and the future. They represent possibilities for the power of community voices to bring about change. They also serve as dramatic reminders of the significance of the voices of young people everywhere to address HIV and AIDS.

Other points

Follow-up interviews can also be important; for example, working with groups often means that the voices of individuals get lost. Where possible, we have tried to follow up with individuals. These follow-up interviews may take on a photo-elicitation format, where individuals are asked questions such as: 'Which photograph are you most proud of?', 'Which photograph that you took says the most about the issue?', 'How do you think of yourself now as a photographer?', 'What difference does this work make?' and 'What difference could this work make?' Some other points are as follows:

1 Take photographs of every stage of the process.
2 If working with photos from point-and-shoot cameras (versus digital), always make duplicate copies.
3 Before giving out a package of photos to a group or individual, remove the negatives and duplicate set for safe keeping.
4 Label sets (and include as much information as possible): name, sex, age if relevant, school or location.
5 Pictures from the collection should be returned to the community itself. Community photographers should have at least some photos from the collection for their own use. Cost will determine whether there is a group set of photos for the institution or whether individuals receive copies of their own photos.

Working with the Data

Many at this point may exclaim: Help! What do you do with the pictures? Does a picture stand alone? It is hard to answer the 'What do you do with the pictures?' question in any definitive way. For researchers who are comfortable with the idea of thick description, the work of Kuhn (1996), for example, on working with a single photograph and our adaptations of that (Moletsane and Mitchell, 2007), suggest the possibility of an in-depth unravelling through work with a small amount of data. It is also possible to carry out codings, as per the work of Rose (2001) with large collections. With some collections of work, we have been interested in the idea of building a digital archive, and from that, developing procedures for engaging community members in participatory archiving (see Chapter 7).

It should be obvious from the description above that there is an abundant amount of data in any one project: the photos, the captions, the analysis carried out by the photographers through poster-narratives and researcher photographs of the process (see Chapter 8) to name only the most obvious data sources. Gillian Rose (2001) argues that coding images is complex and draws on at least three modalities: the technological, the compositional and the social. For example, in addressing production, she poses such questions as: When was it made? Where was it made? Who made it? Was it made for someone else? What were the social identities of the maker, the owner, and the subject of the image? She poses other questions about the image: What is being shown? Is it one of a series? As for *audiencing*, as she terms it, she asks the following questions: Who was the original intended audience for this image? How is it being circulated? How is it redisplayed? Does the image have a written text to guide its interpretation in its initial moment of display (for example, a caption or catalogue entry), or is it free standing? The oral presentations of the photo-narratives are also rich texts. Both data sources, however, are just the tip of the iceberg. Where possible, we have tried to video-record (and photograph) every stage of the process, as well as record audio from participants working in small groups. One might also look at how audiences respond to the photo-narratives.

Conceptualizing the Work of Community-Based Photographers: Another Angle

In various community photography projects, my attention has been captured by the range of photography styles, and whether the focus of the project has been more on the aesthetics of photos and picture-taking (see, for example, the work of Wendy Ewald), reflexivity (particularly in relation to staged photos), or social realism through photo documentary.

On the aesthetics of photos and picture-taking

The programme of the First International Conference on Visual Methods held at Leeds University in September of 2009 was made up of a vast number of presentations on community-based photography and video production, mixed in with critical issues around ethics and power. The question of aesthetics was largely absent, that is until Rosy Martin, an artist, phototherapist, photographer and memory scholar, got up to speak. In her presentation, she showed photographs from various projects she had been working on, including several involving work on her childhood home in a working-class district of London. At one point in her talk, the issue of aesthetics was on the agenda. Martin was showing us images that were works of art. In my own presentation a day earlier, I had been showing images of toilets produced by girls in Swaziland and pictures from an informal settlement as social commentary about the degree of poverty and unemployment as photographed by 11-year-olds. I am not suggesting that photos of toilets or of unemployment cannot be artistic but only that the point of these pictures was to document the social conditions *through the eyes of a child*.

There is, of course, no final answer to the question of aesthetics. Wendy Ewald (1985, 1992, 1996; Ewald and Lightfoot, 2001), in her work with children about photo literacy and aesthetics, covers the full gamut of learning about composition, developing pictures and the aesthetics of display. Indeed,

Ewald would argue that her work with children is precisely not about social documentary, even if it is sometimes read that way (Hyde, 2005). I mention aesthetics because that could be one of the ways of working with community-based photography. Wendy Ewald's work is a good example of this. In the case of researchers who are not professional photographers or people with art history backgrounds, the aesthetics of the work may be secondary – or may not be discussed at all. Does this matter? Should there be more consideration of aesthetics? How would that interfere, if at all, with the process of 'voicing' issues?

On the art of storytelling through performance: The staged photos

Photographers have been telling stories through their art ever since the medium was first invented, staging scenes of one kind or another, and direct-ing the *actors* posing before their cameras. The theatrical photograph has assumed an enormously varied range of forms over the past century and a half, and its interactions with the related arts of theatre, film and video, and the realms of advertising and journalism have taken fascinating directions. One can only wonder why such a rich vein of photographic history has been so little studied. (Theberge, 2006: 7)

In many of the photovoice projects conducted in a workshop format in schools and clinics, the participants, for reasons of safety and lack of access to transporta-tion or cost, must take their pictures on site. Almost all of the projects involving school children, for example, take place at school. In the Southern African con-text, this means that we have thousands of photos (and videos) of school-aged children in school uniform *staging* what they see as issues of stigma, or safety and security, or masculinity/femininity to name only a few areas of focus. In actual fact, throughout our warm-up activities, we often encourage participants to stage photos. As Theberge observes, this is a particular type of photographic practice, and one that can be seen in the work of Jo Spence (1995) and in her collaborations with Rosy Martin (Spence and Martin, 1988).

Staging is also a key element of much of the work of photographer Sally Mann, particularly her photographs of her own children. Similarly, many of the children in the projects organized by Wendy Ewald draw on staging. However, some might see this as a limitation of the work (after all, where is the authen-tic documentation of stigma in a community?). For us, this process has been an eye-opener in the sense that there is often a remarkable level of reflexivity in the process. The story is told both through the dramatization in the picture and through the captions produced by the photographers. In the photo of the staged suicide, for example, in Chapter 6, the provocative image produced by a group of four boys could only be conveyed through staging, and the caption 'He can't accept that he is HIV positive. He feels he has to commit suicide because he would not like to tell people that he has AIDS' powerfully conveys what they think about stigma. Pierre Doyon (2009), in his work in schools (but with video), notes a similar phenomenon represented in student-produced videos in *hall culture*. The videos are all shot on the site of the school because the students are not allowed to leave the school premises during school hours, which is when they have access to the equipment. His argument is that students demonstrate a remarkable level of creativity in how they work with and in *hall culture*, and rather than seeing constraints imposed by school officials as a limitation to this kind of work, we should regard this power differential as a genre in and of itself. Doyon observes:

> This environment will make its stamp on most of the productions for the simple reason that students have been asked to depict their life in it. They will choose locations that represent their existence, some private spaces, some public, some within the very class that they were assigned the task. Where the students chose to film may also give insights to how they perceive these spaces, how they use them, and hopefully they will appropriate these spaces in an attempt to take control of the spaces that they represent. The fact is that many school-based texts representing the lives of students will have the same basic look due to the constraints of shooting within the confines of the school. In the case of the 'baby boomer' school where these productions took place, there is a particular look. Indeed, these 'Hallway Productions' use their schools as a setting for students' productions due to the fact that the cameras cannot be removed from the schools and/or the students are reluctant to use their own time (after school) to create productions. (2009: 82)

Social realism through photo documentary

Finally, there are the photographs produced by community photographers in natural settings (outside of the institutions where students go to school, or workplace settings); for example, photos can be taken at the market, in the informal settlement, on the street, in the shopping mall, or in the home. Some of these settings can of course be problematic from the point of view of ethical clearance and safety. We found the safety issue to be a critical one in the *Friday Absenteeism Project* (Mitchell et al., 2006a) because the children were taking photographs in settings that could be dangerous (see also Chapter 10). In some cases, even having a camera in certain settings might make the photographer vulnerable. At the same time, being able to photograph in community settings is important. In the TIG Xpress project (Larkin et al., 2007) in rural KwaZulu-Natal, we made a point of holding the photography workshop in a community centre, in a village, where at least some of the photographers lived. When they wanted to photograph images of the structural features of HIV and AIDS (poverty, migration, unemployment), they had no trouble finding naturally occurring phenomena such as billboards, lack of sanitation, or other community markers. The resulting photographs and the public displays meant that audiences could identify the particular features of the landscape that were important to them and, perhaps in terms of visual literacy, made the exhibition more accessible to more people.

In another project organized on site, a group of university students and lecturers in Rwanda and several visiting lecturers worked in small groups to document *Challenges and solutions to the social and economic empowerment of women* through a visit to a local market in Kigali. Each group chose a different theme (power, inequalities, intergenerational issues) and focused on different sections of the market (textiles, clothing production, marketing fruits and vegetables) in order to arrive at an analysis of some of the key issues in their own community. Notwithstanding the fact that the photos themselves were beautiful, they conveyed a type of authenticity when they became part of a mounted exhibition. Policy makers, members of NGOs and other community organizations, government officials and university personnel viewed the exhibition. Their engagement with the exhibition was interesting because the audience could identify with images of real people and real places.

Conclusion

It's like a mirror in some odd way – many women in Chajul don't really look at themselves in a mirror often – most of them are living day to day, struggling to put food on the table for their husbands and family and/or supporting their kids as a widow, and/or supporting themselves as orphans, with little formal education and few resources. Yet through this project they began to see themselves and each other relative to each other – and relative to many women who lived in the neighboring villages to which they traveled to take pictures and gather stories – and they began to see the relative 'well-being' of women in the town of Chajul relative to the village women, many of whom still had to grind corn 4 times a day, rather than take it to the mill for milling, as one small example. So the photograph enabled comparative thinking. (Cited in Allnutt, 2009: 60)

From the extraordinary work of Caroline Wang with photography as a critical tool for women with low literacy skills in China in 1996, through to the almost ordinary photovoice projects in qualitative research 15 years later, one can deduce that community-based photography has come a long way. However, I was recently reminded that views of who is marginalized, depicted in a voiceless form, sometimes disappear from consciousness. I had been presenting some of Caroline Wang's work along with the various photovoice projects that I have previously noted, most of which occurred in Africa, to an American university audience of researchers. I was asked this question: 'These tools seem good for Africa, but how would we use them here?' The implication was that we don't have women who lack access to medical treatment or daycare; we don't have people who feel threatened on the street; or there are no 'gaps' in community services – several key areas in Wang's work. At the time that I was doing the presentation, there was a great deal of discussion about whether President Obama's new health bill would go through. I only had to ask what would happen if various constituencies were asked to document, through photography, *Challenges and solutions to addressing health care in the US*. The answer my audience would tell me would surely be some version of the need for a 'through our eyes' approach.

FIVE

Community-based video-making

Introduction

I deliberately use the somewhat ambiguous term 'video-making' in the title of this chapter as a way of avoiding the need to choose from the array of terms that might be used to refer to the process of working with communities to produce videos. I would like to, if I could, avoid using any term to refer to the camera itself because participants may be working with mobile phones, Flip video cameras or camcorders to name only three possibilities. As a result of social networking sites like YouTube or Facebook, the sophistication of mobile phones, and the relative low cost of digital cameras with a video feature as well as the low cost and availability (and usability) of camcorders, there is probably no area of the visual that has so escalated in popularity in the last couple of years than some version of digital video-making. Add to this the significance of Web 2.0 and the convergence of forms of textual production, and there is a fascinating blurring of boundaries between and among media cultures, participatory video and visual research itself that might draw on video. This also means that media-making – what Gubrium (2009) and others refer to as MMP (multimedia production) through website production, digital storytelling, and video production, to name only some of the possibilities – often takes place as part of the everyday experiences of both young people and adults and outside of community projects. This is less obvious in locations that have few resources, and where communities are in some ways marginalized from a high-tech mainstream media-making culture.

However, even in cultural contexts where communities do have access to digital media-making, it does not mean that there is no need to see this as part of visual research – although there may be two types of questions one could pursue: (1) How do participants use multimedia on their own (as a type of DIY culture), and what can we learn from their productions and methods? and, (2) How do participants use multimedia in participatory visual projects and how might their work differ from spontaneous DIY uses of technology? I am aware that even the term 'participatory' applied to video-making may be contentious or at least open to a wide range of interpretations, as Mak (2006) points out, from group members participating in all aspects of the process – from storyboarding, editing and final production at one end of the spectrum to participating primarily in the roll-out of a film that had only minimal involvement of the community, or to participating in an engaged way in the viewing of a video production, as we see in Seshradi and Chandran's work (2006) in addressing masculinity and violence.

Much of the work I describe here involves school and community groups – with the mode of operation being small groups – and so my preferred term would be *community video-making*. Throughout the chapter, I use either this term or participatory video, acknowledging that at least in the UK the term *participatory video* is more formally addressed in the new PVnet guidelines and in the work of large organizations such as Insight.

As with the discussion of community-based photography in the previous chapter, it seems to me to be important to avoid proposing an orthodoxy for participatory or community video. The goals of a research project, the level of sophistication of the research team and the participants, the funds available, the time available, and access to technology and electricity will obviously have an impact on the work. In particular, Shirley White's (2003) comprehensive collection on participatory video makes an excellent case for appreciating a variety of contexts. What is sometimes missing from discussions about community-based video production (in all of its various forms) is the area of 'why video?' and what video-makings offer a research team and the community itself that might be lacking in other participatory visual approaches to qualitative research. In order to explore this set of questions, I divide this chapter into three main sections. The first section parallels the 'Is there a how-to?' section on community-based photography in the previous chapter, detailing 'before the shoot', 'shooting a video', 'after' and 'post production'. The second section of the chapter takes on issues of analysis (sometimes becoming 'Help, what do I do with participatory video data?'), and the third section addresses the broader questions of 'Why video and what does it contribute to community-based research?'

Community-Based Video-Making: Is There a 'How-To'?

As noted in Chapter 1 and Chapter 10, my own experiences of working in communities on film and video production dates back to the late 1970s when, thanks to the National Film Board of Canada's community outreach programme, I worked with Super 8mm with a group of 13- and 14-year-olds in my junior high English class in a small fishing village in Nova Scotia. My next foray into filmmaking was about 25 years later when I started working in rural communities in South Africa with camcorders. Since 2004, this work has included video-making with adolescents in rural South Africa (see, for example, Moletsane et al., 2008; Weber and Mitchell, 2007) and Swaziland (Mitchell, 2004), with community health care workers (Mitchell et al., in press; Moletsane et al., 2007), with teachers (Mitchell et al., 2008), with members of a youth group along with teachers enrolled in a master's course on cinematic and documentary texts, with women principals and vice principals in a leadership programme and with lecturers in an agricultural faculty in Ethiopia (Mitchell and De Lange, in press). The scope of the projects has varied: The filmmaking that I carried out in the 1970s was based on project work that took place over several weeks and involved all aspects of editing – with the students themselves responsible for the editing process – whereas much of the more recent work takes place in one day with a 'no editing required' format (see Figure 5.1). At the other end of the spectrum, Rouch and Feld consider 'the insistence on "live" natural settings and "first takes" with no repetition' (2003: 16) which most of the students routinely carry out because of lack of time. Somewhere in the middle are projects that span a number of sessions and involve participants learning all aspects of the work.

In the beginning: Before the shoot

Even though I may have worked with these groups in the past, the sessions we conduct almost always begin with warm-up activities. What varies is whether the next activity is one that focuses on the technicalities of video-making or one that focuses on the content or issues that are important to the participants.

Brainstorming

In many of the projects I have carried out that are organized around 'in my life', we have started with the question 'What are the issues that are important to you?', and people have worked in small groups to brainstorm the issues. In other projects where there has been a prompt – for example, *Challenges and solutions to the economic empowerment of girls and women* – the brainstorming session has been related to the topic, and there is simply a free flow of ideas, culminating in some sort of voting activity so that the members of the small group get to vote on which topic they would like. The brainstorming usually involves someone writing the ideas (sometimes a facilitator does this), and then participants are given a sticker or marker to check which topic they prefer. From the beginning, then, the focus is more on 'What do we want to say?' than the actual filmmaking process.

Getting to know the camera

As an alternative to brainstorming, however, I have also led workshops where the first activity is working with the video camera. If the group is a manageable size, the facilitator introduces the camera to the group and explains to the first person how to turn it on and off, who in turn passes on the information. When this activity is combined with a participant actually filming the person sitting opposite, asking for his or her name and a response to 'What would you like to film?' or 'What is something that no one in the room knows about you?', it serves the purpose of acting as a warm-up/introduction and gets the participants right into the filmmaking process. I have seen both of these entry points work effectively.

N-E-R (No Editing Required) Video Workshop
Prepared by Monica Mak and Claudia Mitchell

This is a workshop outline for making a 2–3-minute video in one session of about 3–4 hours.

Step 1: Introduction to filmmaking (about 45 minutes)
This includes

- outlining the objectives of the workshop
- talking about the process and the expected results
- giving you an idea of some basic shots
- introducing you to the video cameras.

Step 2: Storyboarding (about 1 hour)
Small groups (4–6) will plan out a 7–8 shot production complete with script. Shots might include

- an establishment shot (the location)
- 3–4 very short interviews on the topic, or a narrative sequence of 3–4 shots
- an ending
- credits.

In order to facilitate the N-E-R approach, groups should decide on their title, which they will film first, and their credits page, which they will film last.

Step 3: Stepping back (about 20 minutes)
Groups return to a plenary session to

- briefly review the process
- review any technicalities about the cameras (especially how to fade from one scene to another
- review issues to do with sound.

Step 4: Groups go off to do the shoot (about 1 hour)

There will be one video camera per group.

Step 5: Viewing the videos
Depending on the technology available, the time and the size of the group, the videos will now be viewed by the group. It is necessary to have FireWire connections, an LCD projector, etc. in order to go directly from video camera to big screen. Because each video is very short, all of them can be viewed in the same 4-hour session if the group isn't too large.

Follow-up: Groups can go back and critique their videos. Each video, if expertise is available, can have a musical soundtrack added, etc.

Note: These are all approximate times. If editing software is used and the addition of musical soundtracks is permitted, the process will take longer.

Figure 5.1   The N-E-R (No Editing Required) workshop

Perhaps the first one, the brainstorming activity, is particularly important in relation to content issues. The technology, then, does not take over.

Once each small group has voted on its focus, the next step is to begin to plan out the shoot through storyboarding. In the case of working with the group over a period of time, it may be that there has been an opportunity to screen various videos. At the very least, with a facilitator, it may be possible in either the large group or in small groups to consider various genres – for example, a public service announcement, an interview, a fictional story, a music video or a social realism documentary. As with discussing camera angles in a photovoice project, I am not entirely certain what the impact of a discussion of genres is (except in the case of a longer period of time and training). I have seen each small group in a session choose a different genre independently of each other, and I have also seen each person choose a narrative based on his or her own personal interest. Clearly, however, choosing the genre will influence the storyboarding process.

Storyboarding

In the one-day event, it is particularly important for the group to develop and follow a storyboard. A storyboard, very simply, is a visual outline or skeleton, made up of a series of drawings or sketches. In the case of the 'video in a day' approach, each sketch or drawing represents one camera shot. The storyboarding is a planning device that participants use to discuss their video production, what it is meant to do and the sequence of shots more specifically. While there are a number of digital programmes that professional filmmakers might use to plan out their shots (see, for example, Oliver, 2009), it is also possible to use a very 'low tech' storyboard consisting of a set of 8 or 10 frames of a rectangular shape (much like a succession of comic book frames) in which a small group can sketch out the basic sequence of events of its story. It consists of a title, shot 1, shot 2, shot 3 and so on through to the credits at the end.

Although this part of the process looks very short and simple, it is actually the one that, from the point of view of research, is one of the most interesting. How does a group arrive at a story angle, and then how do they come up with a storyline? So rich and generative is this component of the process that with two of my colleagues we actually ran a video-making workshop without a video camera. In a workshop in Rwanda with a group of 60 university students and members of NGOs, government officials and lecturers, there was no time and not enough equipment to run a full video-making workshop, so we simply gave groups the storyboarding prompt and page and left it to them to explore and design a five-minute video. As we describe elsewhere (Mitchell et al., in press), the issues taken up by the small groups on the social and economic empowerment of girls and women were fascinating, and the stories – all with a resolution – offered practical approaches to the challenges addressed. As a component to one's research, it is important to try to either video or record the discussions.

Working with the camera

As noted above, the camera activity may happen at the beginning or later in the workshop after the storyboarding. Wherever possible, we try to have each person test out setting up the tripod and experimenting with turning the camera on and

What to do	Check
Train how to use user-friendly video cameras • Setting up tripod • Attaching camera to tripod • Switching on the camera • Opening the viewer and interpreting the information on it • Using the record, forward and rewind buttons • Zooming in and out • Panning	
Allow participants opportunity to practise using the equipment	

Explain 'No Editing Required'
 	
• Each scene/shot video taped only once
• First shot taken is the 'title of the video'
• Ensure that the record button is pressed before the actors read from the script and press the record button once the actor has finished his sentence
• Raise awareness that actors should
 	
   o be near the microphone of the camera so as to ensure audibility
   o face the camera when talking
   o consider interference of surrounding noise levels (and wind) if recording outside
 	
• Encourage participants to practise each scene before shooting (and to keep to 10–30 seconds per scene)
• Final shot taken to the 'credits' at the end	

Allow participants 45–60 minutes to shoot their documentary	
Showing and viewing the video documentaries • Laptop, data projector and screen required and set up • Play video documentaries through the video camera	

Figure 5.2 Guidelines

off, and testing out the zoom lens. This may not always be possible and there may even be some members of the group who do not do this (or who cannot easily do it). The most important point is that someone in the group is ultimately going to be willing to operate the camera. In our work with mixed-sex groupings, we have often encouraged girls and women to work separately from boys and men simply because the work may be taken over by males. This is not always the case as we see in Figure 5.3.

Usually in a whole-group session (or with a facilitator in each group) we also emphasize sound – and the importance of people speaking up if there is to be dialogue – and for the person with the camera to be aware that he or she will need to get as close as possible. In our work with Flip cameras, it is particularly important to have the camera as close to the speaker as possible. One can also emphasize

Figure 5.3 Learning to operate the camera

background noise (especially if several groups are all filming in the same area), external sound and issues of lighting. Obviously, these are major topics that could be the subject of an entire filmmaking course. In community-based work, it is important to at least try to minimize the challenges and problems.

The shoot

We usually allow for approximately an hour for the shoot. This gives groups the opportunity to find a location, to work with props if necessary and to re-shoot the story if there are problems. With more time at the storyboarding stage and also more time to experiment, the product should be better. However, this introduction as an immersion process is often very effective for simply getting groups working. In the N-E-R approach, there is no way of correcting a problem without going back. If a shot doesn't work, someone begins to laugh, or external sound intervenes, it will be necessary to start from the beginning. Although dozens of small groups have operated with this limitation and one might expect that this is a serious challenge, I have never worked with a group that did not manage to come up with a product in the one hour. Sound may be an issue, and in many cases the group may choose to re-shoot the whole two or three minute piece, but the start-stop process has not been a problem. In the case of Flip cameras and using iMovie software, it is even quite easy to reorder the shots on screen.

Immediately after the shoot

As noted in Figure 5.1, in a one-day event, it is critical that everyone gets to view their production, preferably on a big screen. Ideally, the small group will get to preview the video before it is time to show it to the whole group. This first viewing on the big screen and in front of an audience is not usually the time to begin to discuss the technical flaws or 'what the video was supposed to do'. Indeed, the fact that this screening will take place close to the end of the day, and with some urgency to see all of the videos, means that the event is largely celebratory. A member of each group (or the whole group) is given the opportunity to briefly direct the audience to the purpose of its video. For example, in a video project in rural KwaZulu-Natal, the student who plays a teacher in the video *Rape at School: Trust No One* comments on his group's video: 'It is about how our sisters and daughters are raped and how we keep quiet about it.' After the screening, the audience of participants has the opportunity to respond to each other's work. This we feel is important in that it raises the level of reflection and engagement among the community of participants.

Post-production

It is in the post-production process that participants can consider what they would like to have done differently, or can speculate on different types of shots or how they think the video should be used. In our work with different groups, this stage of the process has taken a variety of forms. What I would recommend is that some days or a week later (but at least not the same day as the production) each small group has a chance to work on its own with its own video, viewing it several times and considering various reflective questions. These need not be very complex questions but what they do is provoke discussion and reflection. For some projects, the participatory aspect of the work ends here. For others, this is just the beginning, and going through the entire process of making a video in one day simply sets the stage for a more elaborated process. And even if it does not immediately lead to a more elaborated process in terms of video production, this part of the process ideally will lead to more participation in working with the video, showing it to various audiences and engaging in some of the follow-up analysis. This is a component of the process that is often not discussed (what happens after?), and perhaps one that isn't sufficiently considered by funders: what is the afterlife of the production?

In the *Taking Action* study with aboriginal youth in western Canada on issues of youth sexuality and HIV and AIDS, for example, the youth participants in a weekend-long video-making workshop led by a professional video company were involved much more in the post-production phase than the actual production. While young people participated only marginally in script writing and editing (all of which took place off-site by the production company), they had key roles as actors, and once the final version of the video had been produced, their participation became centred on screening the video with other youth groups and in schools, speaking out about the issues, entertaining questions about youth sexuality and generally being the key spokespersons for the project. This is not to say that they couldn't have done this even if they had been involved in all aspects of the production, but only to say that the final production was of a professional quality and perhaps made it easier for the participants to be the spokespersons (Sarah Flicker, personal communication, April 2010). Similarly, in the *Soft Cover* project on creative arts and HIV and AIDS, which led to the production of the 17-minute video *Fire+Hope* (2004; Mitchell, 2006b), participants from the project were the protagonists in the video, and in working with Shannon Walsh, the filmmaker, participated in helping to storyboard the issues. The production, however, was professionally filmed and edited. The participants, as in the *Taking Action* project, were able to use the video for their own community outreach.

Working with Community-Based Video as Research

What analytic tools can we use to work with community-based video? What counts as data? While there are many different ways of thinking about the texts, and the discourse within the texts, I have been drawn, as I noted in Chapter 1, to the work of John Fiske (1987) and his approach to studying television texts as a way to identify particular components of textuality. Fiske talks about three types of texts: the primary texts (the actual video productions), the producer texts and the viewer or audience texts. As he argues, the three layers leak into each other and as such, they need, as much as possible, to be read together.

The primary texts: What do video productions say?

[Derrida] suggests that we should fasten upon a small but tell-tale moment in the text which harbours the author's sleight of hand and which cannot be dismissed simply as contradiction. We should examine that passage where we can provisionally locate the moment when the text transgresses the laws it apparently sets up for itself, and thus unravel – deconstruct – the very text. (Sarup, 1993: 41)

I start with a consideration of the primary texts. I actually think that as researchers we do not do work enough with the primary texts themselves, which seems in some ways to devalue the work of participants in video-making. So although the process is of course important, the productions also contribute valuable data. Building on the notion of Derrida's unravelling, we see that a critical step in working with video productions is to transcribe them in much the same way as we

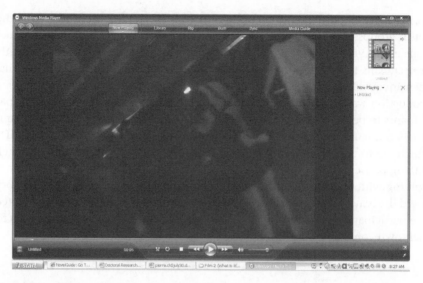

Figure 5.4   Dance scene

would transcribe audio-taped interview data. Because the videos are all quite short (often no more than a few minutes in length), the process is relatively easy. While this may remove the text from the full context of the video, it gives us a chance to look closely at what is being said or told. There is an emerging body of work on engaging in close readings of transcripts that we regard as particularly useful here for acknowledging the limitations on a single reading of any one transcript. Joseph Tobin (2000), for example, proposes that, like the richly textured lines of a Shakespeare play, the transcripts of young people talking about media hold a great deal of meaning, and he argues for what he describes as a 'reading in' process. The titles, themes, special effects, music and types of shots – these all contribute to the overall reading of the primary text. In the context of gender-based violence and HIV and AIDS, for example, the titles created within one video-making day speak dramatically to the issues: *Rape at School: Trust No One*; *How Raping Got Me HIV and AIDS*; *Rape, Effect of Poverty in School*; and *It All Began with Poverty*. Within the primary texts, one can talk about the genre, the basic storyline, particular images or scenes – but also, as I explore in the third section of the chapter, we can also use the analysis of the primary text to begin to look deeper into 'What's going on?'

Pierre Doyon (2009) in a study of girls and video-making in a secondary school in Montreal selects a number of their productions to analyse in some detail. The type of close reading that he uses draws on some of the conventions of a fairly basic film studies approach, but in so doing, he allows us to appreciate the work of the filmmaker beyond simply the process. Each of his close readings are several thousand words in length. The person doing the critique is Doyon himself as the media studies teacher, and he acknowledges his own subjective reading practices. Each of the girls' productions deals with some aspect of school life. Many are graduating from high school the year they are making these videos and their productions very much reflect this as we see in the box below on a 'grad shindig' by 'Stella'.

Stella created an interesting version of cinéma vérité, a documentary of the grad shindig, a ritual held every year by the graduating class as a prelude to the Prom (see Figure 5.4). Held in the school in late October, it takes place after hours and only the grads can attend. It is an opportunity for the girls to show off their prom dresses and serves as a dry run of the actual prom. It was a perfect opportunity for the producer to explore 'representations of womanhood', but since this was never stipulated, and she has a limited amount of time to depict even this, she leaves womanhood out of the equation (though it still exists in the fact that the vast majority of those interviewed are women), in an attempt to truncate an entire evening into a three-minute documentary. She not only sped up the process by reducing an entire evening (and all activities leading up to the event) into just over three minutes, but she literally truncated some of the interviewed, cutting off subjects in mid-sentence as a sense of urgency is manifest in the work.

The velocity of the piece is further accelerated by the speed of delivery: the narrator seems to be racing through the piece which inadvertently adds to the whirlwind sense of the event, giving us an adolescent's gaze of the event. It is here the creator of this film does such a good job of creating a 'filmic truth' and depicts the event as having great energy and speed. The fact she is making a film of the event gives it power, making it into an 'event' rather than just another school dance – an anthropological study of a ritual of womanhood in this school second only to the Prom.

The film begins with titling that splits off in two directions immediately, with driving techno music playing in the background, competing fiercely with the narrator's manic voice over:

> Welcome to the annual West Island High grad shindig, an annual dance which is only open to the students of West Island High. This Halloween dance is the first grad event venue. Several other events follow during the year that we will keep you posted about.

The next shot is of the actual dance, which is generally dark but punctuated by the sounds and lights of the dance, in a style reminiscent of how a filmmaker in the 1960s might depict a drug trip (for example, *Midnight Cowboy* or *Easy Rider*, although these films were not covered in class). We are then abruptly pulled out of the dance to witness the first interview, a record of a discussion with one of the teachers involved. The narrator's manic tempo is finally brought to a screeching halt by the slow pace of the teacher's response. During this interview the interviewer asks typical questions concerning what went into the making of the event:

> Interviewer [off-screen]: What did you have to do in order to organize this wonderful event?

> Interviewed [stands awkwardly with her hands behind her back]: I didn't do very much. It was mostly the ... uh ... students that took care of organizing the events. I just basically called for students to get involved and they ... uh ... they did what they had to do. [pauses] They did not disappoint [nods head].

(Continued)

(Continued)

But here, the interviewer then begins to question a decision made to not allow outsiders to the event, barely allowing the teacher to finish:

Interviewer: Why is it that grads were not allowed to bring guests to this event?

As the interviewee responds, the interviewer quickly dismisses her, cutting off the teacher to ask another, less intrusive question of how much time went into organizing the event, which might have been random, or might be an attempt to downplay the importance of the 'not allowed to bring guests' question. The interview ends abruptly before the teacher can even finish her final sentence.

Interviewed: ... about twenty hours when you consider what went into the event, uh, yes
Interviewer: OK, thank you.

There is barely a second before the interviewer thanks the teacher, all part of the manic speed found throughout the film.

We then return to the lights and music and the film is slowed down somewhat to give us time to actually focus on a few choice actors in the filmic reality before the handheld camera techniques lose focus and wander through the ritual once more creating a sense of urgency.

We are quickly transported to a second interview with another teacher who is introduced using a typical news-style caption (absent from the first interview where the teacher was verbally introduced by the interviewer), but after one question, he is cut off in mid-sentence and we return again to the manic footage of the dance. Whether deliberate or not, the cut fits the mood of revelry and speed associated with the event being documented, but the contrast between the conventions of the introduction of the person being interviewed and then his abrupt departure from the piece is striking and all at once fitting. It is almost as if the interview is truncated to bring us a news flash.

A bright pink caption queries 'The Jonas Brothers?' which fills the screen in reference to the karaoke scene that we witness, but in this scene there is a fascinating example of media convergence and media culture: as the camera attempts to capture the singers, it is blocked by a forest of mobile-phone cameras being used to capture the same event. In a scene that a generation ago would be reserved for politicians and movie stars, this can take place in a high-school setting with participants recording with light-weight digital equipment. The scene is captured, cameras capturing cameras, recording an event and yet the filmmaker herself does not acknowledge the irony of the shot since she is only one of many who are capturing the event (does a goldfish know it is in a bowl?).

The singers are spurred on by the attention of the producers, hamming it up for the cameras. It is an example of reflexivity where the term 'participant observer' has taken on new meaning in this micro-digital world. As the camera becomes less obtrusive, it allows the event to take place more naturally: no one seems aware they are being filmed since camera phones are more commonplace in this culture than traditional cameras (and far less distracting due to the lack of a flash), but in this case, the singers are spurred on by the attention to create this impromptu show.

We leave the paparazzi on the dance floor and are immediately assaulted by a cartoon call-out label 'the students' (in contrast to the earlier interviews of teachers) and a rough jump cut. We now see a shift in the film from anthropological to scripted TV.

The interviews so far have been realistic and generally followed the codes and conventions of reportage, but suddenly the film producer switches genres and we are thrust into a series of scripted (or at least rehearsed) responses to the question, 'What did you think of the Grad Shindig?' The first response is the obligatory 'It was awesome', exclaimed by a young girl in a close-up, followed by a far shot of a second girl who repeats, 'It was awesome!' The next shot is a girl in another hallway (the causeway to the French school) who reiterates, 'It was awesome', and punctuates her comment with a cartwheel. The next shot is two girls who claim 'It was sick' in perfect unison followed by a staccato of positive shots with similar claims that pick up speed and seem more genuine and unscripted than the first two.

This fast-paced depiction of reality is abruptly reduced to a crawl by a jump cut to two awkward teenage girls facing the screen who are asked by the narrator, 'What did you guys do in order to organize this event?' Their names are not presented on the screen as were the teachers, and they are not introduced verbally, but rather their status is implied by the interviewer's question. Obviously unscripted, they list through their responsibilities with an awkwardness that only comes from being totally unprepared, so we have returned to reality (or something like it). A green screen unexpectedly replaces the shot, cutting off one of the students in mid-sentence (obviously this is not a fate reserved only for teachers), and the screen is covered with the caption 'What could have been done differently?'

Now the filmmaker's true agenda comes into focus: the first two teen girls interviewed state that there should have been better music, but then the next three girls agree that 'You should have been able to invite other people', reminding us of the question asked of the teacher in the first interview. The second interviewed student adds, 'other grads from other schools', while the other two girls in the shot shake their heads in agreement. Then there is a jump shot back to the dance footage with the narrator stating, 'Now that we've heard the wisdom of the students …', implying that the last statement is wiser or closer to the 'truth'. The narrator returns to speaking at a breakneck speed so the end of the film is as manic as the beginning, and almost comical. Adding to the urgency of the piece, the credits roll by so quickly they are next to impossible to read.

In three minutes and seventeen seconds, the producer has taken us through the ritual of the dance, introduced us to both the teachers and students involved, and made a point about the rights of the students to bring in students from other schools. The producer of this film understood the possibility of media as a means of making her voice heard, that a political message can be embedded into a text that is seemingly innocuous. When interviewed, she claimed that the desire to have students from outside of the school was a general consensus of the students involved and claimed not to be trying to make a point. Was she afraid of repercussions, or was this an example of cinéma vérité, in which she inadvertently caught the mood of the moment, albeit somewhat constructed? Did she feel that to be a filmmaker one has to manipulate the truth, or given her comment on consensus, did she feel that being a filmmaker means not being able to have an opinion?

Her self-representation was that of a disenfranchised student who had no control over who came to the shindig and attempts to draw attention to what she deems as an injustice. She is empowered by the film and used it as a means to question authority and decisions outside of her power. She represents the school as a place where students have little power over their reality, though it is interesting that most of those interviewed were women, including the teacher who oversaw it and the two girls who were more directly part of the organization. The producer is oblivious to the fact that the event was organized, orchestrated and overseen by women, and since the social aspects of the school are so commonly controlled by women, it goes without notice… (Adapted from Doyon, 2009: 115–21)

We can also look at special effects. In one of the videos produced in a No-Editing-Required format, one of the groups imports music from a mobile phone as part of a soundtrack. And in another video in the same project, the idea of doing an off-camera scene of gender violence so that the audience only hears the cries of the girl from behind closed doors is a fascinating one and, while reminiscent of the film *North Country*, it is unlikely that any of the participants would have actually seen that film.

We might also think of the cumulative aspects of these close readings. As I explore further in Chapter 7 on participatory archiving, the entry point of analysis might be working with a single video, but over the span of several years may also lead to interesting and important comparative data. For example, the N-E-R (Figure 5.1) process described earlier in the chapter has yielded ten videos on gender-based violence, four videos on 'shattering the glass ceiling', three videos on challenges to the social and economic empowerment of girls and women, and at least ten videos on challenges and solutions to addressing HIV and AIDS. In the case where all the data is from one district, it is possible to look across issues of sex, age, theme and time (videos produced in 2004, videos produced in 2010), and to go beyond one district to look at youth productions across settings – Rwanda, South Africa and Canada – all addressing the challenges and solutions of HIV and AIDS.

Producer texts

What can we learn by focusing on groups of young people or adults who produced the video? What do they have to say about their work? In our follow-up work with producers, we have found questions such as the following useful in group discussions:

- What did you like about the video?
- What are some of the images that stay in your mind?
- If you had a copy of the video, who would you want to show it to and why?
- How do you think it could help address the issue you raise (e.g., poverty, gender-based violence)?
- What would help you in the school and community to address the issue?

We also try to have the group talk about how it felt about producing the video:

- What did you like best about making a video?
- Would you like to make another video? What topic would you choose? Why?

As part of studying the producer texts, it is possible in this framework to engage in studying what the process of 'working with the footage' looks like by audio- and videotaping the interaction within the small groups. Indeed, in the case of seeing this work as a strategy for addressing particular social issues such as poverty and gender-based violence, it is the production texts (what the filmmakers and actors have to say before, during and after the production) that are particularly significant in contributing to the self-reflexive stage that Ruby (2000a), Pink (2001) and others discuss. This is also one of the most promising points of interface for bringing about change. Shannon Walsh (2007) highlights this self-reflexivity in her work with a group of young township women who participated in a collaborative video project to produce *Street Fear*. A key component of the video are interviews in which the girls describe (and reflect on) when and why they are afraid to be on the street. However, as noted below, this does not mean that it is a straightforward process and that the results will always be positive (in relation to anticipated change). Making a video does not necessarily alter one's consciousness, and as I describe below in a discussion of the video *Rape*, it is possible that the production even reinforces certain stereotypes and narratives.

Audience texts

Because of the participatory 'workshop' nature of the production and screening, there are rich possibilities for studying audience response, both through observation and fieldnotes, but also, as I describe in Chapter 8, through the use of visual data (photographing and videotaping the audience during the screening). In the one-day video-making workshop, there is time for each group to present its video to the other groups. For many of the participants in these workshops, it is often the first time they have ever seen themselves on film, and the resulting laughter from the whole group at the initial viewing potentially alters the meanings intended in addressing such serious issues. Then there is the question of how different constituencies in community workshops – the teachers, parents and youth – respond to the videos. And how does the research team/workshop facilitators respond to the texts? In the case of *Rape*, a video produced by a group of boys depicting rape (described in more detail in the next section), our research team, as participants in the workshop itself as well as facilitators offering technical support, found it difficult to not participate as audience and to not be somewhat despondent about the message. The boys had insisted in involving a female student from another group to play the part of the girl in the video. We actually attempted to intervene in the video-making process and in particular to try to convince them to not involve the girl, as well as facilitating discussion with the five boys about what they were doing in their video and trying to offer some resolution to the issues in a way that was not simply 'you will go to jail'. What does this look like from the point of view of the girl who is raped, we wanted to ask? What are the underlying issues? When that was not easily possible during the filming, we as a team (behind the scenes) decided that there could be a discussion during the final screenings at the end of the day about sexual relations and alternatives to coercive sex. One of the members of our research team, an isiZulu speaker, led this discussion in isiZulu so there would be less chance for miscommunication.

But one can also talk about the impact of a video on audiences that are made up of males and females of various ages. The video *Trust No One at School*, produced by a group of three boys and three girls, depicts a scene of a teacher (played by a student) sexually propositioning one of his female students. We do not see the actual rape scene, which takes place behind a closed door, but we hear the screams and sobs of the girl. The 'teacher' walks through the door, with his shirt hanging out, and adjusts his clothing. The students are depicting a scene that clearly is 'within their imagination' – a male teacher raping a female student. There are male teachers in the room at the time of the screening, and we look around to see their response. In a later follow-up session, we work with the male teachers in a separate discussion group (Bhana et al., 2009). While we wondered whether there might have been ramifications for the students who produced this video, there seems not to have been.

One of the advantages of video, of course, is that there can be many follow-up screening sessions with many different audiences. In Chapter 9, I highlight the idea of the composite video as a way to present the productions in a contextualized way. Photographs and video can be used but also interviews and even questionnaires. For *Fire+Hope*, for example, we devised a viewer response form so that we could study the responses by different audiences and over time. How does the context change, say, in relation to a video on HIV and AIDS made in 2004 and its impact on viewers six years later? And what can we learn from this in relation to the changing nature of HIV and AIDS?

Viewer Response Form

Viewer:

Age ___

Sex ___

Title of film _____

What did you see as the most important issues addressed in the film?

What did you like best about the film?

Were there any weaknesses in the film? Please explain.

What other issues could have been covered in the film?

Now that you have seen the film, what action would you personally like to take about the issue?

One additional area to consider in relation to the audience text is the response of the producers to viewing and re-viewing their own videos. While the products of photovoice projects occasionally and perhaps more by accident than design turn out to be outstanding in composition or lighting or overall effect, this is much rarer with community video. Although in general participants are pleased with their work, I have encountered situations where the quality is not what the producers expected. The question of quality is a critical one. Jennifer Jenson (2010) argues that perhaps there is a need to counter an over-celebratory approach, 'an anything goes' when it comes to participatory video, highlighting that she has seen one too many shaky camera shots at conferences where researchers show participatory videos based on their field work. She makes the point that we should not give participants a false sense of the worth of their work and that ultimately we should be working with them to strive for higher quality. For some people the idea of making a film means making a Hollywood-looking film. As noted earlier in relation to the *Taking Action* project and the fact that a professional production took on much of the video-making work, there remains a debate about quality vs. genuine participation and ownership and the input of the research team. In the video-making project described in *Our Photos, Our Videos, Our Stories* (Mak et al., 2005), the participants did all the basic filming and even edited their work into a five-minute documentary. Then a filmmaker worked with each of the videos, adding in a musical soundtrack and finalizing the credits.

Video-Making as Strategy – or Why Video?

A critical question in the mind of any researcher is always, 'Why this method?' In the case of doing visual research, what is it about video vs. photography or digital storytelling or drawing that is important? And notwithstanding issues of expertise, cost or access to resources, what can one do with participatory video that one cannot do with some other medium? Sometimes the answer rests entirely with issues of innovation or what the funders will fund, but in other cases, the choice of video-making might be described as a particular research strategy for reaching particular audiences – or as I describe here, it may have some specific benefits in relation to deepening an understanding of the issues under study (for example, violence or environmental issues).

In this section, I focus on addressing gender violence as a theme, acknowledging how gender violence is part of many of the short videos that have been produced in community projects in South Africa, Rwanda and Ethiopia. Beyond the obvious demands of conceptualization (through storyboarding, planning out of shots and so on), there are at least five key areas that may be significant to this work: social constructedness, reflexivity, collectivity, convergence and embodiment. While I do not want to argue that other visual approaches such as photovoice, photo-stories or participatory drama do not include these features as well, here I simply want to draw attention to the ways in which these features might be 'taken as a whole' in understanding participatory video and gender violence.

I focus on the final production of an 'all boy' group in a No-Editing-Required project in South Africa that made a video called *Rape*. Most of the youth groups in the same session elected to focus in one way or another on gender violence, a critical issue throughout South Africa, and given that young women are four to five times more likely to be HIV positive than young men of the same age, it is an issue that is closely related to the high rates of HIV infection among girls and young women. The storyline of *Rape* is organized around the multiple rapings of one girl (G) by her boyfriend (S). The actual narrative is broken up into eight short scenes, four of which directly depict staged rapes. As we see in the box below, the encounters between the boy and his girlfriend start off in a loving way, but the scenes quickly move to forced sex. I focused on rape in an essay that Sandra Weber and I (Weber and Mitchell, 2007) worked on in relation to youth identity in working with digital media. In that essay, I noted that most of the youth groups elected to focus in one way or another on gender violence.

2nd scene

S: *Where do you live now my baby? Give me a hug.* [Girl resists] *No way, let's sit down.*

G: *Take a break and have some fresh air.*

S: [Grabs her]

G: *Just wait a bit. Wait! Stop!*

S: *What is the matter with you?*

G: *I don't like to do it. I don't like it.*

S: *What don't you like?*

G: *To do it. I don't like to.*

S: *What?*

G: *Eh ... eh ... I don't like to do it ... Eh ... eh ... You know what, I'll cry out loud.*

S: *Come on now baby.* [Rape takes place] *But who are you going to cry out to? Come on baby.*

G. reports her boyfriend to the police. He is imprisoned, and as we see below in this last scene of the video, he appears to show some remorse for what he has done, not because of the impact of his actions on his girlfriend so much as what has happened to him in prison, where he himself is subjected to sexual violence.

8th scene

S: *Ei! I am now regretful. I raped my sweetheart. When I get out of here she will not even want to see me. Ei, I raped a person really. I am in prison now. It's tough ... even to eat. It is me that is getting raped now. They mount me. Ei, now regret.*

S: *I don't know what to say. I don't know what to do. I am in prison now. I raped a female person. I raped her and beat her and am in prison now. I don't know what to do now. The men in here mount me and beat me. Just look now, when I get out of here the babes in the location will leave me. I won't get another cherry because I am known to be a rapist now.*

S: *But you my brothers out there, I'm telling you, restrain yourselves (control), be strong, don't rape females because you will be sentenced and grow old inside (prison).*

At one level, the video production can be read as a very disturbing and horrifyingly graphic representation of aggressive masculinity, one which reinforces all of the stereotypes about boys and young men in South Africa. Indeed, in many ways the scenario depicted here is no different from the kinds of testimonies that are described in face-to-face interviews with young people in various South African locations where boys report that it is 'okay to hit your girlfriend', where it is 'okay to expect sex', and where girls talk about the inevitability of forced sex and unprotected sex (Sathiparsad, 2008). In one of the 'all-girl' video groups, for example, the first point that they bring up in the 'in my life' brainstorming is 'We worry about getting pregnant before we finish school'.

But at another level, and why I include it here, the video invites us to consider what difference it makes that this is a 'production' (and not just an interview) and to ask how working with new technologies such as digital video (and not, for example, just performance or just still photographs) contributes to deepening an understanding of identity construction. The availability of relatively inexpensive equipment (ranging from mobile phones, webcams, digital cameras with a video function and inexpensive camcorders) clearly has made this kind of work more feasible, even in a rural school in South Africa, and even where the only electricity is in the principal's office, as is the case for this production.

Constructedness

Working with video production as a group process (from initial concept through to storyboarding, planning shots, shooting and initial screening) offers participants access to a type of socially constructed knowledge that is particularly significant to addressing themes and issues such as gender violence, which are in and of themselves difficult to express through single (and fixed) images. Working with video offers participants an opportunity to engage actively in the idea of 'social construction' in ways that are quite different from photovoice, although perhaps not so different as creating photo-stories or participatory drama.

The group chooses the themes, decides on the images, *constructs* the stage and so on. In the case of video (versus live performance), there is a whole array of techniques that expand the possibilities for constructedness – from shot angles to dialogue to theme music. Participants can stop the process, view and re-view the work – and, indeed, can even easily see themselves in action. Each frame is considered and re-considered. Nothing is accidental. And although we employed a No-Editing-Required approach, so that each scene was shot as a final cut, participants did have the opportunity to re-shoot the whole episode from the beginning if they wished. Several groups rehearsed the entire episode first, offering yet another way of playing not only with the various components of the video but also and especially with gendered identities. In *Rape*, the boys worked to construct the girlfriend as weak and passive, and themselves as cool and powerful. S. appears after each of the rape scenes with his shirt half hanging out, and later in the prison scene appears in one of the cool woollen beanies that boys wear outside of school (but which are not part of the school uniform attire that is mandatory).

Borrowing from the phenomenon of construction toys, one might look at the somewhat playful and more or less deliberate and often creative 'assembling' of role-playing props and film techniques. As with construction block play, you usually start out using the materials at hand, respecting or finding ways to get around their limitations, working with others or alone. Once you have acquired some skills and have explored possibilities, however, you may find yourself improvising and seeking out additional materials to incorporate into your constructions, and find that what you end up with has unintended potential use. Suggested blueprints or models may be included with both toys and media design, but individual and collective interpretations may differ; negotiation, subversion and adaptation are commonplace. Digital production as creative construction in this way embodies the manipulation of gendered, racialized and sexualized identities. Visual evidence of this constructedness can be found in the video production itself.

Reflexivity

Participatory video draws on critical scholarship within feminist visual studies (e.g., Citron, 1999; Knight, 2001) and also has a lengthy history of use by visual anthropologists and sociologists. Jay Ruby (2000a) discusses how reflexivity, autobiography and self-awareness can figure into working with the film-texts, something that is important to keep in mind in relation to working with young people and video on an issue like gender violence. It is particularly important in addressing an issue where the dominant images of sexism and power inequalities need to be challenged. The types of follow-up interventions that draw on reflexivity are extensive. How, for example, could the group 're-vision' their original documentary as a text that explicitly contests the traditional power dimensions – and how does video lend itself to this kind of critical awareness? How would other students (a group of girls, for example) respond to the video, and how could this audience component contribute to the reflexivity of the original filmmakers? How would teachers, other adults and the education officials respond to the video? Like the work of Barnes et al. (1997), who used collaborative video to work with HIV positive mothers, the participants were able to 'reproduce and understand their world as opposed to the dominant representations in the mass media' (1997: 27, cited in Pink, 2001: 86).

Working with the visual is a key component of reflexivity as visual anthropologists such as Sarah Pink and Jay Ruby suggest. In the process of making *Rape*, the boys seemed to be consciously (and insistently) trying on identities that reproduced the masculine-role images that they see around them in school, village and the media; while at the same time, they were also testing out new identities, not the least of which was a type of 'prison hero', as we see in S's final soliloquy. The plea is to feel sorry for him and not to wonder what happened to his girlfriend. Interestingly, in the storyboarding for *Rape*, the boys were adamant that they needed to 'borrow' a girl from one of the other video-making groups so that they could enact the rapes on screen. Although the facilitator tried to convince the group that they could 'suggest' rape through off-camera voices (one other group that also dealt with gender violence used 'behind closed door' screaming, not unlike the school rape scene in the film *North Country*) or through the use of an item of clothing as trace, the boys convinced one of the girls to join their group for the purposes of filming the rape.

Collectivity

Schratz and Walker (1995) argue that a critical feature of various interventions that lend themselves to social change is that they are in fact social in nature in the first place. They involve the group and cannot be managed 'individually and in isolation' (1995: 172). Schratz and Walker go on to explain: 'It [Motivation] requires a collaborative effort and a reassessment of the nature of self in relation to social context, not a submerging of the individual within the collective, but a recognition that the person only exists in the light of significant others' (1995: 172). What difference does the collective process make, particularly in evoking and exploring gender? *Rape* was clearly a group effort. Indeed, as my colleagues and I reviewed the process footage, we saw groups 'in action' negotiating particular scenes as well as working out who would be behind the camera and who would be in front of the camera. While it is quite possible that individual responses may sometimes be overshadowed in this collectivity, we would argue that in the case of gender violence, which is social in nature and multi-layered in meaning, the collective response is vital – a version of 'the meaning is the message'.

Exploring the collective process in video-making may help to deepen our understanding of social construction more broadly. The fact that each of the videos is produced by the group (from group brainstorming to group decision-making about the scripting, planning and filming) complements both the idea of constructedness noted earlier and the idea of negotiation. The technology of the camera and the 'no editing required' constraint means that groups must collectively arrive at decisions about 'who' (will play the rapist, do the filming, play the police), 'what' (the number of scenes, dividing them up and so on) and 'where and how' (choosing location, deciding on props and sound). The 'how' includes performativity. At one point, for example, when one of the groups is still brainstorming the various 'in my life' critical issues, there is a discussion about gangsterism and 'the look' of a local gang member, wherein various group members physically stand a certain way, pull up their collars, put their hands in their pockets and so on. While Judith Butler (1990) discusses the idea of performing gender, we would argue that it is the technology of video-making and, in particular, the group effort that is significant. The fact that most groups rehearsed their scenes before they actually filmed them meant that group members were able to offer suggestions, and in some cases even re-play what the person who was being filmed should be doing. And while this could be true for any type of performance, it is the capturing on film that adds to the identity-in-action process and the possibilities for social action.

Convergence

By convergence, I refer to the converging and blending of technologies – old and new – a process that involves emerging media mixes (see also Jenkins, 2006). Reading digital production within and across examples offers a unique glimpse into the collision of old and new media more generally. In the production of *Rape*, young people 'perform' using traditional forms of role-playing, although one might see parallels to role-playing on the Internet. At the same time, when they use digital cameras they are able to work with an instant replay where they can see if they have caught the scene exactly as they want it. And as noted earlier, at one point one of the group members completely crosses conventional stereotypes of the digital divide by importing a soundtrack from a mobile phone into the video.

Embodiment

There is a tendency when discussing identity in the context of new technologies to forget that identities are always and inescapably embodied (Weber and Mitchell, 2007). One of the most graphic examples of embodiment is *Rape*. In the horrifying rape scene, for example, S is filmed overpowering G with a simulated rape. At other points, we see the various characters 'trying on' identities: rapist, gangster and repentant prisoner. Items of clothing and body gestures become markers of these identities: the shirt half hanging out, the 'cool walk' of the gangster and the beanie of the prisoner. As a reminder that this is 'made up', but also of embodiment, we observe in the video that someone has put down two sheets of flip-chart paper so that G does not have to lie on the dirty cement floor of the classroom.

Constructedness, reflexivity, collectivity, convergence and embodiment are all features that help to frame 'what's going on'. They are by no means, however, the only features that could be used to appreciate participatory video, nor do they begin to capture other aspects of what might be described as the dark side of video. Milne's work, for example, on 'saying "no" to participatory video' (Milne, 2010) speaks to the fact that not all communities want to participate in video projects and to the importance of collaboration that makes it possible for communities to say 'no'. Walsh's (2007) work on 'studying up' in a video project with black township youth in South Africa who are interviewing white youth at a private school about their views on HIV and AIDS and sexuality (see Chapter 2 in the volume) helps to disrupt what is often a one-way flow of power. And Yang's work (2008) on video-telling workshops highlights the politics of working with volunteers and negotiating some of the power relationships within the group. What Milne (2010) advocates is a truth-telling about this work so that participatory video is not seen as a type of problem-free tool that inevitably results in emancipatory practices.

Conclusion

In this chapter, I have highlighted some of the conceptual, process-related, product-focused and social values of video production, with specific examples on addressing gender violence. Recent studies on gender violence in and around schools have called for creative and innovative solutions. I do not regard a one-day video-making workshop as 'the solution', but I do see that the active participation of young people is critical, and that using visual arts-based approaches such as video-making is one way to engage them in 'stepping outside' the everyday. Given the pervasiveness of sexism and gender inequalities, there is a need for solutions that have both a distancing effect – what Margot Ely and colleagues (Ely et al., 1991) call 'making the familiar unfamiliar' – as well as interventions that are potentially engaging and that facilitate reflection. This seems to be in keeping with the stated principle of the recent 'PV-Net Statement on Participatory Video in Research', which puts forward the idea that this work should aim to 'look beyond individual projects and seek to serve community interests and the public good through social learning, partnership and the strategic interweaving of initiatives to meet community needs'. Another principle notes that participatory video work should, 'above all, celebrate the opportunities that the increased availability of new media and technology and the emerging interest in participation in research provides for social learning, and assert a collective ambition to use those opportunities well'.

Perhaps what is also important to hang on to, though, is representation itself, and the significance of communities in determining which images need to be produced. Jan Egeland (2005) writes in the foreword to *Broken Bodies – Broken Dreams*:

> When images of the world's disasters flash across television screens, more often than not, we are presented with a rough sketch of the humanitarian crisis. Rarely do the cameras venture beneath the surface to look at the hidden impact of a humanitarian crisis on affected communities. If they did they would find that virtually without exception, it is women and children who are the most vulnerable. (2005: 1)

Even more rarely, I would add, are the cameras that venture beneath the surface controlled by the very people who are most affected, even though an emerging feature of work related to confronting and combating gender violence and other social issues is a recognition of the importance of the participation of communities in mapping out the issues and, more significantly, in taking action as protagonists.

PART III

On Interpreting and Using Images

SIX

Working with photo images: A textual reading on the presence of absence

Introduction

'Where have all the Swazis gone?' was a headline in Toronto's *The Globe and Mail* (Nolen, 2007). The results of a census carried out in Swaziland in 2007 had apparently surprised everyone in the region, especially the group of demographers who conducted the door-to-door count. They discovered that there were 17,489 fewer people in Swaziland than had been counted in the previous census a decade earlier. Who would expect a developing country like Swaziland, where unchecked population growth has traditionally been one of many challenges to social development, to be losing people? In actuality, demographers estimated that the population was close to 300,000 short of what was expected based on projected population growth. However, those working on the front lines of HIV and AIDS, both nationally and regionally, were not really surprised. The official statistics said that 40 per cent of the population was HIV positive; few had access to anti-retroviral drugs, and all of the conditions were there for a disaster – migrant labour (many of the men working across the border in the mines of South Africa), the low status of women and the public endorsement of multiple sexual partners. The surprise should not have been around how many people were missing but, rather, the surprise should have been about the surprise reaction itself. One traditional healer observed: 'We bury people even in the middle of the week, bury people daily. It is even difficult to remember what life was like a decade ago' (Nolen, 2007). If someone had tried to capture the face of AIDS, the visual images of daily burials, ravaged bodies and empty offices would have told a story that would have left no one surprised about the 17,489 missing bodies.

In her book *The Body at Risk*, Carol Squiers (2005: 13) examines the relationship between health and the visual in relation to an exhibition she curated in 2005: 'Health is not considered a particularly interesting subject of photography, and is often treated as a minor aspect of grander topics such as war, social and political strife, or economic development of decline.' Squiers draws on the visual works of 10 photographers as documentarians and photojournalists, from the work of Lewis Wickes Hines on child labour in the early 1900s to the work of Donna Ferrato on domestic violence in the US, and to Gideon Mendel (2001) and his documentation of HIV and AIDS throughout Africa and around the world. Squiers adds: 'I hope that this project can participate in multiple discussions, among them the growing debates about health policy and responsibility, as well as the role that photography can play in *visualizing what is at stake*' (2005: 243).

The expression *visualizing what is at stake* is an apt one to apply to a recurring question (after 'But is it ethical?'): But what do I do with the images? Part of me always wants to say that 'It all depends' because the content of visual images is only one component of data in visual research, regardless of whether the work is in the context of community-based photovoice, digital storytelling and participatory studies, or in relation to studies of autobiography, memory, self-study and memoir, where working with one's own photo images (e.g., photo albums and family photographs) is the focus. Ways of working with visual images are inevitably context specific as we see in the vast range of photovoice and community-based photography projects, including those exploring perspectives of dialysis patients (Allen and Hutchison, 2009), gender violence and toilets (Mitchell, 2009d), environmental issues (Thompson, 2009), women's access to health care (Wang et al., 1996), youth sexuality (Tao, 2009), teachers and community health care workers' views on challenges and solutions in addressing HIV and AIDS (Mitchell et al., 2005a), girls living on the street (Umurungi et al., 2008), stigma (Mitchell et al., 2005b), teachers' images of hope (Olivier et al., 2009), and disrupting colonial discourses in Namibia (Rohde, 1998). The vastness of this list does not mean there are no common reading strategies. As noted earlier, Gillian Rose's (2001) work, particularly her research on visual discourses, provides an excellent look at the ways in which 'the photo' carries with it particular features for coding. As she observes, coding images is complex and draws on several modalities. In addressing production, she poses such questions as 'When was the picture made?', 'Where was it made?', 'Who made it?', 'Was it made for someone else?' and 'What were the social identities of maker, the owner, and the subject of the image?' She poses other questions about the image itself: 'What is being shown?' and 'Is it one of a series?' As for 'audiencing', as she terms it, she asks: 'What was the original audience for this image?', 'How is it being circulated?', 'How is it re-displayed?' and 'Does the image have a written text to guide its interpretation in its initial moment of display (a caption or catalogue entry)?' At the same time, issues of process are also at stake: engagement, activism, empowerment and so on are all areas that can be studied separate from or alongside the visual images produced. However, it is the images themselves that are more likely to be regarded as problematic, and notwithstanding the fact that I do not think visual images should dominate visual research, I do not think that they should be absent from our analytic frameworks. The images are, after all, the most visible evidence in visual research, although the types of visual images that

can serve as evidence may be more broadly interpreted than just the images produced by participants in community projects or in individual archival projects.

Visualizing What is at Stake: Theorizing the Presence of Absence

The question of absence – 'Where have all the Swazis gone?' – may seem like a
strange entry point to a chapter that sets out to explore analytic frameworks for
working with the visual. However, an underlying theme that is appropriate in
keeping with visual studies more broadly in much of the work that community
photographers address in 'visualizing what is at stake' is that of absence: the absence
of peace and security, the absence of social justice on the playground, the absence
of voice, the absence of access to health care or education or protection, and even
(or especially) the absence of life. Indeed, Susan Sontag writes:

> Ever since cameras were invented in 1839 photography has kept company
> with death. Because an image produced with a camera is, literally, a trace of
> something brought before the lens, photography was superior to any painting
> as a memento of the vanished past and the dear departed. (Sontag, 2003: 21)

As Jay Ruby, among many other visual scholars, has pointed out, absence and the
presence of loss and death are common themes in photography, as both the objects
in photography (memorials) as well as the subject (remembering, grieving, mourning,
recovering and so on). Capturing absence is explored in Jay Ruby's work (1995) on
post-mortem images, in Batchen's work (2004) on photography and hair jewellery, and
in the 'materializing mourning' memento mori studies of Pointon (1999) and others.

The work of photographer, photo-therapist and activist Jo Spence (1986), in particular, serves to trouble the issues of health and culture as read through the lens of the
camera, focusing, as she does in her photographs, on a sense of presence and absence
in relation to breast cancer and finally to leukemia, which killed her in 1994. Susan Bell
(2002), in her essay on three of Spence's photographs (*Mammogram, I framed my ...* and
Untitled or *Jo Spence on a good day*), studies the ways in which her photos work. Bell draws
on what Spence herself says about presence and absence, visibility and invisibility:

> We must begin to question photographs, asking not only what we think they
> show us (and how much of what we think we perceive is in fact based on the
> particular type of visual rhetoric working upon the sitter), but also what they
> don't (can't) show us. (Spence, 1986: 92, cited in Bell, 2002)

Mammogram is a photo of Spence, naked from the waist up, taken at Spence's
request by the X-ray technician. There is something of an irony here of the technician photographing Spence's exterior when the mammogram itself is of course
somewhat removed from the person. Bell writes:

Spence is holding up the plates with her hands, a standard protocol at the time. The photograph is dominated by the machine and the breast. ... To create a successful mammogram, the radiographer must do all she can to separate Spence's breast from the rest of her body, isolating breast tissue from the chest and armpit. ... The four images – the mammogram – taken by the radiographer of Spence's breast will look different from *Mammogram*. Although the radiographer will snap photos for both images, it is the one that we see, *Mammogram*, that reveals the systems of medicine and photography. (Bell, 2002: 20)

Loss and absence give over to absence and (near) death. Jon Prosser's (2007) poignant narrative essay in *Visual Studies*, 'Visual Mediation of Critical Illness: An Autobiographical Account of Nearly Dying and Nearly Living', draws together a collection of visual images from X-rays, drawings (his own and those of his children) and photographs of himself mountain climbing as a young man of 15, all juxtaposed with images of the ambulance that took him to the hospital, an arm of the British Heart Foundation. This collection of images serves as visual evidence of a journey of recovery. The images and narrative are presented in the context of a metaphor of mountain climbing, Prosser's passion. The essay is fascinating for a number of reasons, not least of which is in relation to what he concluded about the use of visual strategies:

Looking back, two visual strategies operated in tandem, acting as instruments of change management. The first, a crude version of art therapy, fed and countered my emotional angst, thereby meeting my psychological needs. ... Taken in moderation and imbued with subtlety, it was visual evidence of a crisis that needed resolving, an emotional outlet and safety valve. Changing emotionally dark images into something contrary was creative and playful. ... The second strategy was a proactive one whose sole purpose was rebuilding what had been lost. This was the 'ape' element of climbing to recovery, since it involved the application of brawn repetitively, laboriously, and grindingly, over a long period and is ongoing. (Prosser, 2007: 198–9)

Carol Mavor (1997), in her work on the materiality of dress and memory (and simultaneously the materiality of photographs), quotes the French artist Christian Boltanski: 'What they [clothing and photography] have in common is that they are simultaneously presence and absence. They are both an object and a souvenir of a subject, exactly as a cadaver is both an object and souvenir of subject' (cited in Mavor, 1997: 49). Mavor's work has been critical in constructing a sense of absence and loss in family photos. Family relations, mothers and especially the absence of any autonomy can figure prominently, as seen in Annette Kuhn's excavation of memory through school photographs:

Sadly, the photograph of me in my newly bought uniform, is now lost, but I retain a clear sense not just of what the picture looked like but also of how it felt to be inside those clothes at that moment. I did not particularly like the photograph; to me, the girl in the too-big uniform looked fat, graceless and out of place. What was there to be proud of? Did the sleeves of my blazer cover my limply hanging hands, as my memory-image insists? Were the shoulder seams several inches past my sagging shoulders? Was the hem of the dress six inches below my knees? Did strands of badly cut hair stick out from underneath an awkwardly placed beret? These clothes, in every sense, decidedly did not fit.

And yet this uniform was proof for all to see that, as an eleven-year old bound for a good school, I was different, cleverer, a cut above the rest; it singled me out from the rest of my contemporaries. The fact that the photograph was made at all is proof that, for a brief time at least, I was once again special, the credit to my mother I had stopped being several years earlier; the photograph was her own idea, and she went to some trouble to arrange it. (1995: 91)

This work around photography and absence extends to play as Jacqueline Reid-Walsh and I discovered in our work on the afterlife of popular culture and the work of bell hooks (Mitchell and Reid-Walsh, 2002), where hooks mourns the loss of a photograph of herself dressed up in a cowgirl suit:

I loved this snapshot of myself because it was the only image available to me that gave me a sense of presence, of girlhood beauty and capacity for pleasure. ... The camera captures me in my cowgirl outfit, white ruffled blouse, vest, fringed skirt, my one gun and my boots. In this image, I became all that I wanted to be in my imagination. ... Losing the snapshot, I lost the proof of my worthiness – that I had been a bright-eyed child capable of wonder, the proof that there was a 'me of me'. (hooks, 1994: 45)

The Presence of Absence: Vulindlela, 2004–2006

Dealing with death is what we all have in common. (Author field notes, September 2004)

When I consider that the focus of the various photovoice and participatory projects in which I have been involved over several years (mostly in Southern Africa and mostly in the context of HIV and AIDS, arguably a topic that, at least until the beginning of the roll-out of ARVs a couple of years ago, had inevitable links to death and dying and absence), the themes of many of the images should not be surprising. Although there is greater access to ARVS in 2010 in Southern Africa, there remain many barriers to people knowing their status (before it is too late), let alone actually seeking treatment or having access to treatment, something that is well documented in Steinberg's (2009) *Three Letter Plague*. The images that I explore here are taken from a collection of 500 or so photographs produced between 2004 and 2006 by teachers, community health care workers and youth in one rural district of KwaZulu-Natal, a district where at the time 66.67 percent of pregnant women were HIV positive and where children were often in child-headed households or raised by grandparents, mostly grandmothers (gogos). What interested me when I went back over many of the photographs, captions, interviews and composite videos that had been produced (see Chapter 9) was that despite an often optimistic sense among participants of 'we can do something' (which is good), there was a correspondingly deep narrative running through their work that spoke of absence.

In a previous article in which my colleagues and I described some of the same visual data that I refer to here, we used the expression 'the face of AIDS' to talk about the types of images that the community photographers (teachers and health care workers) produced. 'The face of AIDS,' we argued, was about empty chairs at a beauty parlour, grandmothers taking care of young children because their own offspring were sick or dead, and community health care workers walking up into the hills to tend to sick patients (Mitchell et al., 2005a). An alternative and complementary reading that I explore here is an examination of the ways in which absence *is* the point. By this I mean that absence is not just viewed in the objects and scenes represented but that it is a broad discourse.

In the following pages, I analyse the photographs in two ways. First, I look at content, noting the ways in which absence cuts across many of the photographs produced by teachers, health care workers and youth in relation to such thematic areas as missing people (according to generations and gender), emptiness, and absence of hope. I then go on to look at several genres of picture taking, noting the ways in which various genres in and of themselves evoke absence.

Themes of Presence and Absence

Absent generations: Where are the parents?

This photograph, as taken by one of the community health care workers, depicts an older woman in the foreground who is more than likely the grandmother. In the background, a young girl is standing in the doorway of her house. She is in her

Figure 6.1 Lost generation

school uniform. While there is no caption for this picture, it speaks to a growing phenomenon in South African families: the raising of children by grandmothers following the sickness and death of parents. As Gideon Mendel (2001) points out in *A Broken Landscape*, in some cases there are grandparents who are caring for as many as 12 or 14 grandchildren, not just the children of their own offspring. In Figure 6.1 the actual parent is absent – and somehow the particular construction of the picture suggests a missing generation. From the perspective of the government departments of Education and Social Development, the situation may be far from ideal. For example, in an interview with an official from the Department of Social Development, the point was made that there is a need to offer parenting skills to these *new-again parents*, particularly in relation to interacting with teenagers and understanding contemporary issues of sexuality, issues of child care and so on. In some cases, communities that have set up drop-in centres for orphans and vulnerable children are offering such parenting skills; however, to date, there are few such services. At the same time, there is another type of absence: the almost inevitable absence of grandparents, who themselves are not well. A UNICEF study a few years ago noted that in addition to children losing one or both parents, they were also sometimes doubly orphaned in that they may have lost the very grandparent (or aunt or other relative) who had assumed initial responsibility for them after the death of a parent, and had to, once again, be relocated (Smart, 2003). Some children who had been orphaned, the report stated, had been moved three and four times because of the death of each new caregiver. Schoeman (2000) refers to this as the 'walking the road' phenomenon, a term that graphically names the unfortunate chain of circumstances that are likely to befall a child from the onset of illness of the parent through to having to care for the parent, arranging for a funeral, moving in with other caregivers and so on.

Clearly, the impact on school performance and school attendance is significant. As one rural teacher observes:

> Learners come and go. … The school recently discovered that a brother and sister (grade four and grade six) were living by themselves. Their mother had died. The girl (grade six) appeared at school in a tight t-shirt and pants. She said her mother was about to buy her a new school uniform. Another day, her brother appeared in the same t-shirt he had worn the day before. When the school investigated, we discovered that they were living by themselves. And then they were gone. Relatives swept in and took them away. That happens all the time. (cited in Mitchell et al., 2009: 122)

Another teacher, working with the images from his own family album, comments:

> As a teacher, I have discovered that the number of child-headed families is rising. Sometimes, I find a child is absent from school. Maybe for a week or two, or for the day or two. When you try to dig deeper about the situation you will find that the child could not come to school for the past two weeks or past two days simply because he or she has to look after his or her dying father. Or both parents are very very sick and the child cannot pull the door

and leave for school. Instead, he or she must remain at home with the aim to prepare food, wash the parent, feed them. And some of the children have witnessed the death of their parent. If the family is not being lead by a child, you find that an elderly person, a grandfather or a grandmother, is now actually responsible for the education of their grandchildren. Those are common cases in my country especially in my environment or in my province – Kwazulu-Natal – so it's a challenge or a calling to everybody. Nobody has to neglect that call. Everybody has to respond positively. (Cited in Mitchell et al., 2009: 122)

The situation is exacerbated by the desperation of adults actually buying and selling orphans in order to get the 190 rand (less than $40 CDN) Child Grant per month.

Where are the girls and young women?

I took this picture in a beauty salon. The chairs are empty. You would expect to see pretty young women sitting under these hair-dryers but they are not there. They are either sick or disfigured and can't go out. Or they are dead.

One of the most poignant *presence of absence* photographs in the collection is the image of empty chairs in a beauty salon. The photographer, a community health care worker, offers one of the clearest 'gendered readings' of the AIDS pandemic through her careful attention to the beauty salon setting. As Stephen Lewis, the UN Special Envoy for HIV/AIDS, stated at the International AIDS Conference in

Figure 6.2 Empty chairs in beauty parlour

Bangkok, 'It's a pandemic within a pandemic' – with girls and young women making up 75 percent of all those between the ages of 15 and 24 who are infected. (In KwaZulu-Natal, the estimates now are that between 37 and 47 percent of all women are HIV positive.) The use of prevention methods such as condom use appears to be extremely low. Young women between the ages of 15 and 24 are five to six times more likely to become infected than young men of the same age (UNAIDS, 2008). From other work that we have carried out in the area of gender violence, we know that a girl's first sexual experience in this region is likely to be non-consensual (Jewkes et al., 2002). When we conducted interviews with school girls in the district about the issues that most concern them, their response was 'We just hope we don't get pregnant before we finish school', a statement which suggests that many are engaging in unprotected sex – and, of course, an indicator of their risk of infection.

Where are the children?

I took a picture of this bus because it represents for me what AIDS is doing to our community. This bus is taking a group to a funeral. Another AIDS-related funeral.

The photograph below was taken by a teacher. In his commentary about the photograph, he notes that the school bus is full of mourners on their way to a Saturday funeral. The bus, he says, is following the undertaker. The choice of subject (a bus) is significant for its representation of absence. One would normally expect to see children on a bus like this. Perhaps he is also commenting on the fact that the bus should be on the road on a weekday and not on a Saturday.

Figure 6.3   School bus taking mourners to funeral

Figure 6.4 Empty desks

Figure 6.5 No children crossing

Where are the learners?

A teacher and a principal took these images of emptiness in two different schools. Although there is no caption for the 'empty-desk' image, it offers a visual contrast with what one might expect in rural schools, where there is often overcrowding and

DOING VISUAL RESEARCH

not enough desks for students. The image of the empty desks takes us back to the idea that children may be sick themselves. As Moletsane (2006) has observed, school-going young people who are on ARVs may have to miss school in order to actually comply with the regimen. Or, as we have noted earlier, they may already be caring for a sick parent. And if they themselves are already heading up the household – a situation that is not uncommon – then they may need to be taking care of younger siblings, following up with all of the legal aspects of applying for a social grant, or are too poor themselves to attend school.

A school principal took the image of children crossing on an empty road. In his comments on the picture, he notes that there is a certain irony about a 'children crossing' sign at a time when attendance at school is so erratic. His choice of a long 'pan' shot of the road evokes emptiness.

Absence of hope

He can't accept that he is HIV positive. He feels he has to commit suicide because he would not like to tell people that he has AIDS. (caption translated from IsiZulu)

Figure 6.6 Staged suicide

Figure 6.6, a staged image of a suicide through hanging, was produced by a group of boys as part of a larger collection of photographs taken by eighth- and ninth-grade learners in one school. Their focus was on representing stigma, a theme that came out of initial photovoice work with their teachers, who felt that this was something that was critical to address at the school. While many students chose to show images of metal bars and fences to represent the effects of being shunned by the community, and although some of their photographs offer images of a way forward in terms of programmes to fight stigma, this horrifying image of the staged suicide might be read as a representation of despair and an absence of hope.

Clearly, it is a provocative picture. The boys' staging is reminiscent of Sally Mann's controversial photographs of her children. In her work where she has photographed her own children as sexualized subjects, she has caught elements of childhood that most adults do not want to see. Anne Higonnet observes: 'Mann's work is not easy to look at. Whether in confrontational or visionary modes, her images upset cherished conventions of idyllic childhood' (1998: 204–5). Overall, though, what is striking about the image of the staged suicide is the fact that this entire composition, from conceptualization to creation, was completed in a matter of minutes. The students would have had very little time to 'think up' the images, and it is significant that this particular image came so quickly to their minds. We have argued elsewhere that the 'sick of AIDS' phenomenon in South Africa has often left young people feeling powerless, both because they are tired of hearing about AIDS and because they are literally sick of AIDS (Mitchell and Smith, 2003). The absence of hope is arguably the most critical absence.

Genres of Absence

It is also useful to look at the actual photographic genres, which are integral to meaning. In previous work on school photography that I carried out a few years ago with Sandra Weber (Mitchell and Weber, 1999), we wrote about picture day at school and the resulting portraits. Drawing on interviews with children and beginning teachers, we explored the conventions of this type of photography: the 'sitting', usually in front of a backdrop such as a rainbow, a forced pose for which the child is required to hold a pen or a book or some other school-related artefact and is often required (by the parents) to dress up (Mitchell and Weber, 1999). Photographic subjects are usually required to smile, regardless of how they are feeling. What is often present in these images is what a consuming parent would want to purchase: a package of school photographs of a child posed cheerfully, neat and tidy. What is absent is what the child really feels about the moment, and perhaps some sense of the child's autonomy. Years later, as is evident in the interviews, photo subjects still look back on some of these sittings with dismay. Added to this dismay is the fact that their photos are sometimes still being displayed, years later, on the wall of their school, on a mantel or on a television set of a parent, aunt or grandparent. To take up Gillian Rose's (2001) point about where and how photographs are stored and displayed, these lasting impression images are usually out of the control of the child. In one case, we had a photo taken by a community health care worker in which an adult is caught in the act of lining up a group of children for a picture.

Another type of portrait is what Marejka Du Toit refers to as the environmental portrait (Du Toit, 2006; Du Toit and Gordon, 2007). In her photo work as part of the Durban South project, where she has been looking at the effects of the oil refineries on the people living in the area, she has amassed a collection of photos of smoke stacks belching out pollutants, of chained fences and so on – landscape photos that position the residential area against the backdrop of the refineries. The photos are devoid of people, but the impact of person-created pollution is everywhere. In the collection of photos dealing with HIV and AIDS, the image of the long, straight and empty road leading up to the school with its 'children crossing' sign (Figure 6.5) could be read as an environmental portrait. The photographer-principal has made the point that if nothing is done about the AIDS pandemic, there will be no one coming to school.

Others in the Durban South project used scenes and images metaphorically. A photograph of an empty bed, the teachers said, is symbolic both of death and of unprotected sex, central to a popular sex-equating-to-death discourse. Bulletin boards in schools were photographed because they had been appropriated by learners for the posting of 'love notices', with students recording their affections for another. While on the one hand it was important for teachers to recognize the vulnerability of youth, our team was also at the same time struck by the 'them and not us' feature of their work, and could only speculate how this might affect their interactions with young people. In a more positive way, some teachers arranged a collection of T-shirts bearing AIDS prevention messages as symbolic of youth activism, and also took photographs of AIDS awareness posters and images from an AIDS awareness day in which young people were clearly engaged (see Chapter 3).

Staging as a photo genre

It is the staging genre that participants in the Vulindlela study used most extensively in their work. And while Figure 6.6 is perhaps the most dramatic, there are many other examples in the collection. During the warm-up activities in setting up the photovoice project with the teachers and community health care workers, our team encouraged them to experiment with the cameras, using the prompt 'Feeling strong, feeling not so strong'. As noted in Chapter 4 with reference to the idea of the 'theatrical photograph' (Theberge, 2006), staging might be read as a particular genre of photograph. Drawing from the work of Jo Spence, who used staging as a device to interrogate her own schoolgirl memories and went so far as to dress up as an adult in a school uniform for the poses, we invited participants to act out various scenes. The main point was to give everyone in the group a chance to use the camera.

As researchers, our interpretation of the staged playfulness with the cameras was that it was a matter of necessity because there was no time to go out into the community to produce more realistic portraits. Whether, as discussed in an earlier chapter, it is because of this introduction or whether staging simply fits well as a type of performance/storytelling, we are not sure. Where Jean Stuart used a visual arts-based approach to addressing HIV and AIDS in her work with beginning teachers in South Africa, she found that many of her participants chose a photo-story approach, an important genre within South African popular culture (Stuart, 2007). Lori Pauli (2006), writing about Figure 6.6, states that the staged hanging scene can be read as an example of a long-standing photographic practice:

> In 1840 Hippolyte Bayard created a highly unusual self-portrait: a photograph depicting himself as a suicide by drowning. We see the 'corpse' from the knees up, his tanned hands crossed in his lap, his torso bare, and his damp hair combed back. … The photograph is accompanied by a text lamenting in piteous terms, the failure of the French government to recompense Bayard adequately for his role in the invention of photography.

> Bayard's *Self-Portrait as a Drowned Man*, with its theatrical props and implied narrative, reminds us that the creation of fictitious images or 'staged' photographs has been a part of photographic practice from the very beginning. (2006: 13)

Another photograph 'staging' death is Figure 6.7, in which a young boy depicts himself lying dead in a bush. Interestingly, we see that it is almost identical to an image produced by Sally Mann, *The Ditch*. However, where the young photographers use the image of a body in a bush provocatively to represent death, Mann's photograph, according to Anne Higonnet, is actually one of birthing. Higonnet writes:

> A boy, Mann's son, presses head first along a narrow channel in the sand, furrowing through the matter extending out from the photographer's, the mother's, position. At the end of the passage, the child will reach open water. Already he belongs to crisp light and defined forms, not to the mother's inchoate blur. Anonymous figures loom on either side, silently waiting for the child who leaves the mother's place. The scene is neither grandiose nor epic; it lodges the universal at the level of the ordinary incident. (Higonnet, 1998: 204–5)

While we are quite certain that the boys who constructed the stigma image are unlikely to have ever heard of Sally Mann or to have ever seen *The Ditch*, it is fascinating to see the overlaps between composition and meaning.

Although there may be a variety of interpretations made about the 'almost hidden' body in Figure 6.8, a common one would be the sheer *invisibility of AIDS*. People do not talk about the disease, and although the effect of the pandemic is

Figure 6.7   Stigma

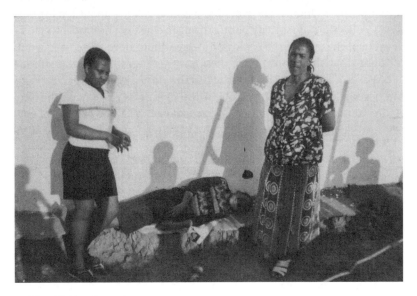

Figure 6.8   Hidden from view

all around, it is not as dramatic as one might expect. People don't suddenly die of AIDS – they become ill over a period of time, and they often have other related illnesses (TB, other opportunistic infections, etc.) and may also be carrying on with work and community events in a limited way.

Presence, Absence and Future-Oriented Remembering

Much of this work about presence and absence has a future-remembering angle to it, and although I have emphasized the ways that photographs can be read according to loss and absence, I do not mean to suggest hopelessness. In doing the background research for *Reinventing Ourselves as Teachers: Beyond Nostalgia* (Mitchell and Weber, 1999), I became interested in how various people, starting with my mother, used photographs in a future-oriented way. Living all of her adult life in the same small prairie town and close to many relatives and family friends, my mother's 'on the ground' training in visual methodologies spilled over into taking action. Her brand of this, over the years, was nothing short of subversive when it came to getting people to take serious family photographs. She would know, for example, of an elderly person in the community who had died and of her bereaved family who might not know what to do with all the personal effects, especially the photographs. Aghast at the idea that the family in its desperation would throw out the photos along with the leftovers in the refrigerator, my mother would jump in and offer to take care of the photos. And she would not just rescue the photos but would spend time going through them, sorting and shifting in a way that is reminiscent of the work of Richard Chalfen (1987) or Martha Langford (2001) with other people's albums. She would sometimes tell me about having gathered together a collection of (sorted) photos from the boxes or albums to pass on to one or more of the survivors. 'Wade and Percy should have these,' she would say, 'it isn't right (that they don't) have these pictures,' and before you knew it, she would be passing a parcel of photos back to the surviving family.

I had never really thought much about the significance of my mother's actions until I interviewed a teacher, Deborah, who spoke of this same practice of engaging in what she described as stirring up memories and forcing others to live historically:

> This turning to pictures for comfort was, and still is, a need I have. When a close relative or pet (I become very attached to my pets) passes away, I need to know that they are somehow still visible to me. I need to assure myself that they really did exist. A photograph somehow fills a void for me.

> Perhaps not all people feel this way. I guess I should keep this in mind: As I have often given pictures I have taken of others as gifts to their family. For example, I often take pictures of my girlfriend's little boy, and later have given them to her in a frame as a gift because I am afraid his growing-up years will be lost to her. She does not take pictures, nor does her family, and it bothers me that they don't. In another example, I came across a picture of my aunt

and uncle from years ago. I had never seen it before and was sure my cousins hadn't either, but I took it upon myself to have this picture mounted in an old-fashioned frame and gave it to my cousin for her birthday. She had lost her mother (my aunt) as a teenager, and I thought she would appreciate an old memory at this point in her life. However, I don't think the picture carried the same meaning for her as it did for me. (cited in Mitchell and Weber, 1999: 110)

Although she recognizes that the photographs may not have as much meaning as they ought to, Deborah nonetheless persists in stirring up memories and carrying out an activist agenda through photos.

Presence and Absence in Framing Photo Analysis

The discussion in this chapter may seem to fly in the face of community-based research and participatory process. After all, aren't the meanings that the participants themselves come up with through their captions, and other produced texts, the ones that are most important? What I have tried to show here are, in a sense, two layers of participant engagement – first, choosing the subject and taking the photos, and then, at a second level, producing captions. What I have offered from my readings of the participants' work is a broader interpretation of what the images might mean 'taken as a whole' – or if not taken as a whole, because I have been selective, I have offered a reading of some of the images in the context of statistical and social data on the situation of HIV and AIDS in one rural district between 2004 and 2006. These photographs can be read in a variety of ways and, depending on the audience, may have different effects. Gideon Mendel's (2001) very powerful visual text *A Broken Landscape* is a recent example in Southern Africa of contesting these invisible spaces of HIV and AIDS. Marilyn Martin (2004) poses the question, 'Can the visual arts make a difference to HIV and AIDS in South Africa?' However, beyond this very specific photovoice project in rural South Africa, I want to suggest that *the presence of absence* can offer a framework for working with other collections, including family photos and community-based photovoice projects.

Invisible photographer

W. T. J. Mitchell (2005), in his essay on the work of American photographer Robert Frank, discusses some of ways in which the photographer typically becomes isolated, disembodied and, at most, a shadow image. Mitchell writes: 'The still photographer is in danger of becoming a spy, ghost, spook, specter: a shadow flitting among the surfaces of things, a vampire sucking out the pink juice of human kind, leaving nothing but a gray residue' (2005: 288). He goes on to describe the one 'family photo' that Frank includes in his 1950s collection *The Americans, U.S. 90 en route to Del Rio, Texas*, highlighting the notion of presence and absence:

In *U.S. 90*, Frank shows his family cut in two. A one-eyed car holds a sleepy May and Pablo, his wife and son, in the early morning hours in the middle of nowhere, piles of laundry in the back window echoing the profile of the distant mountains. The frame of the photograph bisects the car, so that the driver's seat, the place of the father, the photographer, Frank himself, is amputated. Every American father knows this: they rarely appear in the spontaneous family photos, only in the formal ones. Otherwise, the father is himself the photographer, the absent presence, a shadow cast on the image, frame, screen, or medium itself. (W. Mitchell, 2005: 288)

Mitchell's analysis seems to me to offer an approach that makes visible some of the ways in which any photos (including photos in community-based studies) can be read in the context of presence and absence.

Immoveable furniture

One of the first analyses I ever carried out with a set of family photographs I called 'Immoveable Furniture' (Mitchell, 1996), drew on memory work and photo analysis to interrogate 'What's there and what's not?' or presence and absence. One aspect of this work was reviewing the site of so many family photographs: my parents' dining-room table, always with a large portrait of my grandparents and my father and his brother as little boys in the background. The portrait in the years following my mother's death became a contested one. Which of the three siblings in my family would get the portrait? My awareness of its dominance in so many photos made me also aware of its immovability and then its absence in my own family, and yet even if I had been the one to inherit the portrait, I am not sure what I would have done with it. It belongs on the wall of a dining room in a Manitoba farmhouse that no longer exists. Another popular site for family photos in my home as a child was to be posed standing near the piano, which was itself a site for displaying photos (similar to what Hurdley, 2006, discusses about the role of the mantel in British homes as a place of display). The piano's presence in so many photos, however, still conjures for me another type of loss or disappointment, symbolized in my mother's inscription on the back of a photo of me at age 7 sitting at the piano: 'Claudia practising' is what the caption says, but it is a type of wishful thinking on my mother's part. The piano eventually went to one of my brothers so that his children could start learning, and thus there is a new generation and a new place for the piano – and still, it is in family photos that are sent to me. How do my nieces and nephew regard this piece of furniture? Is it immoveable for them, as well?

When I first began to think about where photos were taken in my family, I became aware of the fact that there was not one single photo taken in a bedroom. Even allowing for the fact that most of the early pictures from before I was born were taken outdoors to accommodate issues of lighting, picture-taking sessions with the Brownie instamatic (with flash) in the 1950s and 1960s and beyond still did not go into bedrooms. What were the taboos of North American family snaps that precluded photographing certain domestic spaces, and how have they changed over time? These presences and absences in the photos of the domestic spaces of my childhood, while far from the 'life and death' discussion of the photovoice images from rural South Africa discussed earlier in the chapter, nonetheless complement something about the visual itself, as Susan Sontag reminds us.

Conclusion

As a metaphor for social activism, studying the presence of absence offers communities as well as researchers and policy makers a point of entry for getting underneath and beyond some of the statistical accounts of the pandemic noted in this chapter. Might the participants themselves go back over the images with the question, 'What's there and what's not there?'. Ford and colleagues (2003) argue that the most effective messages and campaigns for change come from inside the community, when the participants themselves create the messages. The examples shown above offer powerful evidence that solutions brought about through campaigns of awareness are not 'out there'; rather, they are intrinsically in and from the community itself. To date, the photographs explored in this chapter have had only limited 'systematic' use within the community from which they emanated. However, it is possible, as I highlight in the next chapter, to extend the 'afterlife' of these photos and other visual data, such as drawings and video, and to deepen the possibilities for interpretation by building community-based archives.

SEVEN

Data collections and building a democratic archive: 'No more pictures without a context'

Claudia Mitchell and Naydene de Lange

Introduction

What can the study of technologies and the practices of coding (including coding by participants), storage and retrieval contribute to visual research? How can we fully mine collections of visual data? Our interest in these questions comes out of a recognition of the generative aspects of using visual methodology tools, such as community photography, participatory video and drawings; the challenges of fully mining the resulting (and expanding) sets of visual data; and the potential for new developments within the field of digital technologies to provide opportunities for social science researchers and those working within information and communication technologies (ICT) to collaborate and to develop metadata systems for analysis. With the popularization of the image-sharing website Flickr, anyone with access to the Internet can engage in sharing family photographs, social tagging through folksonomies, and the various other uses of social networking sites to interact with visual data. Hence, it is assumed that we as visual researchers are making good use of new technologies to manage and extend the use of visual data, and that we engage participants in this process as well. However, as Miller (2007) points out, the work of visual researchers often appears rather haphazard. Commenting on the extensive data sets of photos taken by missionaries in the nineteenth and twentieth centuries, and the potential for these images to capture historical change, he observes:

> Despite their scholarly potential, the usefulness of these historical photographs has been limited by their fragility and by their unorganized state and inaccessibility, distributed as they are across many separate repositories. Researchers

who have sought to tap into these resources have typically had to travel to the places where the photographs are held and then thumb through the collections in the hope of finding just the right photos that will illustrate a text, illuminate some scholarly theme, or provide visual confirmation or disconfirmation for an argument or empirical claim. Some collections have been scanned and catalogued for use on-sight in the archives, thus achieving the goal of protecting the originals from handling and making the photographs easier to work with. More often than not, however, the success of a search through the paper files has been a function of the sheer persistence and good luck of the investigator. (Miller, 2007: 85)

Miller is referring to historical documents and ones where neither the photographer nor the photo subjects are likely to be alive. However, as the subtitle of this chapter, 'No more pictures without a context', suggests, how much more might we do with images if the photographers themselves and those representing their various communities could be more involved in working with their own visual productions through participatory analysis? The statement 'no more pictures without a context' comes from a manifesto created in 1988 by the AIDS activist organization ACT UP. Dismayed at the way that photo images of People Living with AIDS (PLWA) were being taken (by outsiders), and responding to the catalytic event at the Museum of Modern Art (MoMA), New York, where photographer Nicholas Nixon was exhibiting photos he had taken of PLWAs, ACT UP developed a manifesto, which stated the following:

> We believe that the representation of people with AIDS (PWAs) affects not only how viewers will perceive PWAs outside the museum, but, ultimately, crucial issues of AIDS funding, legislation, and education. The artist's choice to produce representational work always affects more than a single artist's career, going beyond issues of curatorship beyond the walls on which an artist's work is displayed. Ultimately, representations affect those portrayed. In portraying PWAs as people to be pitied or feared, as people alone and lonely, we believe that this show perpetuates general misconceptions about AIDS without addressing the realities of those of us living every day with this crisis as PWAs and people who love PWAs ... The PWA is a human being whose health has deteriorated not simply due to a virus, but due to government inaction, the inaccessibility of affordable health care, and institutionalized neglect in the form of heterosexism, racism, and sexism. We demand the visibility of PWAs who are vibrant, angry, loving, sexy, beautiful, acting up and fighting back. STOP LOOKING AT US; START LISTENING TO US. (Grover 1999: 113)

While the manifesto predates the idea of the participatory digital archive, it is important as it raises awareness of the 'othering' that photo images can perpetuate. Furthermore, it might simultaneously be read as a precursor to the idea of the participatory archive. 'Start looking at what we see' could be the new manifesto.

Unlike the photos in Nicholas Nixon's exhibition at MoMA, the images included in the previous chapter were produced by the community members themselves in a rural district of South Africa over a specific time (2004 to 2006). This period was characterized by relatively little access to ARVs or to voluntary counselling and testing (VCT) services, and attitudes of stigma played a key role in how communities regarded the issues surrounding HIV and AIDS. Thus, notwithstanding the various ways that one might read a set of images, it is critical to regard them as being from a particular era.

In this chapter, we consider two types of data sets: photos collected as data in a photovoice project in South Africa and drawings collected as data in a project on gender-based violence in Rwanda. In the first part of the chapter, we report on our work with digital archives. We then go on to offer two case studies. The first case study concerns the development of a community-based archive. The second case study looks at the ways in which drawings produced by children, as a commonly used data source, might be explored in the context of a participatory archive. In this case study, the participants themselves are involved in the coding and interpreting of their own data.

About Digital Archives and Social Research

A digital archive, as Pearce-Moses (2005) writes, is a collection of data in digital form that are stored in a way that is accessible by software applications and that support restoration of part or all of a system. Digital images are described using a metadata protocol and are saved in a database for retrieval, access and preservation. As outlined elsewhere (Park et al., 2007), in the actual digitization the activity of connecting original materials and their apparent 'objective' and 'subjective' descriptions with newly created digital surrogates forms a database (Hughes, 2004). Digital archives are used in the field of information management and, of course, hold value for the present and the future generations of researchers, as well as the public at large (Park et al., 2008a). However, the full potential of such material can be only realized if the resulting digital archives are easily accessible, have a suitable search function, and are accompanied by sufficient metadata to support the use of the data (Linden and Green, 2006).

In his essay 'Reading an Archive', Allan Sekula (2003) observes that archives are far from neutral. He cites numerous examples of the ways in which both the content and management of archives shape what knowledge (and ultimately whose knowledge) is stored in the first place, how it is coded and categorized, how it can be retrieved and who has access to the archive. But if archives are far from neutral, they are also far from one-dimensional in relation to their meanings. But more than this, they do not have to be static. We became more interested in how we might use technology to work with collections of visual images in communities.

A few years ago, we secured funding for two studies: 'Giving Life (to Data) to Save Lives (in the Age of AIDS)' (Park et al., 2008b) and the 'Social Uses of Digitization' (Park et al., 2008a). These studies emerged from our concern related to the sheer size of our collections. What we saw as the challenge, as noted in the introduction of this chapter, was doing more with the data. Although a variety of metadata schemes have been developed and used for improving teaching and learning within public collections, the development of protocols for documenting and using visual images and metadata within team research in the social sciences is less well developed.

Visual ethnographers such as Marcus Banks and Gillian Rose observe that developing protocols for working with visual data is a complex process. Rose (2001), for example, draws attention to at least three modalities related to photographs: the technological, the compositional and the social.

Although we encountered work with many different metadata systems, we found only a limited amount of work that had been done in working with community-based images, particularly in the context of health issues, and almost no work in such areas as HIV and AIDS and gender-based violence. Unlike the work described by Miller (2007), which related to hundreds of thousands of photographs taken by missionaries that are in the public domain, our focus, for ethical reasons, has never been to establish a large public archive accessible to a global audience. Rather, we have been concerned about the management of collections (countering Miller's 'thumbing through'), particularly because we have been working in one community over a period of time; because we have been able to work more strategically with images in ways that were longitudinally significant; because we have been communicating about the fact that communities themselves, especially in rural areas, may have had limited access to their own images; and, finally, because we want communities who have identified critical issues through their own participation in taking the pictures to be able to continue to work with the images.

Obviously, these communities were dealing with different social issues (see, for example, the work of Du Toit and Gordon, 2007, in Durban South on the impact of industrial pollution on the health of local participants). The catalyst for our own work in the area of HIV and AIDS came out of an acknowledgement of what Barnett and Whiteside (2003) refer to as the 'long wave effects' of HIV and AIDS, and the changing face of the epidemic (see Iliffe, 2006). Of the set of images, for example, produced in 2004 and 2005, one might ask the following questions: If those were the images produced during that time, what images are being produced in 2011? Are there generational differences? Would 15-year-olds in 2011 produce the same images produced five or six years earlier by their brothers, sisters and friends? Will teachers and community health care workers who produced the images in 2004 – many of which touched on death – produce the same images six or seven years later? We suggest that questions such as these are best answered in a context where we have comparative data, mechanisms for coding, technologies for storing, and retrieval systems. Furthermore, we recommend that those who are affected, and who produced the images, have some say in how the images are coded and stored, and even who has access to them.

Case Study 1: Building a Community-Based Archive in Rural KwaZulu-Natal

Vulindlela, the location for much of the photovoice work we describe here, is a rural district in the lower foothills of the southern Drakensberg in KwaZulu-Natal, a district, as noted in previous chapters, ravaged by the AIDS pandemic. Over the past six years, our use of participatory visual methodologies in the community has been in response to the failure of HIV and AIDS prevention programmes in the AIDS crisis (Campbell, 2003) and the importance of engaging community members as protagonists in addressing the issues in order to stem what has been described elsewhere as a 'sick of AIDS' phenomenon (Mitchell and Smith, 2003). Therefore, we have worked closely with the community of participants, which has included teachers, community health care workers, parents and young people. We have used drawings, photovoice and participatory video work to engage the participants in addressing the issues surrounding HIV and AIDS.

Various data sets gathered by teachers and community health care workers, for example, consisted of drawings (de Lange et al., 2007), several hundred photographs representative of the issues and solutions in addressing HIV and AIDS (Mitchell et al., 2005a), and photo-narratives of their discussion of issues and solutions in addressing HIV and AIDS in their community (de Lange et al., 2006). Young people, too, generated a data set consisting of photographs related to their understanding of stigma and how to address it (Moletsane et al., 2007). Working around issues affecting the participants' lives as they occur in their community has also generated a number of short video productions (see Chapter 5) as well as several composite videos about these issues (see Chapter 9). To date, work with these data sets has included two parts: (1) building the archive, and (2) developing a participatory component to the archive. The digitization process is explored in relation to the data sets in more detail elsewhere (de Lange et al., 2010; Mnisi, 2010; Park et al., 2007, 2008a). In this chapter, we briefly outline the stages of the project.

Process

Stage One

In adopting digitization techniques, we have scanned each photo item of the data set into a digital form. The first stage involved developing a scanning protocol for an entire photo collection, along with a database protocol for storing digital images. In working with a vast amount of data, accountability is always of the utmost importance, and as various postgraduate interns worked on the project, each intern was required to open a folder and indicate it with his or her name and the project title. Ascribing names to the collections of processed images allowed for a method of working through the hard copy collections where each intern could see which photographs had been digitized (i.e., what work had already been done), a procedure that avoided duplication and improved efficiency.

Stage Two

Second, the data set that was scanned in was carefully scrutinized to ensure that the visual data was clear, and to determine whether cropping and cleaning of the images was necessary (by using a software programme such as Corel PHOTO-PAINT or IrfanView). Following this, an identifier was added to the set of photographs (e.g., *Learning Together*), and, to each individual photograph (e.g., lt001, lt002, lt003). Once the preparation work had been completed, each photograph was scanned, converted to joint photographic experts group (JPEG) format, the resolution set at 300 dots per inch (DPI), the output type set as 'millions of colours'. Once the full scanned image was visible on the computer screen, the photograph was cropped to remove any unwanted elements; the image was re-sampled (by adjusting the physical size of the photograph (e.g., 15 × 10 cm)) and was then saved as a JPEG image in the allocated folder. To ensure that the scanning process had been done correctly, the size of the current image was compared to that of the previous image because the objective was to compress each image to a similar file output size (e.g., 300kb). In this way, the quality of the scanning process and the digital image was ensured. Finally, the folder containing the collection of digital images was then ready to be uploaded into the Greenstone digital library software.

Stage Three

The third stage involved producing a metadata schema. Metadata is merely data about data and describes and documents the subject matter; for example, metadata provides information about when, where, and by whom the data was generated, about the format of the information, and about whether access and copyright is provisional. However, regardless of the number and type of steps involved in creating a database of images through participatory archive methods, building such a database is always ongoing, and should be tested out for its effectiveness, especially with respect to the requirements of each project for which the data is used.

Much time has been spent on thinking about which elements to include in the metadata schema to facilitate the optimal use of the data by not only the various researchers but also the participants from the community. This has required careful reflection on the purposes for which we would use the metadata, who would be using the metadata and, of course, ethical considerations. Our first attempt at creating a particular standard for participatory metadata included information about the creator of the image, the title, the date the photo was taken, the date the digital image was created, historical information, holding information, call number, size, type, colour, rights, access restriction, sex of participant, cultural group of participant, content of image, age of participant (e.g., people or things, group or individual, girls, boys, family, father, mother), location of image, and the caption for the image (usually created by the photographer).

In coding these images, we also saw the necessity for different and specific types of metadata that might be relevant to systematizing our participants: their sex, age, cultural group (e.g., Zulu, Afrikaans, English-speaking), location (e.g., school, community, home, rural, urban), subject (e.g., school objects, landscape, cityscape), themes (stigma, virginity testing, orphans, poverty, gender-based violence), stance (e.g., candid, posed, composed), and caption, as well as the prompt we used to stimulate the participants to generate the visual data attached to the photograph. This metadata would therefore contextualize the 'making' of the data.

We decided on the Dublin Core metadata scheme (2008), which contains only 13 elements and would easily allow us to enter the data into the Greenstone digital library software (see below). We added two further elements: (1) the prompt we used to initiate data generation, and (2) the captions accompanying the data.

During the initial research process, we uncovered a number of important issues that would help inform our research as we progressed. One such issue was the need for immediate and methodological documentation of all the necessary elements required for the metadata set. A second critical issue was recognizing the importance of creating some sort of web tool where the images could be stored and accessed by all members of the team in both countries. Following this, the issue of ethics was also raised, as our initial plan was to put the digital data sets on the Internet for all persons to access and use. However, although having already acquired informed consent from our participants, the consent form did not explicitly outline to participants that we would be uploading their photographs onto a public website. Therefore, we decided to restrict access to the researchers only through a password-protected system.

Using Greenstone software for building and distributing a library collection

Central to the aims of our community-based research was the desire to highlight the fact that the aim of the Greenstone software itself was to empower users, particularly in universities, libraries and other public service institutions, and to help them build their own digital libraries. One way that digital libraries are radically transforming how information is disseminated and acquired is through UNESCO's partner communities and institutions. This is occurring all around the world in the fields of education, science and culture, particularly in developing countries. Greenstone's developers received the 2004 IFIP Namur Award for 'contributions to the awareness of social implications of information technology, and the need for a holistic approach in the use of information technology that takes account of social implications' (www.greenstone.org/factsheet, accessed 7 March 2008).

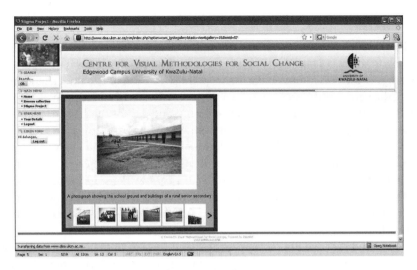

Figure 7.1   Example of a data set in the digital archive

Stage Four

Once the data set was organized into particular photo folders, with the metadata elements agreed upon, Greenstone Suite was loaded on the computer and was set up to begin creating a new collection (see Figure 7.1). Training for Greenstone Suite was provided by Digital Imaging South Africa (DISA), our collaborator and the eventual host of the database. Through the 'Gather' function, and the entry of the metadata for each photograph through the 'Enrich' function, the user-friendly software allowed for the easy uploading of the scanned photograph data set (see Figure 7.2). The photographs and the metadata were then combined to form the new collection by clicking on the 'Create' button.

Figure 7.2   Example of a photograph with its metadata

The participatory archive

Jay Ruby writes that '... the study of images alone, as objects whose meaning is intrinsic to them, is a mistaken method if you are interested in the ways people assign meanings to pictures' (Ruby, 1995: 5). His point is a critical one to understanding the idea of the participatory archive. Data mining and the use of scanning, digitizing and the development of metadata systems tell only one part of the story. However, we did succeed in building an archive containing drawings, photographs and videos, and we managed to pilot a data set of 125 photographs generated by young people on the issue of stigma. Further, we thought that the data set could be strengthened by asking the participants (community health care workers and teachers) to add captions. Each caption highlighted what the creator(s) felt the photograph depicted about stigma, and in so doing explored and deepened our understanding of HIV-related stigma.

We realized that having participants expand the visual data (adding captions) provided us with a tool to see how the participants constructed meaning from the images. We asked ourselves the following question: what would happen if the archive could be reconfigured so that community members themselves could participate in accessing the archive? Greater participation would democratize the user space, changing it from being an archive managed and used primarily by researchers to one that invited community members as participants in its (re)making. Hence, participants could assist with the coding and creation of categories, and they could go beyond analysing individual images to explore the archive's broader uses within health care and education. In this way, community photographers would be agents in the construction of knowledge.

A digital archive that is compiled in such a manner is known as a participatory archive. The participatory archive, as Huvila (2008) and Shilton and Srinivasan (2008) note, is a relatively new concept that refers to the ways in which users can be engaged in designing the archive as well as in coding and recoding the data. As Shilton and Srinivasan observe, the reason for creating a new participatory method is to prevent as much as possible the distortion of cultural histories of marginalized populations. A system that allows various marginalized groups to become engaged in the entire archiving process permits a community to ensure the authenticity of the individual pieces, with the archive depicting a more accurate history of the community. While much of the current literature about participatory archives links to the use of public archives in such settings as libraries and university departments, the nature of interactivity offers promising developments that could very well be incorporated into the participatory work of community-based archives in innovative ways. To go beyond more conventional forms of coding and working with the data with adults in participatory ways, how might children and young people as producers of images relate to, for example, their own sexuality, and how can they become their own agents in the construction of knowledge through the process of participatory archiving?

To date, there are few intervention strategies that regard the functions of technology as part of the solution to addressing critical social issues. Yet, we have written about one example of technology-based solutions. It involved a group of teachers from the Vulindlela community working with the digital archive of stigma photos produced by young people. While this was a small pilot study, we were interested in the teachers' engagement in the process and their practical ideas on how such an archive could contribute to addressing sexuality education (de Lange et al., 2010). However, we were not entirely focused on the actual process of engaging with the system. What particularly struck this group of teachers – and what drew us to this work on technology in the first place – was the sense of urgency. As Steinberg (2009) found in his work in Eastern Cape Province in South Africa, community members often refuse to be tested for HIV and AIDS when they are just a few steps away from a mobile clinic. We offer this point as one that could have an impact on how best to use a community archive. Who should have access to it, what ethical procedures need to be in place, and finally, what is the responsibility of the team itself to ensure the least harm to its participants?

Case Study 2: Working with A Participatory Archive of Children's Drawings

Another way to think about who or what constitutes a community is in relation to a particular demographic or social group. In this section of the chapter, we consider the ways in which children and young people interact together within a community. Our focus here is on the utilization of drawings as visual data. The use of drawings in visual research, as has been explored elsewhere (Prosser and Burke, 2008; Weber and Mitchell, 2007), can be a very efficient and engaging approach to obtaining the perspectives of communities, particularly communities of children and young people.

However, as with other visual methods, there are both strengths and limitations to allowing participants to become the researchers. One danger is that of 'tokenism', particularly in the case of children ('There, we have consulted; we asked them to draw a picture'). On the one hand, the low-tech aspect of using drawings as data makes it a very popular approach, particularly in development contexts. And while there are still many ethical issues with which to contend, the technical expertise of the participants may mean that there are fewer ethical issues in terms of anonymity and confidentiality than there are when working with photo or video images.

The work described in this section was carried out between 2005 and 2007 in Rwanda (Mitchell and Kanganyara, 2005; Mitchell and Umurungi, 2007) more than a decade after the genocide, where various ministries and NGOs have been tasked with determining the issues that need to be addressed. Combating violence against women and children has been an important issue for some time now (see Mitchell and Kanganyara, 2005). As part of a study related to testing out participatory approaches to addressing gender violence in and around schools, a large-scale consultation with children and young people in every region of the country was set up. One of the data collecting tools was the production of drawings on gender violence and the children's experiences of *feeling safe and feeling not so safe*. The initial data collection, which took place in 2005 (Mitchell and Kanganyara, 2005), yielded more than 1000 drawings, and a related study two years later, in consultation with women and children throughout the country, yielded another 500 drawings specifically about gender-based violence.

Most of the images produced included written captions and very extensive narratives, written in Kinyarwanda, the local language. For this reason, we worked with a local translator who became a co-researcher (Mitchell and Umurungi, 2007). However, we became even more attune to the limits and challenges of interpretation when a graduate student at McGill University helped with the organization and categorization of the drawings. The task proved to be a difficult and frustrating one because she felt so far removed from the context of the actual collection of the drawings, and the context of contemporary Rwanda, that the research process itself became lost in translation.

She offered the following observation at the end of the process:

> My ability to read scenes of men and girls with cars and cell phones as prostitution was inhibited by my lack of familiarity with this type of exchange in my urban North American childhood, where cell phones and cars were forevermore a 'natural' part of middle-class life. So, too, was my ability to interpret scenes of children in forests as a commonplace threat to a Rwandan child's safety impeded by my cultural estrangement from having to cross wide-open, unpoliced spaces daily without the provision of a trusted adult.

Engaging young people in the process of interpretation

The participatory archive addresses the issue of interpretation and can facilitate further dialogue and discussion. In terms of process, the first step is digitizing the full collection of drawings and developing a basic coding scheme. Further, the data can include references to the figure (e.g., people or things, group or individual, girls, boys, family, father, mother), subject (e.g., school objects, landscape, cityscape) and themes (teacher violence, peer violence, family violence, community violence, orphans, poverty), as well as the prompt we used to stimulate the participants to generate the visual data.

How might the producers who drew the images interact with an archive containing the very same images? Would putting images in a digital archive alter their meaning? Would the process of re-viewing their own images and those of their peers be traumatic, given that the images express very dramatic instances of violence? How could the whole process of dialogue and discussion help young people to re-imagine a new future? These are all questions that require further study and, of course, are embedded within larger questions related to digital technology.

In the same way that there are some strategic areas to think about in relation to participatory archiving and photo work related to HIV and AIDS, particularly in relation to the long-wave effect of the disease, there are also some strategic areas to consider in relation to participatory archiving and children's drawings.

Figure 7.3 Drawing of forest danger

The celebration of the voices of children and their drawings is a common one. If you perform an Internet search with the key words 'children's drawings', you will come up with references to a fascinating array of collections – from the drawings

Figure 7.4   Drawing of girl being propositioned by male

at the Jewish Museum in Prague that were produced by children in the Terezin concentration camp to the drawings at the World Awareness Children's Museum, whose mission it is to 'foster curiosity, awareness, understanding, and appreciation

Figure 7.5 Drawing of unwanted pregnancy

of worldwide cultural diversity for children and adults' (www.worldchildrens-museum.org). One can even access virtual collections, such as the drawings pro-duced by children during the Spanish Civil War (http://www.columbia.edu/cu/lweb/eresources/exhibitions/children/).

References within these archives generally include the size of the collections; for example, Paintbrush Diplomacy includes 2000 pieces of art created from over 100 countries; Stone Soup Museum of Children's Art contains over 1300 works; and the Jewish Museum contains 4500 drawings from Terezin children. If you ever visit these virtual collections, you will discover some of the coding and categorizations that lend helpful and unanticipated information about the participants, such as age, sex and location of the child producers, and sometimes even their names.

The circumstances in which the drawings were collected are often part of the information provided. For example, in the case of the Terezin drawings, Mrs Friedl Dicker-Brandeis taught art class to children at the camp before she was sent to Auschwitz. She was able to hide two suitcases full of the children's drawings. Some

Figure 7.6 Drawing of unwanted pregnancy: baby in toilet

of this work complements what is also present in published book collections, and can be seen in Volavkova's (1994) *I Never Saw Another Butterfly: Children's Drawings and Poems from Terezin Concentration Camp, 1942–1944* or in Geist and Carroll's (2002) *They Still Draw Pictures: Children's Art in Wartime from the Spanish Civil War to Kosovo.*

This work on children's drawings in the public domain is interesting for a number of reasons. First, it highlights the ways that children's drawings serve as evidence of some of the most horrific moments in history. As Colin Rhodes (2000) points out, the whole movement of children's drawings dates back to Jean-Jacques Rousseau in 1900; and then in the late nineteenth century, the notion of the raw primitivism of children's drawings spoke of a natural expression that is 'outside the complex social structures that govern the lives of most adults' (2000: 26–7).

A second reason for highlighting the existence of these collections is one that is methodological: these collections can be read as a validation of children's drawings as a method in and of itself. Notwithstanding the many debates and discussions about the truth value of images, and of course the challenges of interpretation, the sheer volume of drawings produced by children in response to so many different social justice issues suggests that we need to take the genre seriously – though not uncritically. If so many images exist, how were they collected? Under what circumstances, in whose interests and with what questions do the drawings point back to the responsibility of adults to not trivialize the time, the hopes, and the dreams and safety of children?

What are *we* doing with all of these images? This last question is particularly critical because so many children's drawings have been collected during times of war. What is the impact of these drawings, if any, on adults? The existence of so many public collections also raises the question of why we do not make better use of already existing collections. By this we mean, that if, for example, we are interested in studying the effects of conflict on children, do we not have a responsibility to seek out other collections that are in the public domain (on websites, in museums, in published collections) so that we can continue building on and adding to new knowledge, rather than simply collecting more data?

Thus, a third reason for making reference to collections of drawings relates to the idea of fully mining the 'collections' of drawings that we ourselves create in our field work with children. While there are collections of children's drawings of images of war and online material that informs about the uses of drawings in addressing domestic violence, we are not aware of any public or private archives of drawings that are specific to addressing gender-based violence in its various manifestations of physical, psychological and sexual abuse, particularly in and around schools in conflict and post-conflict settings. Glynis Clacherty's (2005) work with the drawings of refugee children emphasizes the need for us to employ technologies, techniques and methods that allow us to fully honour the faith and trust that young artists bestow upon researchers.

As researchers in the social sciences, we glibly speak of data collection in our research studies, but what do we really think of the 'collections' in the data collection process? What are some of the ways that we can apply this research work on collections (extracted from museums' websites and other online sources) to our own collections (of data)? When drawing on new developments in the area of digital technology, how can 'users' and 'producers' (including children and young people) become more engaged in working with/interpreting and translating the data?

Some Final Reflections on Archving

'Can the visual arts in South Africa make a difference?', asks Marilyn Martin (2004). What we have learned from our work in research settings in South Africa and Rwanda is that a digital archive holds vast potential for researchers and the participants (and also the communities from which they come) to explore a range of social issues. The whole area of participatory analysis is one that remains under-studied within community-based research, and yet, as Flicker et al. (2007a) and others highlight, this is a critical area of study. The participatory nature of building the archive offers opportunities for researchers to extend the data by adding metadata, and also to re-use it; for graduate students to use the data to extend their own research projects; and for participants to both access data (that is rightly theirs) as well as to engage in new ways with the images produced in their community.

As we have suggested here, ICTs hold great potential for revolutionizing our field work, but they also pose many challenges, particularly in relation to ethical issues and community ownership. How public should an archive be? Who should have access to it and for how long? How do we, as researchers, negotiate with the ethics boards of our institutions regarding the need for data longevity? Can we anticipate ways in which archives might be misused? We believe that the community itself (in whatever way community is defined) can and should be involved in addressing these kinds of questions. Dyson and Leggett's (2006) work with indigenous communities in Australia, which sought to create a participatory archive with an aboriginal population for an aboriginal population, highlighted the importance of local decision making and the need for Research Ethics Boards to become more attune to the challenges and expectations in community-based research. Further, we need to consider whether local communities in rural areas, especially those possessing limited literacy skills or access to technology, actually desire to engage in this type of work. In the pilot study with the teachers noted earlier we found that there was a great deal of enthusiasm for this kind of engagement. In another small-scale study working with some of the same photographs as part of a blogging initiative, we saw that participants were interested in working with the data in a playful manner. For instance, when we observed how girls in Vulindlela had interacted with the online images, we found that despite their limited access to the Internet (even in 2008 and 2009), and despite the fact that the girls were participating in a crash course on using the Internet (learning how to create an email address and how to blog), there was a great deal of potential for them, within a participatory culture framework, to express their views and perspectives in relation to key areas of health and sexuality.

Therefore, we recognize the many challenges, acknowledging that there is still a great deal to be done in terms of ensuring that rural communities have access to the Internet. In studying girls and media-making (see, for example, the work on video-making by Bloustien, 2003; Kearney, 2006), issues relating to girls and identity are critical. However, much of the previous literature on girls and blogging looks at the idea of private writing in public spaces as an overarching idea that reframes the extensive body of work on girls and diary writing (Bell, 2007). We recognize that engaging in work with local data has a great deal of potential, particularly as it is framed within a youth-as-knowledge-producers context (Mitchell et al., 2010).

We regard the potential for community-based archiving to enable participants to work across collections that are in the public domain, as well as within their own collections. In the area of visual images and HIV and AIDS, for example, we might think of how local collections can be interpreted in the context of such global collections as Griffin's (2000) work on representations of HIV and AIDS, Mendel's (2001) photographs in *A Broken Landscape,* or images from the various photographers offering 'an insider's view' on living with HIV and AIDS, as described in Grover's (1999) essay (see for example Albert Winn's *My Life Until Now* or Michael Tidmus' work).

Perhaps the most important point to think about is the likelihood that in this work passive one-way communication is less effective than interactive or participative communication. We cannot talk about participatory visual methodologies that increasingly rely on innovative technologies and then turn around and ignore the use of technology in how we work with communities. This does not mean that we have to abandon thumbing through paper copies of images (when they exist). Indeed, after having extolled the virtues of digital cameras and PowerPoint presentations in working with photo and video data, we remain fascinated by the materiality of photo images and the way people prefer to physically hold onto a photograph to talk about it. New gadgetry, such as the portable printer (battery operated, if necessary), makes it possible to print out digital photographs right on site. We are reminded of the significance of the materiality of photos by Edwards and Hart (2004) and also by Packard (2008), who writes about the ways in which his participants, homeless people in Nashville, often physically held their photographs when they spoke about them (as opposed to having their photographs presented by the researcher). He writes:

> ... when I interviewed Terry about his images, he physically took hold of the pictures so he could control the pace of the interview, flipping through pictures much more quickly than I would have liked, and providing less detail than I had hoped. Several times during the interview we had to back up so I could ask a specific question about an image. Sometimes, however, my requests and questions were simply ignored, as Terry continued to flip through the images at his own pace. (Packard, 2008: 73–4)

Packard notes that Terry and the others were not accustomed to having their voices heard and therefore found it difficult to engage in the process of talking about their choice of images. When we read this, we interpreted the process differently, and we imagined how Terry and other onlookers would take control of the images, moderate the speed of looking at the photos and indeed physically hold on to the photos. We felt that this extract speaks volumes about ownership, the collaborative process of participatory archiving, and the potential of participatory archiving to enrich the possibilities for 'hanging on' to one's own images, whether they are real or digitized.

Acknowledgements

We gratefully acknowledge Eun Park for contributing her deep understanding of metadata and participatory archiving. We also want to acknowledge the significance of Thoko Mnisi's field work in the area of participatory archiving with teachers in rural South Africa and Lukas Labacher's work on reviewing the literature on participatory archiving. A significant section of this chapter first appeared in a themed issue of *E-Learning and Digital Media* (de Lange et al., 2010).

EIGHT

Look and see: Images of image-making

Introduction

A few years ago, Kathleen Pithouse and I embarked upon studying the engagement of participants involved in taking and looking at pictures in a community-based photovoice project (Pithouse and Mitchell, 2007). What interested us in particular were the expressions of intensity on the faces of apparently disengaged youth looking at the photos they had taken, the body language of participants as they engaged in picture taking and image-making, and even the relationships between and among the photographers as revealed by their proximity to each other. Our sense was that visual images of people engaged in image-making could reveal something about the process as well as something about social change.

We were particularly interested in what kind of evidence we could find for engagement. The pictures that we were examining had not been taken specifically for this purpose. Rather, they were 'just pictures' that had been taken in an effort to help us to document the process of photovoice – and later the process of participatory video.[1] The 'looking' process, as Richard Chalfen (2002) points out in his discussion of family photographs, is one that raises some critical questions. Chalfen discusses the phrase 'how they looked' in his exploration of home media and suggests that the domestic snapshot is more concerned with how we look or how we look *to* (someone else) than how we look *at*. As he notes, 'family members are much *less* likely to make evidentiary claims for how they looked *at* their lives than how they appeared *to* people in their lives' (2002: 143). He suggests that there may be resistance to being 'critical viewers of our own family pictures. … People may experience a kind of security in not having to treat their own snapshot collections as problematic' (2002: 144). Social scientists on the other hand, he contends, bring a different perspective; they seek the 'social and cultural practices and processes' (2002: 143) embedded in the snapshots. As Chalfen rightly suggests, this is a separate area of study, and one that is often missing from studies of domestic photos and from photovoice and photo documentary studies where the focus is often on 'the products' (what the resulting photographs mean) or the ways in which the photos are their own prompts.

In looking back, I see the *looking at looking* work as the beginning of compiling another type of visual evidence – what John Fiske (1991) would describe as examples of production texts – and the beginning of document- ing something that otherwise remains elusive in relation to such questions as the following: What is going on in community-based photography? What can we learn about looking and seeing and the gaze? How does one docu- ment social change? Increasingly, I find myself more and more drawn to looking closely at two types of pictures of looking. The first are those that have an explicit 'third party' component. Typically, in community-based visual projects these are the photos that have been taken by members of the research team on the research site (of participants taking pictures, making videos, and selecting and sorting photos). They are photos that I encourage all visual researchers with whom I work to take when they embark upon a visual studies project, and regardless of the quality of the photos and the skill of the researcher, these are images that reveal something of the process of that particular project or site. However, more than that, they serve as visual field notes, and in the same way that written or audio taped/tran- scribed fieldnotes become part of the evidence (the data), visual fieldnotes can be read, examined, used as reflective pieces and studied as data in their own right. At some points, I have wondered if adding this *looking at looking* dimension runs the risk of adding a hyper-reality where the work is more about the looking and not the doing. However, I take some encouragement from the work of W. J. T. Mitchell and what he calls his 'showing seeing' project (Mitchell, W. 2005). Interested in 'vernacular visuality' (2005: 356) and 'everyday seeing' (2005: 236), he asks his undergraduate Art Appreciation class to show and/or tell about seeing, thereby adding a layer of conscious- ness to what counts as visual. Showing, seeing and looking seem to me to be complementary processes.

The second type of images are the ones taken by the participants themselves, which in their content and composition, either spontaneously or in a more deliberate way, reveal something about the visual and the image-making process. These could include images of a camera or of picture-taking itself in the photo- graph or video (through, for example, the use of mirror images, shadows, and so on). As we see in Figure 8.1, images produced by participants might be regarded as a particular genre, one that brings with it a type of reflexivity. The picture taken in Figure 8.1 was produced by a group of women in Ethiopia who were visually exploring some of the challenges and solutions to revisioning the curriculum in higher education in the context of gender and HIV and AIDS. Their mirror image of the photographer and camera is accompanied by the caption 'know yourself' and the idea that taking pictures can help one reflect on the issues.

DOING VISUAL RESEARCH

Figure 8.1 Looking at looking: know yourself

Both types of images are interesting for what they can reveal in relation to deepening an understanding of the uses of visual evidence in visual research. This is a relatively under-studied area within visual research, although this is not to say that there are no studies in this area. Interestingly, a few years ago, Barbara Harris (2002) embarked upon a study about people's engagement with photos in shopping malls in Britain when they picked them up at a photo-developing outlet. She interviewed people as they opened up their envelopes of snapshots of vacations, weddings, birthdays and so on. She was interested in not only what they took photos of but also how they regarded the products. Her study gives rise to many questions about looking. For example, if there are pairs of observers or whole families, who holds the photographs and how do people rifle through the envelopes of photos? And, of course, new questions about looking are raised by the popularity of digital photographs and looking at the tiny screen of the camera at the time of taking the photograph (or later showing the collection to others) or looking at the photographs later on the computer screen. Thus, this chapter is all about looking at looking. What visual and reflexive data (either through the lens of the researcher or of the participants) is available to researchers when a *looking at looking* component is added, and what can we do with this data?

Looking at Looking Through the Eyes of the Researcher

The data set that forms the base for this section of the analysis draws from what was initially a somewhat haphazard collection of hundreds of photos taken from various photography and video-making projects over a period of several years. The collections contain mostly the photos that end up in PowerPoint presentations for conferences or classes; these images lend authenticity to some aspect of 'well, this is what we did'. Some of the images are of participants producing images; some show participants working with photo or video images; and still others show community audiences viewing a video, looking at photo exhibitions, and so on. Occasionally, these images also appear in a photo exhibition, but somewhere close to the curatorial statement. Their purpose is typically to give context for the photography project, showing where the pictures were produced (and how), more than as images that have a meaning unto themselves. Indeed, until Kathleen Pithouse and I (Pithouse and Mitchell, 2007) wrote the chapter about *looking at looking*, as noted at the beginning of this chapter, I didn't actually have a category for filing these images, either digitally or as material objects: they were just there. There are a number of explanations for this, ranging from the question of 'What counts as data?' (our focus on what the participants produce more than on what we produce ourselves in a photography project) through to the place of the researcher-as-photographer/filmmaker in community-based research.

Several areas of *looking at looking* help to illuminate the potential of this work:

1   the engagement process itself, arguably one of the most crucial in using and studying visual participatory methodologies in working with youth
2   the study of gaze and the question of 'What does looking look like?'
3   the area of gender and the revealing data within images-as-research, a critical feature of much social research.

The engagement factor

There is probably no area of investigation in the area of community photography and participatory video that is more celebrated (and perhaps more romanticized) than engagement/participation. At the same time, however, it is an area contested (by researchers, funders and indeed the communities themselves) in relation to the question 'What difference does this make?' and the related question 'How do we know?' There are many areas where one might want to study engagement (from school-based literacy programmes to working with street youth to participants in a health-related programme). In the study of youth and sexuality in the age of AIDS, for example, there is a great deal of rhetoric related to 'participation' and 'doing'. Ford and colleagues (2003) go so far as to say that unless young people are given more say in finding and applying solutions to critical aspects of HIV and AIDS in their lives, programmes are doomed to failure. This analysis can be seen across a broad range of interventions in Southern Africa (Chege, 2006; Mitchell, 2006a, 2006b; Mitchell et al., 2006b, in press; Raht et al., 2009) as well as in North America (Flicker et al., 2007a). The term *youth as knowledge producers*, which is borrowed from the work of Lankshear and Knobel (2006) and which helps to conceptually frame this work (see also de Lange et al., in press), draws attention to the need for tools that help us identify, describe and evaluate engagement within knowledge production.

Further, while the *engagement factor* appears in some of our previous work (Mitchell et al., 2005b, 2006b) and most recently in Moletsane et al. (2007), it was in our chapter on looking (Pithouse and Mitchell, 2007) where method became critical and where we applied the approach of working with a single photograph (Moletsane and Mitchell, 2007) to *looking at looking*. The idea of working with a single photograph within the interpretive process of analysing visual data comes out of the work of Annette Kuhn, whose book *Family Secrets: Acts of Memory and Imagination* is a critical text within autobiography, memory and visual studies. She writes that a single photograph can serve as a basic tool, 'the raw material' of self study (Kuhn, 1995). For Kuhn, a single photograph offers a rich entry point to autobiography, to socio-cultural history, and to broader questions of class and gender. Kuhn's ideas mesh nicely with the work of Clifford Geertz (1973) and the idea of 'going thick and deep'. Figures 8.2 and 8.3, both taken from Pithouse and Mitchell (2007), highlight this approach.

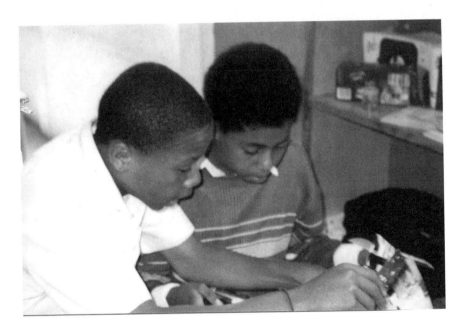

Figure 8.2 Two boys looking

Figure 8.2 comes out of a small collection of photographs taken by the research team. At the time that we took the photographs, we thought we were simply documenting the process of children engaged in a photovoice project, and as such, we have photos of the children 'in action' taking photographs of each other as well as photos of them actually working with their pictures. In *Two boys looking*, the children have completed their own photographic work and, in groups, are going through their 27 or so pictures, first scrutinizing them and then selecting some to include in small photo albums. We are not quite sure which part of the looking process is documented in Figure 8.2. What interests us, though, is the total absorption of the two boys, and the contrast between this absolute engagement or absorption and what we ourselves have seen of one of the boy's participation in other school-related activities. In our contact with the class as a whole over several weeks, this boy gave us the impression of feeling uncomfortable in the school environment. He appeared to be the type of learner who was often classified as 'disengaged', yet in this photograph there is no hint of disengagement.

Figure 8.3 shows a group of teachers and community health care workers after school and after work looking at the pictures each of them took of challenges and solutions in addressing HIV and AIDS in their neighbourhood, a rural district in KwaZulu-Natal. Like the two boys, they appear to be deeply engaged in looking. For both the teachers and the community health care workers, the pleasure of looking is not something in which they have often engaged. Most of the participants noted that they had never taken pictures before (something that could account for their engagement), but it was their rapt attention to the particular images they

Figure 8.3 After hours

had produced (then and in their discussions later) that intrigued us. We know of no definitive features to measure in these photographs of looking (or of the embodied participants looking), but the photos cause us to ask how we might begin to look at looking in relation to change itself, an important feature of our work with photovoice. Here, our attention is on 'the gaze', and we could look at such markers as the position of the body, the intensity of expression, the fact that the participants are oblivious to the person taking the photograph, and so on.

The two images just discussed are taken from photovoice projects where the participants used simple non-digital point-and-shoot cameras: they were working with photos that had been developed in a photo studio and that were very much in the form of photos as material objects, as described by Edwards and Hart (2004). With greater access to digital cameras and mobile phones, are there differences in the engagement process, both at the time of taking the pictures when the individual photographer or the whole group (in a community-based project) can review an image and during the 'working with the photos' process? In a photovoice project in Ethiopia for which we had no printer, all of the images that groups wanted to work with had to be reviewed directly on the small digital camera screens and then later were projected onto a large screen through the use of an LCD projector. For the small groups producing the photos, this lack of instant gratification meant that there was no direct handling of the images (a disadvantage if one thinks of the materiality of images); further, for the audience and other members of the project, the viewing was on a huge screen, so that the images took on a 'larger than life' format.

In my view, there was more engagement of the audience in the interpretive process using this approach, although this is hard to prove because it was predominantly about what was said than about what was done. To illustrate, many of the images presented on the big screen evoked a great deal of discussion and controversy about meaning. The photographers themselves would offer their interpretation of a photo they took by saying something along the lines of 'We took this photograph because ...' only to be told by members of the audience, 'No, that's not what that means. This photo shows ...'. In another photovoice project, which also relied on digital cameras but where there was a portable printer available, the images were printed out almost immediately in a 'snapshot' size format (3" × 5") on larger sheets (so that there would be several prints on any one sheet) and then cut into snapshots by the group members before they started working with them to produce captions. In many ways, the engagement potential is more significant in this last approach, and offers participants many more entry points for decision making, reflection and discussion than other forms of photographic image production.

Finally, there is the connection between engagement and dispelling some of the mysteries of photography through the use of digital cameras. In our earlier projects where we only used disposable or point-and-shoot cameras, there was inevitably a delay between the taking of the pictures and working with them. The photos magically appeared already processed on matte or glossy paper, and in the photo study, in pouches or envelopes. Working digitally, as previously noted, altered the element of timing and, at the same time, has added a dimension to the looking process where participants are able to 'look and see' their images before they are even printed or before they are edited using sophisticated image manipulation software technology.

The gaze

Whose eye is looking and where does it focus? Questions about gaze are located within several discourse communities: colonial discourses on photography and the making of 'the other' (see, for example, Harris, 1999; Lutz and Collins, 1993; Sekula, 1986), and film discourses on contesting the male gaze (see Carson and Pajaczkowska, 2000, and Mulvey, 1989). While both discourse communities are vast, one critical feature of work around the gaze focuses on trying to understand relationships of power and dominance between the photographer (the colonizer) and the subject (the colonized). Harris notes the following about his work on the colonizing gaze within colonial photography in Namibia from the nineteenth century up to the mid-twentieth century: 'By definition, colonial photographs depict images and scenes from the colonial setting. They were taken almost exclusively by colonists or their agents and beneficiaries ... intended largely for circulation in a Western metropolis. ...' (Harris, 1999: 20). Harris goes on to write about the way in which the photographs were used: '... to illustrate physiognomic and phrenological theories which held that the shape and size of the human body, particularly the human head, served as an outward indicator of inner characteristics which helped to define the deviant and the pathological "other"' (1999: 20).

Much of the work on the gaze draws on film theory and, in particular, theories of what is taken in the pictures and whose eye is privileged (Mulvey, 1989). Carson and Pajaczkowska observe: 'In visual culture, the materials of textual deconstruction and historical reconstruction are subject to particular techniques of analysis which are responsive to the different forms taken by visual representation. Materially, the technologies of the image have significance for feminist research' (2000: 11). They go on to cite the work of Laura Mulvey, noting that 'the most crucial structuring of sexual difference through vision and visible differences in visual culture is through the "gaze"' (Carson and Pajaczkowska, 2000: 12).

Arguing that filmmakers (primarily male) had offered a particular gaze on the (in)visibility of women (as subjects), the work in the 1970s on the female gaze served to interrogate the idea of who is looking and what is seen – and the possibility of women filmmakers and photographers creating images that challenge a masculinist view of the world. Indeed, the question 'What can a woman do with a camera?' as taken from the work of Jo Spence and Joan Solomon (1995), Caroline Wang (1999), and Brinton Lykes (1989) is precisely one that suggests that we need to try to understand the gendered gaze in community-based visual projects (see also Moletsane et al., 2007); of course, one way to do this is to look at the media productions themselves, and another way is to look for gaze in the image-making

Figure 8.4   You can be raped in the bushes

process itself. What does the gaze look like when those who are typically the subjects and not the agents are behind the camera? While much of the discussion in earlier chapters gives a good idea of what the photographers, who are often marginalized, think should be seen (according to the various categories and prompts), what can we learn when we add in a *looking at looking* dimension?

You can be raped in the bushes (Figure 8.4) is the picture that was produced in a photovoice project (as opposed to being taken by the research team). We do not actually see the photographer (or photographers, because there may have been two girls taking the picture), but we nonetheless have a sense of the presence of the photographer by virtue of where the camera focuses and by the positioning and expressions of the girl subjects. The picture was taken in a peri-urban school in Swaziland as part of a photovoice project called *Feeling Safe/Feeling Not So Safe*. The group of girls who were involved in producing this image chose to enact a rape scene, and although in this case we do not actually have a picture of the photographer(s), what is interesting about this picture is the way it evokes the presence of the photographer. While acting out something that is (unfortunately) within their imaginations and perhaps their everyday realities, given the high rates of sexual abuse and sexual violence in Swaziland (Mitchell and Mothobi-Tapela, 2004), the girls demonstrated, through their more amused expressions, that they are also at play with the photographer(s). And although there is no audiotape of their transactions in co-creating this photo, there is nonetheless a sense of a female gaze.

Figure 8.5 depicts three girls participating in a video-making project on teenage pregnancy in a rural school in South Africa. The topic of teenage pregnancy was the idea of the girls who participated in the filmmaking workshop conducted by Dorothe Raht and colleagues (Raht et al., 2009). As the work of Kearney (2006), Bloustien (2003) and others looking at girls and media demonstrates, the idea of a girl behind a video camera is an uncommon image not only in South Africa but also in North America and Australia. Thus, the idea of trying to get at what the

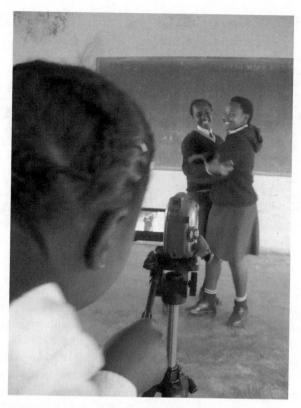

Figure 8.5 The girl behind the camera

gaze might look like is a critical one. Figure 8.5 highlights the position of the girl behind the camera as well as the relationship between the photographer and the two girls who are being filmed. Like the *You can be raped in the bushes* image, there is no indication, in spite of the topic, that the girls are not enjoying themselves.

What does gender have to do with it?

I ask the question 'What does gender have to do with it?' but, of course, there may be equally fascinating questions regarding other categories, including age, geography, economic status, urban/rural, and youth in/out of school, that might help to frame looking at looking. Building on the work that has already been done on various cultural contexts for studying gender in relation to curating family photographs (see Langford, 2001; Kuhn, 2002) as well as in the area of gender and media representation more broadly as previously noted (see Bloustien, 2003; Kearney, 2006), is there anything to be said about the ways in which males and females actually take pictures or look at pictures in community photo and video-making projects? And if there is, how might we study the question through

12, 14 years old

Taking picture session at RUHENGERI

Figure 8.6 Girls taking pictures in a photovoice project

images that depict *looking at looking*? In the various video and photo projects in which I have been involved in Southern Africa, it would be strange not to ask that question. Thus, we have been interested in the ways in which gender is linked to the kinds of images produced. In the *Feeling Safe/Feeling Not So Safe* photovoice project in Swaziland, for example, the boys were much more likely to produce images related to pollution and the environment and the ways in which safety issues have an affect on the environment; the girls were more likely to produce images that pertained to their own personal safety and security. In a video-making project in South Africa, where almost all of the video productions had something

Figure 8.7 Group photo of girls with a video camera

Figure 8.8 Boy taking pictures of boys: 'feeling strong'

Figure 8.9 Taking a picture at the market

Figure 8.10 Reflecting on the video

to do with gender violence, the boys produced scenes of actual violence whereas the girls focused more on 'off camera' scenes (either behind closed doors or referring to something that had already happened).

But what might process pictures reveal? Many of the photo and video studies I am reporting on involve participants (male and female) who may never have used a video camera nor a digital or simple point-and-shoot camera. The visual representations of the ways the girls have positioned themselves suggests a more collaborative approach to taking pictures (than that of the boys), although many of the images come from projects that only involved girls in any case. The picture of the two girls in Rwanda (Figure 8.6), for example, was taken by a researcher carrying out a photovoice project with girls living on the street in a city in Rwanda, and separate from any sense of how boys and girls might take pictures differently, many details in the photo speak to the relationship between the two girls: the hand of one girl gently resting on the shoulder of the other, the foot of one girl touching the foot of the other girl, the two girls looking together through the view finder. At the same time, there is the solitary image of the young boy taking a picture in the market (Figure 8.9) and the image of the boys *feeling strong* (Figure 8.8), taken as part of the same project as Figure 8.7 where the girls position themselves together.

These are all images of young adolescents in Southern Africa and may say something about how males and females position themselves differently in this cultural context. One may see completely different gender relations in other cultural environments. Finally, there is Figure 8.10, which depicts two beginning teachers working on a participatory video project related to HIV and AIDS. It is an interesting image that depicts something of the reflective process, in which the two participants went immediately from shooting some footage to wanting to see if they had really captured what they sought. In a heterosexual dyad, it may not be appropriate for the two to be trying to look through the lens of the camera at the same time or in such proximity as occurs in the girl-only photos shown previously.

A word about *looking at looking* with a focus on audiences

Looking at the *looking of audiences* in community-based visual projects can also be very revealing, and could pertain to any of the three areas noted in the preceding sections: engagement itself, the gaze and, of course, gender. If one considers the idea of getting the word out, and the reach of the images that are produced in visual projects (*Where Do We Feel Safe?*, *Challenges and Solutions in Addressing HIV and AIDS*, *Addressing Poverty*, and *Challenges and Solutions in Addressing Bullying*), then understanding the reception of the production of texts is also important. I have endless regret in not taking pictures of a photo exhibition that took place at the University of KwaZulu-Natal a few years ago.

The exhibition was part of the TakingITGlobal (TIG) Xpress project at the University of Toronto, which engaged youth in Canada and South Africa in taking pictures of how they saw the structural features of HIV and AIDS (gender, geography, poverty and so on) (Larkin et al., 2007). The exhibition was set up in the foyer outside of the gymnasium, where the plenaries for a follow-up conference were being held. Although it was well received by those attending the conference, and was the focus of a plenary presentation that included some of the youth, the real reach of the exhibition was only observed towards the end of the first day when eight or ten members of the cleaning staff were all gathered around the exhibition. They were very clearly enjoying it; in an animated way they were debating the meanings they each saw in the various images. Many of the cleaning staff had only limited levels of literacy and probably never had been involved in the programming of a conference. It was a stark reminder of the ways in which photography serves to democratize research. Alas, I have no photographs of that scene, and when I want to make a point about the benefits of visual research in relation to reaching a range of audiences, I am left with only words.

In Figure 8.11, the audience is made up of 30 or so people who participated in a day-long video-making session. They were clustered together in a small space (the only one in the school with electricity) at the end of the day to view all six of the short videos that had been produced. On the one hand, it was hard to capture in such a small physical space the full context of the screening. On the other hand, the only thing that is really going on in terms of gaze is the single *all eyes* focus on the video that is being screened on a blank cement wall five feet away. While television makes regular use of pan shots of audiences (e.g., at a concert or a public hearing) or close-up shots of an audience member (e.g., of a contender for an Academy Award), there is probably no picture that captures more of the intensity and single focus of an audience than this one. Other photos of community viewers in which the attention is clearly on the images serve as a reminder of the appeal

Figure 8.11 Community video-makers viewing their video

of local community productions over those that are produced with large budgets but with no personal connection for the audience. This is something that could be of particular significance for NGOs or researchers contemplating the value of putting money into local productions (of photos or videos) rather than investing in a video that could reach a broader audience. While it is not necessarily always the case that local is better, the kind of engagement and intensity of gaze seen in Figure 8.11 is a powerful demonstration of how important the local can be, with less sophisticated sound, lighting and so forth being accepted by very forgiving audiences.

Looking at Looking in the Images
Produced by Participants

Examples of *looking at looking* photos produced by the participants themselves might be regarded as a particular genre of photography, one that brings with it a type of reflexivity and self-consciousness through various approaches, including self-portraiture and shadows, as well as explicit images of people taking pictures. In James Hubbard's book *Shooting Back from the Reservation* (1994), for example, 11-year-old Cindy Stout includes a picture of two of her friends with cameras: *Photographing the Pueblo*.

Wendy Ewald, in her work with child photographers, has devised specific writing and photographic activities around self-portraiture. As she observes, there are practical challenges when it comes to the use of photographs in self-portraiture, particularly because the cameras she used did not have timers. 'The simplest solution,' she writes, 'is for the students to take a close-up self-portrait by holding the camera in front of their faces. They must hold the camera with their arms stretched out in front of them. This is an awkward solution, can make for some tedious framing' (2000: 40).

What I have been interested in are the ways in which community photographers have spontaneously (or accidentally) incorporated a portrait of the self as well as the camera. While the number of photos that I have in this category of collections is somewhat limited, it is worth noting the limitations of producing this genre in the first place. The key ways of doing this would be through the use of shadows, or through the use of mirror images, either by means of actual mirrors (including mirror-image sunglasses), plate-glass windows, shiny metal or bodies of water.[2]

Figure 8.1, *Looking at looking: Know yourself*, is probably the most successful (intentional) example I have seen of this genre. As previously noted, this image was produced by a group of Ethiopian women at Jimma University in a photovoice project on challenges and solutions to addressing gender and HIV and AIDS; these women relied on a plate-glass window for the intended effect. Specifically, they used digital cameras rather than non-digital point-and-shoot cameras and projected their images onto a large screen using an LCD projector. Most importantly, the image presented to the audience (Figure 8.1) was one that caught the attention of the entire group of 30 or more participants and eventually became the centrepiece of a large poster that was produced to highlight the significance of participation through photovoice in revisioning the curriculum.

Another *seemingly* self-conscious image produced as part of a photovoice project by a group of students at a university in China also relies on the use of a window for mirror effect. The picture, part of a photovoice project conducted by Ran Tao (2009), has an intriguing story. As Tao observes in a close reading of the photo:

> It was accidental that this boy was reflected in the glass. They kind of snuck around the police station to take this picture for fear of being caught. They did not write a caption but they explained why they would take this picture in their presentation and I kept a note. What they said is that the spread of STIs/HIV in entertainment sites should be, at least partially, attributed to the inadequate function of the police. In some cases, the bosses of entertainment sites buy off the inspectors, who would give the green light for the sex business, which is illegal in China. Sex workers, who are also illegitimate and unprotected by law, have no agency in negotiating condom use as most clients want sex without a condom, and neither do they have access to health services. In such situation, STIs/HIV infections transmit without any obstacles among sex workers, sex buyers, their sexual partners and wives. (personal communication)

Tao's (2009) explanation above says something about the term *seemingly*, and whether the photo, even in accidentally revealing the mirror image of the photographer, does mean to say more. She goes on to observe:

> This picture was taken by the group of participants to represent how they see HIV and AIDS in current Chinese society. They related social problems surrounding AIDS directly to the police. In their photo presentation, they sharply pointed out that what the police have done is far from what they are supposed to do to fulfill their duty of keeping society in positive development. A participant revealed that some local police, subject to bribery, collude with lawless businessmen in the sex industry for profit at the expense of the health of sex workers and people involved. The participants' photo and presentation show that these young people do not confine themselves to the ivory tower but rather give concern to social issues outside it.

Finally, she comments on the photo in relation to the idea of *looking at looking*:

> Looking at this photo and especially looking at looking in the image, I felt a strong sense of youth agency and youth voice in social issues. In the face of this picture of the façade of the police station, my eyes were drawn by the red banner with a conspicuous slogan of 'solve prominent problems, establish good atmosphere for police operation.' However, regardless of the encouraging call or promise given by the police, young people took critical attitudes towards how

the police actually operate in dealing with the prominent problem of HIV and AIDS. The reflected image of the young man shooting the police station conveys to me a message that young people put social institutions and social issues under observation and hold commitment to changing them.

The shadow image of the photographer, as noted in Chapter 6 in a discussion of the work of the American photographer Robert Frank, also offers an interesting angle on looking. In the case of Frank, as W.T.J Mitchell (2005) indicates, the focus is the shadowy feature of the semi-absent father-photographer, suggesting the effect is intentional. In other cases, as can be seen in many community projects, the effect may be accidental, though no less provocative in hinting at the presence of the photographer. In James Hubbard's *Shooting Back from the Reservation*, for example, there is an interesting image of the photographer, 9-year-old Tashina Martinez, as a shadow in her photograph titled *Ladder and child* (Hubbard, 1994: 8).

Studying our own work with participants, shadows are used in a few of the images from our various photo projects. Figure 8.12 was taken in a rural area in South Africa as part of a project involving ninth-grade students taking pictures of stigma.

Another way of looking at the mirror and shadow effect in images is to read them in the context of 'me and my shadow image' and the notion of the double or doubling in nineteenth-century photography. As Lindsay Smith observes

Figure 8.12 Shadow of the photographer

in *The Politics of Focus: Women, Children and Nineteenth Century Photography* (Smith, 1998), while the interest in the concept of doubling fell away with the advent of camera, there remained, nonetheless, some fascinating experiments within this genre.

Looking at Looking: A Case for Visually Verifiable Data

What can we learn from including a *looking at looking* component in visual research? This chapter is meant to extend the 'field' of visual studies, drawing on the potential value of the investigator's visual contributions to deepen an understanding of the visual in community-based research, as well as drawing on the complementary *looking at looking* data produced by participants themselves. As a component of enriching our understanding of the practical value of this work, there are a number of possibilities. In the case of *Two boys looking* (Figure 8.2), the photo begins to open our eyes to new possibilities of reading what youth engagement or youth participation really means. Any measures of youth engagement are often 'after the fact' and do not necessarily take account of what the moment of engagement really is. In a sense, as researchers or educators, we are not quite sure what we are even striving for when pursuing projects that address sexuality and HIV and AIDS, for example.

While there is an inherent anticipation that behaviour change is possible through these projects, as defined by participants delaying sexual debut or engaging in safe sex through condom use, the idea that young people who might otherwise be bored or disengaged can be so engaged in something that has a critical 'insider–outsider' component to it suggests that we need to find new ways of expanding this engagement. New avenues of participant engagement can synergistically complement other work in Entertainment Education and help inform ways of understanding why artful engagement is a powerful component of the process of influencing a change in behaviour (McKee et al., 2004). In a current UNESCO-funded review of arts-based approaches to HIV and AIDS prevention in which we are involved, we already see that the evaluation of the projects could very well benefit from a specific analysis of the engagement process itself (Mitchell et al., 2006b).

Viewing (looking at), like reading, is a complex process. At the same time, however, we, as researchers and educators, look to the visual as evidence for things that are otherwise thought to be intangible and not possible to study. More than anything, though, we see that this kind of work adds to the possibilities of what Schratz and Walker's *Research as Social Change* (1995) can mean for understanding images as evidence of social behaviour. In photos like *Two boys looking* (Figure 8.2), it is the very moment of engagement that we are seeing. While there may be many meanings attached to this moment (and we are acknowledging that this is just a 'moment in time'), the image suggests that there is far more (than meets the eye) to be looked at in photovoice and other participatory works done through visual methodologies.

Again, John Fiske's (1991) work on textual analysis is particularly relevant here. As previously noted, Fiske talks about primary texts (the photos or videos produced by the participants), the production texts (what the producers themselves say about their work), the audience texts and how audiences (and other members of the production process) respond. In television research, the audience texts can be in an immediate form (as in the case of a live audience) and can vary in reactions from applauding to the famous arm gestures from audience members during the 1990s nightly-aired television programme *The Arsenio Hall Show*. In a less immediate form, fans can respond through websites, blogs, Facebook – or create their own fan fiction.

Typically, documenting audience response is limited to conducting interviews, using surveys or polls, or collecting written accounts, although with blogs and websites there are new forms of data collection that can facilitate this process. However, using visual images to document the ways in which participants are engaged in producing images, working with images, or responding as audiences to productions all provide additional layers of textuality to the data collection process and demonstrate new ways of using the visual as evidence in visual research.

As an example of this, a few years ago, my colleagues and I screened *Fire+Hope* (2004), a video I produced with Shannon Walsh (the director), which deals with a group of young people in two townships near Cape Town who were involved in Soft Cover, an HIV and AIDS awareness project devoted to studying youth participation and creativity. The video was meant to be fast-paced and youth-friendly, consisting of interviews with several of the youth; images of AIDS-related graffiti; a hip-hop soundtrack; and a performance by the Common Man, a local spoken-word poet. Produced in Cape Town, this video has an urban vibe to it. The video is in English, except for one scene in which a very cool young man named KK recites a poem in Xhosa. When we screened the video in rural parts of KwaZulu-Natal, specifically to rural youth (many of whom did not have access to learning English as a second language), we were struck by how restless the audiences were. However, when KK recited his poem, the audience's attention became suddenly rapt, and again, thinking of missed opportunities, we would have been able to document the visual signs of their undivided attention if we had brought a camera.

What difference does it make that we have images of the audience clustered together, as they are in Figure 8.11, viewing their videos? And does it matter that there is no visual evidence of the audience's engagement with KK's poem? Does it matter that there is no visual image of the cleaning staff viewing the TIG Xpress exhibition? I would argue that it does matter, and I maintain that what this kind of work suggests is that as visual researchers we could draw more effectively on collecting and using visually verifiable data as evidence. As previously noted, in the case of the cleaners, there are arguments to be made for using work with the visual to democratize the research process. However, if one wants to make that claim, where is the evidence to support it? As part of a training exercise in visual ethnography and visual studies, we might emphasize the value of visual documentation in all aspects of the research process, and we might make particular reference to studying and documenting audience responses visually rather than through conventional interviews or surveys.

In her books on working with children and photography (*Portraits and Dreams; I Wanna Take Me a Picture*), Wendy Ewald (1985) includes pictures of the process. Olivier et al. (2009) do the same in their work with teachers in *Picturing Hope*. Beyond including images that document the steps, however, we can also hone our skills in reading the evidence and using these process images to do more than simply show the reader that 'this is what we did'. In each of the three sections in this chapter on reading the data – on engagement, on the gaze and on gender – the process of analysis really only scratches the surface of what we consider using in the future.

In 2008, Phil Borges exhibited an international collection of photographs on women and empowerment in Pretoria for National Women's Day. The exhibition was made up of images of hundreds of woman around the world taken by a photographer who was looking to capture *empowerment*. Empowerment is another one of those elusive terms similar to engagement and participation – celebrated and romanticized but hard to document. And yet, as the audience viewed the exhibition, it was unlikely that any of us had difficulty in seeing empowerment. The issue of documenting engagement is similar. If one of the goals of community-based visual research is to engage participants, then can we use the visual to document that? Can we use visual evidence to also satisfy funders during the reporting process? On a related note, can we add a visual dimension to the evaluation process? As Raht et al. (2009) highlight, evaluation of arts-based visual research in such areas as HIV and AIDS is clearly a challenge (and hence the question 'What difference does this make?'). How can the visual *looking at looking* data contribute to the evaluation process?

Setting an Agenda for *Looking at Looking* in Visual Research

On the one hand, it may be misleading to draw too many conclusions from the images I have presented in this chapter. Was there something, for example, about the girl groupings that caught our attention as we were snapping photos? Is it easier for female researchers to perceive gender when it comes to working with girls? On the other hand, perhaps this *looking at looking* work needs to be read within the context of some broader social issues, such as girls and media production, and the visibility of the gaze of the girl. It is worth noting that *looking at looking* was catapulted to fame in the United States right around the time of the swearing in of President Obama in February 2009, when the press began to notice the picture-taking practices of Malia Obama, the president's 10-year-old daughter.

Mary Celeste Kearney (2006) discusses this media hype, what I would regard as *looking at looking*. As the author of *Girls Make Media*, Kearney based her own (*looking at looking*) study on the public images of Malia Obama taking pictures. Kearney notes that there are many meanings that can be made of this phenomenon, including a consideration of the significance of the idea of a black girl being seen in a position of agency in making the images (and not just being the object *within* images). She writes:

> ... The lure of Malia the Photographer does not just result from her relationship with the President of the United States of America, and thus her ability to capture images of one of our most public and powerful figures in his most private and perhaps vulnerable moments. Certainly, those factors pique our interest about this girl photographer. Nonetheless, I believe the primary reason Malia's photographic practices have garnered so much attention is their juxtaposition with a young, female African American body. Most individuals in the U.S. are simply not used to seeing a black girl in a position of such agency. Stereotyped as crack whores and teen moms on welfare, black girls are more commonly constructed in the media as victims than heroes, 'at-risk' rather than 'can-do.' Thus, it seems Malia is attracting attention not just because she's a girl who takes pictures or because she is a First Daughter who takes pictures, but because she's a black First Daughter who takes pictures. Malia Obama's snapshotting has captured the public's attention and thus encouraged a barrage of photographs of her in response. In addition to acknowledging contemporary girls' technological agency, one of the most significant consequences of these images is that our whitewashed notions of girls, girlhood and girls' culture are beginning to disintegrate. With numerous cameras ready to

Figure 8.13   Malia Obama as Photographer1 (6 July 2009)

Figure 8.14 Malia Obama as Photographer 2 (6 July 2009)

capture her every move over the next four years, Malia is helping to alter the dominant image of American girlhood through her place in front of, as well as behind, the lens. (http://flowtv.org/2009/02/malia-obama-girl-photographer-mary-celeste-kearney-university-of-texas-austin)

Notwithstanding the fact that these images are within the domain of the public media, their meanings can be read (and debated), as Kearney (2006) demonstrates, within a research mode, and so can the images of image-making within community-based visual projects. Reading agency into the images of Malia Obama as photographer, along with reading the significance of the gaze of a black girl who typically is in the gaze of white, masculinist media and policy makers, suggests some of the ways in which this work can inform visual studies.

Finally, I return to the reflexivity of the visual researcher. Elsewhere, I have drawn on Lyn Mikel Brown and Carol Gilligan's (1993) idea of the Listening Guide to break down (and interrogate) the process of women researchers interviewing girls and young women, and Holland et al.'s (1997) notion of a feminist reading on data through team discussions (see Mitchell et al., 2004b; Moletsane et al., 2008). It is critical that as visual researchers, we take into account and indeed theorize our own subjectivities in relation to what aspects of the process we actually record and document. More than anything, the visual representations of our own work (particularly if we work in teams) may be one of the richest entry points to engaging in our own reflexivity and self-study as researchers. Do we all see the same things? Do we all make the same interpretations on the process of pictures? If and when we see things differently, how can we fully mine differing interpretations? In their work with postgraduate students, Ebersöhn and Eloff (2007) contribute another layer to the idea of *looking at looking* by considering the rich possibilities for discussion between a master's or doctoral supervisor and student when there are photographs of the field work process. At the risk of having this meta-work being read as hopelessly recursive and never-ending, W. T. J. Mitchell (2005), in his work with the *Showing Seeing* project, concludes that

> visuality – not just the social construction of vision but the visual construction of the social – is a problem in its own right that is approached by but never quite engaged by the traditional disciplines of aesthetics and art history or even by the new disciplines of media studies. (2005: 356)

Adding a dimension of 'look and see' can be critical to unravelling a more complicated picture than we might first have thought of when taking pictures.

Notes

1 I gratefully acknowledge the contributions of Kathleen Pithouse in the work that we first published in 2007 on 'looking at looking' (Pithouse and Mitchell, 2007).
2 Interestingly, much of the work that I do is where 'none of the above' would apply. The schools in rural areas often do not have window panes, much less mirrors; more importantly, these schools are geographically situated inland and away from many water sources. Because small workgroups are often working with just one camera and away from other groups, the genre of photographing a camera in use is almost impossible.

NINE

What can a visual researcher do with a camera?

Introduction

In this chapter, my focus is on an essential question: what can a visual researcher do with a camera?[1] The question may seem to be misplaced; after all, many visual ethnographers and visual researchers are already photographers or filmmakers who use the visual as their main means of doing research (see the work of Banks, 2001; Wagner, 1979; Harper, 2001, 2002; and many others whose own visual work is the data). However, the role of the visual productions of the researchers (as opposed to the participants) working in the area of community-based research is a grey area. Yet as I have suggested in the previous chapter on the study of images of image-making in visual research, the camera work of visual researchers during field work has a great deal of potential as an analytic tool. Beyond this, there is also the challenge of how we might use our visual productions to engage participants in analysis, to communicate with their constituents from governments, NGOs and so on, and to discuss with other researchers. Moreover, it is critical to evaluate how we use the work ourselves within our own research teams. In this chapter, I consider that the visual work of visual researchers is under-studied and argue how because visual work is often very much a feature of the research, it warrants further study.

In writing this chapter, I was particularly indebted to Jay Ruby (2000b) for his book *Picturing Culture*. Ruby acknowledges that the visual anthropologist's main use of film has been what he calls cine fieldnotes. He notes the advent of the use of low-cost Hi8 video cameras and their use in field work, but he laments that their most common usage is for filming cultural events and material objects and that because few anthropologists have formal training in film production, the resulting work is of low quality and 'often resembling the footage taken by tourists' (2000b: 51). He goes on to comment:

This work is seldom edited into finished films and has gone largely unstudied even by the people who produced it. ... Only a small percentage of this film has ended up in an archive. Little is known about this vast body of work. It is almost never presented in public as part of the field-worker's 'publication'. ... Like written notes and photographs, the film footage produced during field-work is a private document. Fieldworkers discover upon their return that it is unprofitable to subject the footage to close and detailed analysis or to edit it into a finished film. (2000b: 51–2)

Ruby notes the difficulty of transforming much of this footage into anything that would be of interest to anyone except other anthropologists who might share expert knowledge in the area. Peter Loizos (2000) seems to agree with Ruby:

(T)housands of video recordings are made in community research settings, but many of them are probably never watched seriously, and may have the status of research and action 'fashion accessories' and have been a waste of time and money. No doubt, future historians will be grateful that these videos were made. ... (Loizos, 2000: 106)

Sarah Pink, in her work in the area of visual ethnography, suggests that there are different roles for the ethnographer as video-maker; she highlights the distinction between 'objective' video footage and 'creative' footage and makes us aware of the debates that date back to the 1970s:

Some (e.g., Heider, 2006) argued that ethnographic film should be objective, unedited, and not 'manipulated'; it should be guided by scientific, ethno-graphic principles, rather than cinematographic intentions. Such footage was intended to be stored as a film archive and screened to anthropological audi-ences; it was part of a project of recording an objective reality. During the same period others produced more creative expressive films intended for public consumption. (Pink, 2001: 78)

However, Luc Pauwels (2002) offers a few cautionary notes on what a visual researcher might do with video:

All in all, visual scientists could make much better use of technology now that it is within reach of even small-scale highly specialized and moderately funded projects. But having more expressive means and signifiers (text, image, layout, sound, movement, non-linear structures, etc.) compared to traditional scholarly 'texts' may also provide hazards. For it could lead to instances where the incompetent applications of those means may become counterproductive, e.g., by affecting the legibility or readability, or by adding a 'look and feel' that contradicts or diverts from the essential line of reasoning. Ultimately such inconsiderate choices may even subvert or invalidate the scientific state-ment, e.g., by implying relations that are not supported by research findings. The most severe and widespread sort of disruption is caused by thoughtlessly adopting an established visual or (new) media culture that does not serve the scientific goals one seeks to attain. Such an incompatible style (e.g., flashy edit-ing, unusual camera angles and movements) is particularly misleading since audiences and producers often consider this a quality of the product (a sign of 'professionalism' or creativity) rather than a flaw. (2002: 152)

The Composite Video: An Overview

Composite: A complex material, such as wood or fibreglass, in which two or more distinct, structurally complementary substances, especially metals, ceramics, glasses, and polymers, *combine to produce structural or functional properties* not present in any individual component. (The Free Dictionary)

Heeding Pauwels' warning, the focus of this chapter will be on the creative side of researcher-initiated production and the development of what my colleagues and I have come to call 'the composite video' (Mitchell et al., in press). While there may be other terms for what a researcher-produced data-driven video text might be called, we regard the composite video as a specific genre: a research video, a research tool, a communication tool that is more than simply video data (or visual data captured on video). The composite video is a production in and of itself, with a clear beginning, middle and end. It includes a narrative (conveyed either through voice-overs, captions, subtitles or textboxes), samples of the actual visual data (pho-tographs, participatory videos, drawings), plus the contextual data in the form of video footage taken during the research process and often a musical soundtrack in some part of the video. What is critical is producing something that allows for the various layers of work to come together as a composite. Marcus Banks (2001) dis-cusses multimedia projects that might aid visual researchers; he draws on the work of Fischer and Zeitlyn (2003) to elaborate on the idea of layering:

In this model no object or set of objects is necessarily primary, nor does the object or object-set necessarily have any definitive organizational structure or predetermined sequencing. Instead, a set of objects are linked to one another in (metaphorical) layers – a group of photographs, a set of field notes – and also linked to objects in other layers: A photograph of an individual in one layer is linked to a genealogical diagram in which the individual features in another layer, and also to half a dozen field notes that concern that individual in yet another layer. The linkages within the layers may be tight and sequential (for example, all the frames in a length of digitized film footage may be viewed randomly, but are probably best appreciated in sequential order) or loosely linked (for example, photographs of all the inhabitants of a village could be clustered into household or kin groups, but there is probably little to be gained by viewing the photographs in any predetermined order). (2001: 163)

The composite video can serve a variety of purposes. It can be a reflexive tool that provides an opportunity for the researcher or research team to sift and sort and to get an in-depth look at the data (responding to both analysis and representation). It can also be a reflexive tool by providing an occasion for the research team and participants to work together. Indeed, as a genre, it is useful to present back visual data visually – as a type of extended data collection – to the communities with whom we work, to other researchers working in the same area of research (e.g., HIV and AIDS, gender and identity, and gender-based violence), and to those working in community-based research more broadly. As I argue in the previous chapter, opportunities for working reflexively within our research teams are critical, and the production and use (including multiple screenings) of these composites can be part of that reflexive process. These are not videos that would necessarily ever be broadcasted publicly, or even shown at a film festival (except, perhaps, at a composite video film festival), but they may be ideal for use in a conference milieu and depending on the technical sophistication can have a much broader set of uses. Typically, they draw on community-based photo or video projects. In the case of several of the composites described in this chapter, there are various scenarios in relation to the involvement of participants. In some cases, the composite video may simply involve the researcher interacting with her visual data and not involving the participants directly. In others, some or all of the participants may be closely involved in all aspects of the production.

The composite video can serve as a communication tool, which both the research team and participants might use in their respective communities. Interestingly, however, it can also serve as a data-generation tool within the recursive process of research. As I describe in more detail in the following sections, for example, the responses of the participants to 'their data' reconfigured within the composite may be read as data, and, of course, the responses of local communities to the composite can yield further insights into the issue under investigation. The composite video contributes, in a sense, to the afterlife of a research project.

Some defining features of the composite video

In this section, I describe the composite video and direct the reader to viewing several of these videos, which are posted on the website www.cvm.org. The defining features of the composite video, at least in relation to what we have developed so far, include the following:

1 Length of no more than 18–21 minutes (linked to audience engagement and attention span and manageable even within a conference slot)
2 Narrative format that has a beginning, middle and end, and either offers a point of view or non-neutrality (not unlike a conference paper)
3 Orientation to the process and context, as well as content, so that it includes images of doing while also including primary texts (the photos and videos produced in a participatory video project)
4 Intent (or multiple intentions), which can include (a) serving as an organizing and reflexive tool for the research team; (b) its contribution to the participatory process; and (c) acting as a communication tool, communicating back to

the community participants and to the broader audiences of planners, other researchers and community leaders (hence it needs to represent some aspect of the visual data in an engaging way)

Clearly, many of these features are somewhat subjective: What counts as an appropriate narrative format? How much of a point of view is represented? And, of course, in the context of limited operating budgets and oftentimes limited technical know-how, both concerns of Ruby's as well as mine, what counts as an engaging video? Finally, as Pauwels (2002) asks, when is a video so engaging that it loses its place within the process of visual research? In the work that I describe here, audience engagement is critical. Even though not all of the examples I offer are within a southern African context, several are. However, the idea of what is *engaging* or *compelling* in one cultural or regional context may vary. The addition of a musical soundtrack is a case in point: all of the composite videos that we have produced include music, something that perhaps locates *point of view* and *non-neutrality* in the videos. However, Pauwels questions this:

> Music, unless it actually is performed during the recording, and is thus an integral part of the reality conveyed (i.e., synchronic sound), indeed can have a disrupting effect on the process of knowledge transfer. Sound that is added afterward can set a particular mood and thus impose a certain interpretation upon the viewer, for which there may be no scientific grounds whatsoever. Or it will at least distract some of the viewer's attention, which otherwise would be focused on the actual material. Likewise, whether the use of commentary may be guiding or not, remains a hotly debated aspect of audio-visual productions by social scientists. (2002: 126)

The question of whether the absence of a soundtrack contributes to non-neutrality is an interesting one within broader studies of audience research and viewer response. Given that the composite video serves double and triple duty (and is not meant to be 'the analysis' but only a contributing piece), I would argue that the engagement factor is a compelling one in community-based research, and the community of scholarly inquiry might have greater expectations for the product, as can be seen in recent debates and discussions within arts-informed inquiry (see, for example, Knowles and Cole, 2008).

Overall, one might also add another defining feature of production: acknowledging what is not – this being the genre of text that would inevitably overlap with the type of 'pure' ethnographic footage described by Pink (2001). Notwithstanding this, though, the composite video is not meant to be pure entertainment. Pauwels observes: 'Compared to productions in the entertainment industry, a scholarly discourse will always have to be more reflexive and explicit in its ways of thinking and doing, so that the statements it makes can be shared and integrated in an ongoing process of constructing or deconstructing knowledge' (2002: 159).

There are, of course, different ways to approach the production of a composite video according to cost and technical support, ranging from a fairly basic digital storytelling/PowerPoint (or MovieMaker or iMovie) format to a more elaborate construction produced with sophisticated software and the technical support of a videographer/filmmaker. Significant to the earlier discussion by Pink of what is (and is not) ethnographic video, the genre of the composite is geared more towards the creative than the objective, with the potential to appeal to not only other researchers but also the participants themselves as well as various stakeholders.

Some Examples of Composite Video

This section contains several different genres of composite videos, ranging from those which serve to frame participatory video-making projects – the area where we first applied the term *composite video* (Mitchell et al., in press) – to composite videos that serve as video collages (drawing together in a creative way a variety of interrelated data into one video production) and, finally, to an example taken from a former doctoral student/colleague who was presenting her field work to her doctoral committee as well as the participants.

Izindaba Yethu (Our Stories)[2]

From the various projects I have been involved in with community-based participatory video, three composite videos have been produced: *Our Stories, Seeing for Ourselves* and *Shattering the Glass Ceiling*. Each of these three videos is based on community-based video production, and an approach called No-Editing-Required (NER) as described in Chapter 4, involving participants making short videos in small groups over the course of a single day. In all three of the video projects, production is carried out with participants who may have never used a still camera and who certainly have never used a video camera, and yet, at the end of several hours in a video-making workshop, they have something to present. The resulting video productions are usually 2–3 minutes in duration and include a title, a storyline and closing credits. Occasionally, if someone in the group has the idea of downloading music from a mobile phone, the video may include a musical soundtrack.

What can be accomplished in such a short time may not be very sophisticated. However, because we have worked out a very tight format, and due to the fact that we always make sure that there is at least one facilitator working with each group, we have never encountered a situation where a group has not created a video production by the end of day. Although there are many opportunities to use the videos in reflexive ways in small groups, the productions do not stand on their own. Indeed, the general rough-cut quality of the productions and the limited integration of actors external to the immediate video production group are limitations of the No-Editing-Required, one-day video-making activity. As a research team, we therefore reflected on how the individual videos could be used to continue community engagement. While we did not want to tamper with the actual video productions, which in themselves say a great deal and certainly exist as research data, we felt that in their raw (and very short) state, they might not *travel well*. At the same time, in the video project described below, in which young people produced videos, the issue of gender violence was so dramatically (and urgently) presented that we felt an obligation to develop a strategy or tool for taking the videos further.

Our formula for producing composite videos organized around participatory video takes the following pattern:

- Include a title for the composite video (e.g., *Our Stories*).
- Provide a context for the issue (i.e., statistical data on the issues being addressed: rural teaching, gender violence, youth and HIV and AIDS, for example).
- Capture footage during the video-making that shows each step of the process (explaining the process, brainstorming and voting on the issues to be addressed in the video, creating a storyboard, filming, and viewing the finished copy).
- Self-contain the short videos (making sure to include title, credits and English subtitles if necessary).
- Wrap up (using a text box, captions or a voice over).
- Include credits.

As previously noted, the finished composite should be no more than 18–21 minutes.

In the case of *Izindaba Yethu* (*Our Stories*), a videographer working collaboratively with the research team compiled a 17-minute rough cut composite video, complete with a musical soundtrack, text boxes containing statistics on gender violence, footage for the workshop itself where the videos were produced, English subtitles for each of the short videos (all filmed in isiZulu) and credits. The storyboarding for the production started with the research team. We knew that we wanted all the videos produced by the young people – all clips were about gender-based violence – in one video. We also had some statistical data that we were able to pass on to the videographer. As for the process, we decided that we wanted to include video clips that would represent all phases of the one-day video-making workshop: opening group activity; brainstorming about the issues and including images of the participants voting on the particular issues on which they would focus; storyboarding; filming; and, finally, screening the videos. Our storyboarding process was a reflexive tool for the research team, and the preliminary rough cut was an opportunity, as we discovered, to engage community members more fully in the process.

The rough cut of *Izindaba Yethu* was taken back to the participating school a month or so after the video-making workshop was conducted and the initial screening for viewing and discussion had taken place. After the screening of the composite video, the participants were asked to reflect on such questions as 'What did you like about the video?', Who should see the video and why?' and 'If we hadn't finished editing the video, what would you like changed or added?' The participants clearly highlighted the importance and need for their own engagement in the process. They felt that the video work opened up opportunities to engage with issues that were seldom talked about, but also to envisage how the composite video could be used as a tool to inform and encourage further debate. The first question, regarding what the participants liked about the video, led to the following responses: 'Acting about what is hidden beyond the school walls'; 'That it teach[es] and show[s] us what is happening to our community'; 'What I like most is that it was made by us'; 'We were together and sharing our ideas'; 'Learners were participating actively'; 'An opportunity to talk about how you feel'; and, finally, 'That we as learners we should not trust teachers that much.'

The above confirms the agency of the participants in bringing out into the open 'what is hidden', and not talked about or addressed in their schools and community. Furthermore, the responses affirm the possibility of meaningful participation. Reflecting on images that linger underscores the impact that gender violence has on the community, particularly on young people and on women, as the following responses show: 'The door, what was happening behind the door'; 'It's the part where the teacher rape[s] the child'; 'When the learner was crying [after the rape] … looking so sad'; 'Women and female learners are vulnerable'; and 'All young people'. These comments have an immediate quality in relation to the effects of gender-based violence on the victims as well as on the witnesses, and there is a sense of urgency of doing something because 'all young people are vulnerable'.

Taking up the issue of extending the debate around gender violence in the context of HIV and AIDS to other audiences, the groups referred to the school community, family, friends, church, community, the department of education and the government. The responses to the 'Why?' question confirmed the urgency of addressing the issues: 'They must help' and 'To stop … abuse in this community'. The video also raised awareness about the vulnerability of students in spaces traditionally seen as safe: 'to show them how easily a child can be raped in the school'; 'to teach about abuse that is taking place in homes, schools, even in the workplace and churches'. The participants did not only think of their own vulnerability, but also of the vulnerability of youth in a collective way: 'I want them to see … that our generation is in a situation'; 'I want them to know how dangerous [it is] to go alone … if you are a boy or a girl.'

Turning to the key issue of addressing gender violence, and how the composite video could help, participant responses foreshadowed the need for information and communication (e.g., 'understanding violence because it can teach other people', 'many people they know nothing about it' and 'the community would inform police about the stories and not to take law into their hands'). In asking what would help to address gender violence in schools and in the community, viewers stressed information, support, a sound value system and punishment for the criminals. Teachers felt the need for it to 'be explained in subjects, different media should be used … to teach respect to women and men'. Finally, for the question of what participants would like added to the video, one of the participants raised this thought-provoking comment: 'How is life after rape?' The question is an important one and serves as a prompt for a follow-up project on gender-based violence that considers the importance of the effect that such an act of crime would have on the life of a victim and a community.

Beyond the responses of the participants, we were interested in how the composite video could help to engage the community in exploring and making visible the issues about which people are silent – those that remain *hidden* – and in deciding where community action is required. We were encouraged by the comments and suggestions of the participants to take the video to a wider audience, and to create an opportunity for engagement between them and us. For us, the importance of getting the story out (White, 2003), to look at it and reflect upon it, is critical, as is demonstrated in the following response: 'What I like the most is that … eh … this is now being spoken about. It even appears on video and yet it was not spoken about. It was hidden. If you spoke about it you would close everything you were doing.' The importance of the composite video (based on participatory video work) is in bringing the hidden issues out in the open to be discussed and to be viewed from different perspectives.

Our Photos, Our Videos, Our Stories

The production *Our Photos, Our Videos, Our Stories* (Mak et al., 2005) might be described as a hybrid in relation to what constitutes a composite video. On the one hand, it offers a composite of several settings and several different visual approaches (photovoice, participatory video and personal albums based on family photos), and it has served as both a reflexive tool (in producing it as well as screening it to various audiences) and a tool to engage participants and communities. At the same time, because it was produced with the assistance of professional filmmakers, its quality arguably puts it in a different category. Perhaps the deciding point is to consider its chief function in the community and within the research team, and, in that respect, it functions very similarly to *Our Stories*. Below, I include the ciné fiche prepared for *Our Photos, Our Videos, Our Stories*.

Ciné fiche: *Our Photos, Our Videos, Our Stories*

Our Photos, Our Videos, Our Stories is a 22-minute documentary about South African educators who share a common experience: using visual technology to reflect on the impact of HIV and AIDS on their community, their learners, and in many instances, their personal lives. The experiences described in the video inform the way teachers and health care workers work with youth to approach these issues. The film takes us on a journey from university grounds nestled in a peri-urban industrial zone to schools dotting the vast sun-scorched rural regions of Vulindlela. In these contrasting settings, we encounter individuals who have used digital and analogue media to focus on the subject above.

First, we meet Thembinkosi. He is a primary school teacher who just completed his honours degree at UKZN. Completing a digital photo-essay project about his family, the

(Continued)

(Continued)

assignment helped him to cope with his sister's AIDS-related death. His fascination with visual representation to grapple with his own personal loss has triggered his interest in its use as an introspective learning strategy, and one that he has an interest in exploring in relation to his own teaching methods. In place of digital photography, he has been encouraging his sixth-grade students to create an art collage about the impact of HIV and AIDS in their daily lives.

Next, we move on to Gobindlovu School in the heart of the Vulindlela midlands, where a group of female secondary teachers speak about their use of digital photography to document the effects of HIV and AIDS on their village. We witness the moment in which their explanation of their photos turns into a discussion on the myths or problems of the tribal practice of *virginity testing* in relation to female teens and the HIV and AIDS epidemic.

Moving onward, we meet Zama, Nobuhle, Zola, Nolwaze and Rokam, who make up the *2010: We'll Be There* troupe, a collective of teachers whose intensive one-day workshop on digital video-making technology inspires them to create a one-minute video. In the video, they explore their feelings about HIV and AIDS from the perspective of educators, community members, close family friends or relatives, and parents; they use South Africa's 2010 World Cup event as their piece's thematic backdrop.

At a later point, Nolwaze, a principal at a primary school, talks about how his sixth-grade class embarked upon their own photovoice project, in which they exposed the difficult conditions of their community that gave rise to the Friday Absenteeism initiative about children working in the market instead of coming to school. Throughout the film, visual media in the form of a still camera, video camera, or art collage play a central role in repositioning their users – South African educators and youth – as active agents of social progression, especially pertaining to HIV/AIDS awareness campaigns.

The educators' potential to instigate positive social change begins with understanding their own views about HIV and AIDS. In this case, working with visual media is a vital way for them to engage in self-study. At the same time, working with visual technology helps them to encourage youth, the country's most vulnerable population, to use visual media to engage with the same issue at a personal level. Haunting black-and-white still photos of educators' respective modest neighbourhoods combine with mesmerizing travelling shots of Kwazulu-Natal's urban cityscapes and rural horizon to complement the many voices and faces featured in *Our Photos, Our Videos, Our Stories*. (www.iirc.mcgill.ca)

Although there was more than one community that was involved in the participatory work represented in these videos, all of the work took place in the province of KwaZulu-Natal, particularly in the rural parts of the province. In post-production screenings, we brought together various community members at the district community clinic in one community, including a community activist, an *induna* (advisor to one of the chiefs of the district), respected elderly women, teachers and community health care workers. We explained about the origin of the video, screened it, and then created an opportunity for audience engagement through focus-group discussions. Because it is a rural district and many members of the audience were only able to communicate in isiZulu, much of the discussion occurred through the medium of isiZulu, with some code-switching to English. The discussions were recorded, transcribed and translated to allow a deeper access to the richness of the text. Next, we referred to a number of key issues arising from the focus-group discussions and related to the theoretical framing of community-based video work.

First, the audience highlighted their sense of being a community (Visser, 2007). The audience members reiterated the idea that people in the community respond better when messages, such as those that address HIV and AIDS, originate from the community and are created by the community, as highlighted by Ford et al. (2003). Comments by audience members show this more fully: 'The person from the location has to speak to people of the location and the one from the rural areas speak to those of the rural areas'; 'We saw our places in the rural areas and how many things happen there'; and 'I like the way that you acknowledge everybody that participated because in most cases you see [only] the project coordinators... I think that was a wonderful idea'. The role of the community health care workers, and how much they are valued, is closely linked to this sense of community (described above):

> It is a surprise because we do not take things in rural areas seriously because we do not have much knowledge. It is like being a health worker, we from the rural areas did not get them soon enough. Their movement into the rural areas is good because many women now know the purpose of clinics through the health workers because there are health workers. We don't quickly get many things and we don't know about them.

The audience members commented that people from within the community could improve the quality of their own lives by drawing on their individual and collective assets: 'A person gets a chance to do things that are relevant to the environment that you are in'; 'Because I think it's good that if a person has found a better future ... share it with others in the community so that the community may benefit. We are grateful because most of the time when people get educated they flee ... they have developed our rural area because ... we realize that the future is bright in our area.' Kretzmann and McKnight (1993) concur that the strengths within a community are rich assets from which individuals can draw strength, even when the community seems under-resourced.

The participants commented that they saw a use for the video in their community: 'I think it would encourage the community if it was to be seen by the community'; 'In my opinion there should be groups that are there, that go around visiting families, teaching them about this thing'; and even 'The owner of the tavern ... [can] show the cassette in order for the community to listen intently about this thing that is here'.

Another important issue raised relates to the difficulties of communication between and among different generations, as illustrated by the following responses: 'It is easy for us young people to speak when we are on our own ...'; 'If they assemble together, it is good for them to hear the grown ups ... why don't they allow the youth and adults to assemble with them in order for us to beat the virus that is here ...'; 'It is easy for an old person to understand a thing if it means you sit with him/her and talk about the matter. He/she understands better that way, rather than standing in front of them.'

Messages of teaching and preaching were deemed less useful whilst collaborative video was seen to help equalize power relations. It was interesting to note that the HIV and AIDS epidemic was conceptualized by the audience as not only affecting adolescents and adults. For example, one audience member saw the importance of including 'small children like those in crèche since they are also important ... I don't know, adapting to small children in order to entice them to understand better'.

An issue that I take up elsewhere (Mitchell, 2006a) pertains to what I perceive to be a never-ending story in the use of these composite videos, and how they continue to elicit data. Indeed, the idea of having multiple screenings of a video, as opposed to the single life of a conference presentation, has been an important lesson learned in this research. *Our Photos, Our Videos, Our Stories*, as noted above, has been screened among many different communities where it was produced (with the help and support from community health care workers, teachers and learners) as well as in many other venues in Southern and Eastern Africa. When I showed it to a university group at Jimma University in Ethiopia, staff were interested in the methodologies (photovoice, curated photo albums, participatory video), but what most interested and shocked them were the living conditions of rural life in South Africa (they had not imagined that South Africa was so rural and so poor) and the statistics on the rates of HIV and AIDS, which are much higher than in Ethiopia. When I showed the film to an aboriginal group in rural Nova Scotia, Canada, their response was that 'this is just what our conditions are like'. Instantly, the group educators from a seemingly developed country felt a bond with the participants in rural South Africa.

Dress Fitting

Ciné fiche: *Dress Fitting*

Drawing on in-depth interviews with women remembering their high school prom experiences, *Dress Fitting* looks at the ways in which 'the dress' operates symbolically in the interplay of popular culture, mother–daughter relationships, body, and age. The video's group interviews, which were conducted over a month, might be read both as markers of 'the pleasures of research' as well as evidence of the significance of memory work in research. (www.iirc.mcgill.ca)

Dress Fitting is a 25-minute documentary-style video that uses the topic of the high-school prom (graduation dance) to explore issues of dress and identity. As part of a research project on body, dress and identity, we had been collecting *dress stories* (Weber and Mitchell, 2004), some of which centre on the high-school prom (see also Chapter 3). We had been interviewing women (individually and in small groups) who were 17 or 18 years of age and getting ready for their prom. We also included women in their early 50s, who related from their memories experiences of anticipating, preparing for, and attending or not attending their high school graduation dances or proms. The actual production of the video came out of a recognition that the stack of video tapes that had piled up were just 'sitting there', and that somehow just transcribing them didn't seem appropriate, whereas viewing them again with all the participants in the study seemed very worthwhile (see also Mitchell, 2009a).

The production of *Dress Fitting* really came about as a result of the complexity of trying to 'show' the links between popular culture (images of the prom in *Seventeen* magazine, *Barbie* music, and various Hollywood movies organized around the senior prom), the materiality of the prom dress, various prom artefacts, and then the lived experience of the prom (before, during and after) – in the conventional written format of a conference paper, journal article or book. Even though other scholarly work on the prom, such as Amy Best's (2007) book, is insightful, the approach did not convey fully what we had in mind. As researchers, we wanted a way to show the interplay of popular culture, domestic relations, romance and identity, and, perhaps, as much as anything, we did not want to be left out. In a sense, *Dress Fitting* is auto-ethnographic; as researchers and producers, we are present in the film.

In 2003, Norman Denzin explored some of the levels of identity creation that people go through in an era where cinema and television increasingly provide us with reflections in which we locate our own identities. He comments that 'members of the postmodern society know themselves through the reflected images and narratives of cinema and television' (Denzin, 2003: 142). In the case of producing *Dress Fitting*, we ended up gathering together many of the women who had been video-taped in the interview situation and sat down with them to watch the tapes, to discuss them, to make notes and to seek commonalities and differences between women's responses. Watching and discussing the tapes in a group gave rise to a new sense of the interpretive experience.

From there, we began the actual production. *Dress Fitting* draws on more than 20 video-taped interviews (some close to an hour long) and was developed according to a number of topics and themes common across the interviews – going shopping for the dress, the dress itself, the prom dinner, after the prom and reflections on the whole experience. In many of the interviews, a participant would bring in her prom dress or photographs of the dress, or both, providing visual features that the video genre allows for. At many points during the video, one is aware of the presence of the research team, sometimes in an oblique way (laughter in the background as one of the participants speaks) and sometimes directly (when we talk about our own proms and then at a later point when we draw attention to what the research process is and why we are studying *dress* this way).

Choosing the music for the production was also a critical feature. Music speaks to both the producers and audience, but it also adds to the overall effect. This process was contentious at times since Sandra Weber and I were working with young filmmakers who had a different idea about which particular pieces of music were appropriate for the project. We were not specifically looking for music that represented our own prom days from the 1960s, but neither were we seeking a 'right now' musical representation. In the end, we chose several pieces of music including a cut from the film *The Commitments* ('Try a little tenderness') (1991), which we thought conveyed something of the romance and nostalgia of the topic. In one segment, we included images of Sandra's young niece playing with several Barbie dolls and 'dressing up' herself in adult-sized prom dresses. As a backdrop to a spontaneous dance, we included some tango music. As with the other composite videos described in this chapter, the video has been used in a variety of ways. These include conference presentations at academic conferences linked to methodology, such as those hosted by the American Educational Research Association (Mitchell and Weber, 2000) and the Popular Culture Association (Mitchell and Weber, 2000); a presentation at an international conference on fashion, dress and consumption (Weber and Mitchell, 2003); part of a plenary at a symposium on dress (Mitchell, 2009a); and part of training with graduate students on data collection and data analysis.

On the supervision of new researchers and the use of the composite video: *Over The Rainbow*[3]

As noted in the previous chapter, Liesel Ebersöhn and Irma Eloff (2007), in their work 'Lessons from Postgraduate Studies Employing Photographic Methodology', offer a compelling set of arguments for having master's and doctoral students include process-based visual data in their field work, regardless of whether the actual study involves visual work. As the authors argue, supervisors are often not present on the research sites of their students, so visual data can help to provide a context for the work. Drawing on narrative data from their students, Ebersöhn and Eloff include a rich discussion on the benefits of including visual images. These encompass the sheer 'joy of capturing the research process', critical components such as 'anchoring' the student and providing a sense of security, students' ownership of the data, the handling of visual data as either primary or second data, and increasing clarity and reflexivity experienced by both the students and the supervisor. To this set of arguments in support of visual data (especially photographs), one might add in the possibility of a composite production serving a variety of uses, starting with many of the same reasons outlined above (especially the fact that the supervisor may not be present on the site). The composite video can also help the (novice) researcher to get a better understanding of what constitutes the data set and can offer rich possibilities for eliciting critical and engaged commentary on the study.

Paula Charbonneau-Gowdy, as a doctoral student at McGill University several years ago, produced a short composite documentary called *Over the Rainbow* about her fieldwork involving a military group from Eastern Europe enrolled in a residential language programme in Canada. The video, about 22 minutes in length, combines a 'talking head' narrative with edited 'cinéma vérité' scenes of her classroom at the military base where the course is offered and where the students live. The opening scene shows Paula, the narrator/talking head, holding the microphone and speaking directly to the audience. She tell us about some of the difficulties of second language teaching and something specific about the group of NATO officers from Eastern Europe who are currently in Canada and learning English.

Paula is the reporter/journalist that we are used to seeing live and on location. She speaks firmly – no nonsense – but a little haltingly in places, and we think of her as someone who knows about and cares about her teaching. No actor could play her any better. From the opening scene, we enter into Paula's classroom, where a group of six or seven men in military uniform are sitting in a semi-circle around Paula. In the scenes in her classroom, she explores a number of issues – themes in the data that she has been collecting, that she sees as barriers to effective language learning. Specifically, Paula explores teacher control and the marginalization of students from their own learning (and from each other), and she demonstrates, too, the ways that status and rank, in particular, enter this picture. We hear the men laughing, talking among themselves, groaning at the types of assignments they are required to do and lamenting their test scores by expressing 'how dumb they are'. At one point, we see them making fun of one of their colleagues who is struggling with the language tasks, and they demonstrate what might be regarded as typical excluding behaviour (derogatory comments directed towards Vlad or meeting in a group for coffee without him), something that Paula sees as a feature of the classroom she controls. As she demonstrates (and interrogates) in the video, there is something not quite adult-like about some of the classroom scenes. While the men do not misbehave, they are in some ways not unlike a group of adolescent boys. And Paula, who may be the same age as her students or not much older than some of them, is 'the mom' – a situation that in itself may be a barrier to learning.

At another point in the film, we visit the men's dormitories, which, as Paula narrates, are spartan in appearance – nothing on the walls, no ornamentation, but nothing out of place either. Clearly, it is important that we understand where her students are located when they are not in class. But then in the last scene, we see something else: the men are all sitting around the table in the cafeteria, chatting and laughing with Paula, who is in her coat and ready to leave for the day. Class is out. A Keith Jarrett rendition of 'Somewhere over the rainbow' from *The Wizard of Oz* (1939) plays in the background, and we are drawn in to seeing that notwithstanding the built-in barriers to learning in these kinds of government-run programmes, there is, after all, a strong bond between Paula and these fellows. They have all – teacher and students – 'let their guard down'.

When Paula first screened the video for the Textual Approaches to Research graduate class (close to the end of the 13-week course), not only were her classmates enthusiastic about the visual quality of the work but also, and more to the point, were all fascinated by what she had done with her data. During the course, she had spoken extensively about this group of learners. Her classmates and I knew of her frustrations in trying to understand them and vice versa. We had already been made aware about their dormitories, and how they refused to transform these rooms from anything other than army barracks. These rooms were not homes to them. From hearing about the students for most of the course, it was as if we already knew them quite well – or so we thought.

Somehow, seeing these learners – grown men in their military uniforms – as real people who laughed and joked, but who were also clearly worried about their progress, put a different spin on the project. Paula's description of the making of *Over the Rainbow* was illuminating. (I didn't edit the punctuation so as to keep the original sound of the interview.)

> The filming was all done in a day. We [my daughter and I] used two powerful cameras: One we kept stationary in a corner of the classroom; the other my daughter and I used to film outside the space of the classroom – the halls, student rooms, the school layout. The moveable camera was also used for close-ups while the class was in progress so that when a student spoke or was involved particularly in some way, my daughter would focus in on that particular student. Finally, I gave this camera to my students for them to film what they thought was important to document. Some students were initially shy but, as the day wore on, they seemed to forget the cameras and became very natural. It felt to me, judging from the way we interacted, that it was a 'normal' day. After the day of filming, I spent three 10-hour days preparing the video. It involved looking at the enormous amount of footage from both cameras and deciding what was important to clip for the sake of my argument or thesis. I, with my daughter's help, used Final Cut Pro 3 for this process. After compiling the clips, I then decided on a storyline – when I would speak and generally what I would say and what clips would fall under each section. Encouraged by my daughter to speak spontaneously rather than from a prepared speech, we filmed my short blurbs. Then I gathered, arranged and cut the clips into even smaller bits. Next, I chose a title and typed it in along with the credits at the end. I chose first names and a picture of our group to ensure that they would be acknowledged and be recognized for their participation. Finally, I chose the song ['Somewhere over the rainbow'] and added it to the credit timing.

Living with Kidney Failure:
Filmmaking in participatory action research

Finally, I want to refer to a video production titled *Living with Kidney Failure* that was produced as a feature-length documentary by several of my colleagues at McGill University. It was directed by a well-known documentary filmmaker, Garry Beitel, and produced in conjunction with a study on kidney disease that only partly drew on visual methods (participants engaged in photovoice to exhibit their experiences, especially in the dialysis unit). Dawn Allen, a qualitative researcher who was involved in the study and part of the filmmaking, observed:

> We have seen the video as a consciousness-raising project/product that developed from our PAR study on quality of life. I was committed to PAR, but was feeling a bit desperate to find a way to take action that reflected the needs and interests/goals

of the patient-collaborators. They loved the camera, they loved being heard, they loved that 'what they said mattered' and so I went with film as the medium. That we were able to develop our data into a moving, almost feature-length documentary is due largely to Garry Beitel's [filmmaker] good eye, a calm and open demeanor, patience and compassion; of course, a film-maker's aesthetic and sensitivity to that which is most 'compelling'. (Allen, 2009, personal communication)

Ciné fiche: *Living with Kidney Failure*

Living with Kidney Failure is a film about the lived experience of seven individuals of different ages, disease histories and cultural backgrounds. The stories of their dialysis dependency highlight some of the quality-of-life issues faced by people living with chronic kidney failure. While their experiences are in some ways specific to their disease and treatment, the issues of family strain, unemployment, uncertainty, vulnerability and mortality will be familiar to all those who live or work with chronic illness.

This film is the product of a two-year participatory action research project, which involved researchers from McGill University and patient-collaborators from two university-affiliated haemodialysis units.

This film has several different goals: (a) raising awareness about kidney disease in the general public; (b) exploring quality of life and chronic illness issues with health care students and professionals; (c) providing chronically ill people with a larger sense of community; and (d) offering administrators and health policy legislators a window into the needs of this rapidly growing patient-population. (Directed by Garry Beitel with Dawn Allen and Tom Hutchison)

Living with Kidney Failure, it seems to me, fits nicely into the idea of the composite video – allowing for length – because of the intended outcomes and the ways in which it draws together the various data sources.

Conclusion

This chapter has highlighted a creative side of visual research, and in tandem with the next chapter of this book, which is on influencing policy-making and 'changing the picture', suggests some ways that our research can have an afterlife. One of the areas to continue to think about is, of course, the issue of informed consent, and how data collected at one time and place can continue to be used beyond the life of the project. In the research teams in which I am involved, we have been testing out various aspects of composite video over a period of years, and increasingly, we have tried to anticipate the possibility of composite video production from the beginning and have informed participants of this. It is rather difficult to anticipate a one-size-fits-all approach, with the contexts varying from Paula's doctoral research, for example, to the *Our Photos, Our Videos, Our Stories* production, which drew together data from several projects. This is a critical area to explore, however, particularly alongside the more public domain questions of distribution in relation to social networking sites.

Notes

1 Elsewhere, I have considered several other versions of the same question based on the formulation in the title of Jo Spence and Joan Solomon's (1995) edited book *What Can a Woman Do with a Camera?* I have asked (and attempted to answer) the following questions: 'What can a teacher do with a camera?' (Mitchell et al., 2004a; Mitchell and Weber, 1999); 'What can a child do with a camera?' (Mitchell and Reid-Walsh, 2002) and 'What can a girl do with a camera?' (Mitchell, 2009b) I have even taken the liberty of adapting Spence and Solomon's formulation 'What can a woman do with a camera?' to become 'What can a women do with a (video) camera? Turning the female gaze on poverty and HIV and AIDS in rural South Africa' (Moletsane et al., 2009).

2 This discussion of *Izindaba Yethu* is adapted from Mitchell et al. (in press).

3 This discussion of *Over the Rainbow* is adapted from Mitchell et al. (2004a).

TEN

Changing the picture: How can images influence policy-making?

Introduction

The year was 1977 and I was a junior high English teacher in a small consolidated school (kindergarten to Grade 9) in a fishing village in south western Nova Scotia, on the east coast of Canada. Many of my students were the children of local lobster fishermen. For some, though not all, Grade 9 was the exit year. Some of the boys would take up fishing alongside their fathers, uncles and older brothers. Some of the girls would leave school and then marry. The art teacher came to see me one day and asked if I would like to be involved in a filmmaking project with my Grade 9 students. Now, in retrospect and in the context of budget constraints, I am surprised that we actually had an art teacher. The National Film Board of Canada, flush and expansive in its regional office in Halifax, was prepared to provide (free of charge) a Super 8 camera and a small hand-editing machine to process all film (free of charge) through a special outreach programme. When I would need it, they would send the camera down to the school on the Acadian Lines bus and would cover all shipping costs. I could send back the film on the bus to be processed (again free of charge). 'Would I ever,' I said, though I knew nothing about the process of filmmaking.

My students in the ninth grade were very excited, of course. Although we had watched lots of artistic and documentary films thanks to the wonderful film library of the National Film Board of Canada, no one had ever imagined making a film; no one (including me) had ever used a film camera. The actual operating of the camera is now a bit of a blur in my mind, but given that the students operated it, I can only assume that the art teacher must have helped us out. As for editing, I recall that one of the students, Kevin, was a whiz at this. He had the artistic sensibility, technical know-how and patience required to succeed. Now I am not sure whether this project lasted for more than that one semester, but I do still have the visual evidence of the three main pieces we produced: two shot at the school itself (including *Death of a Fly*, a one-minute narrative shot with the opening bars of Elton John's 'Funeral for a Friend' [John, 1973] in the background) and then a rousing, rollicking three-minute bank robber type film, which among other things involved my own car as the getaway car. I am assuming that because no one in the class had a driver's licence, I was probably the person who drove the getaway car. For that film, the music of Scott Joplin was key. And finally, our pièce de résistance was a 'feature length' 8-minute high art piece that we shot on Port Maitland beach and for which we selected John Denver's 'Calypso' (Denver, 1975) as a musical backdrop. The film is full of fade-ins and fade-outs, deliberate out-of-focus mistiness, and an evocative mood of memory and imagination. Clearly, my students were greatly influenced by the various NFB shorts we had viewed for a semester. And in response to a technical challenge, none of the three videos had any dialogue – only music – and now might be regarded as precursors to the music video of the 1980s.

Given an era of progressive education (the age of Paul Goodman, Jonathan Kozol, A.S. Neill and Paulo Freire) during which there was a great deal happening at the government level in Canada by way of support for the arts, or at least that is how it seems now, I don't think I questioned too much why the National Film Board of Canada was making this film equipment available to my little school, or whether anyone else in the province was doing anything like this, or really what happened after that semester. Notwithstanding the fact that we made the films, I really had not given a lot of thought to this project – despite much of my work over the last decade being entirely given over to visual methodologies and community-based visual research, and much of it with young people and their communities. Indeed, it was only when I was reading Shirley White's (2003) description of the Fogo Project in Newfoundland, which was part of the National Film Board of Canada's *Challenge for Change* programme of the 1960s up to the early 1980s, that I started to connect the dots and realize that my students and I were probably part of this same programme:

> This year [1966], The National Film Board of Canada launched an unprecedented project called Challenge for Change. This project, which lasted until 1980 and enjoyed its most active years between 1967–1975, represented an innovative approach to citizenship education in Canada during the boom years of state funding for social services and cultural productions. ... Designed to popularize film and video production in order to illuminate the social concerns of various communities within Canada, Challenge for Change was funded by eight different departments of the federal government. It ran on a considerable budget divided between English and French-language programming (in Francophone Canada, the program was known as Societé Nouvelle). The impetus for the program was the belief that film and video were useful tools for initiating social change and eliminating poverty, and initially entailed filmmakers entering what were considered marginalized communities to document everyday realities and struggles. Among the most notorious of the projects made were Colin Low's twenty-seven films about life on Fogo Island, Newfoundland,

produced in 1967. While the Fogo Island projects were actually preceded by earlier Challenge for Change films, their notoriety helped to launch the program, which went on to produce over 140 films across the country. (http://legacy.oise.utoronto.ca/research/edu20/moments/1966cfc.html)

Although *Challenge for Change* was very much intended to bring about social change, its success in doing this has been critiqued by a number of scholars (see Waugh et al., 2010). And Druick (1998) writes:

> Janine Marchessault, in her 1995 book *Reflections on the dispossessed: video and the 'Challenge for Change' experiment*, argues that the program delivered 'access without agency'. While communities represented themselves, the program did not challenge power relations and few of the videos went beyond a 'social reproduction' of 'difference' as essentialized by the liberal government. Marchessault suggests that the dialogical process that Challenge for Change claimed to initiate was rarely found and that most of the films instead represent a packaging of 'difference' for an outside audience (Marchessault, 1995: 140–2). Challenge for Change has also been criticized as a liberal nationalist project that served to essentialize group identities and attempted to conquer difference by 'framing differences as typical of our shared nationality' (Druick, 1998: 1). (http://legacy.oise.utoronto.ca/research/edu20/moments/1966cfc.html)

These criticisms may well be valid, but the point that was emphasized in the *Challenge for Change* mandate was process and not the quality of the films. In the case of our little project, I am pretty sure that neither *Death of a Fly* nor the other films ever made it into the line-up of 140 films across the country. However, in the context of engaging a group of 20 or so 14- or 15-year-old students for whom Grade 9 might have been their last year at school, it probably doesn't matter whether these films become part of any collection. This work, and now the memory of it, acts as a prompt: to think about its meaning in relation to doing visual research, and to consider ideas of process, and as Shirley White notes, transformation and empowerment.

With this rather long and meandering introduction, what I want to consider in this final chapter are the questions 'So what?' and 'What difference does this work make?', particularly in the context of the impact of this work on policy makers. Much of the work related to visual methodologies is organized around claims of being liberatory and directed towards social change. From the 'grassroots policy-making' of photovoice to the promise of emancipatory practices in participatory video, there is an inherent sense that this work will have an impact – and thereby 'change the picture'. In the absence of retrospective data from my junior high students from 1977, who all now must be close to 50 years of age, what I consider in this chapter are two aspects of studying impact: (1) several short case studies that explore some of the outcomes of a number of recent projects using visual methodologies; and (2) a practical look at reaching audiences. What I explore here are some of the challenges of trying to review this kind of work in the context of policy, and I consider what it might be about the visual that is important. In looking at reaching audiences, my focus is on what might be termed the politics, aesthetics and technicalities of display.

Where is Policy?

> In reviewing [the] assessment of the contributions of qualitative work to the policy process, it is apparent that the contributions are more in the realm of the potential than the actual. There is no broad-based and sustained tradition within contemporary social science of focusing qualitative work specifically on policy issues, especially given the real time constraints that the policy process necessitates. Yet it is also clear that the opportunities are multiple for such contributions to be made. The issue is chiefly one of how to link those in the research and academic communities who are knowledgeable in conducting qualitative research studies to those in the policy arena who can commission such work and who will make use of the findings. (Rist, 2003: 641)

In the section that follows, I look at several projects where it seems obvious that there has been some policy movement in relation to a project involving visual methodologies. While I have written about each elsewhere in this book, here I look at some of the cross-cutting themes and issues.

The *Feeling Safe/Feeling Not so Safe* project (Swaziland)

In this project, seventh-grade students in a school just outside of Mbabane in Swaziland participated in a photovoice activity in which they were given disposable cameras and asked to photograph where they felt safe and not so safe. The photovoice component of the project, part of a larger study on participatory methodologies with youth in addressing issues of sexual abuse, was carried out in three short stages. In the first stage, the 30 or so young people gathered in a group and were given a short explanation of the purpose of the project, which was to find out where they felt safe and not so safe in school – particularly in the context of sexual abuse. They were also given a short demonstration on the use of disposable cameras and were placed in groups of three or four of the same sex. In the second stage, which lasted for approximately 40 minutes, they were free to go anywhere on the school premises to take photographs. The third stage was the 'looking at photographs' stage. The students gathered in small groups on the playground and were each given their envelopes of photos to look at and to choose several for which they wanted to add captions. In the process of the children viewing their photographs and developing captions for them, their teachers had an opportunity to see what the children photographed. Many of the teachers were surprised – not at the conditions of the toilets, because obviously they must have known that the doors were broken, but at the danger experienced and expressed so directly by the girls. I remember a few of the teachers offering comments: 'Why did you take a picture of that [a toilet]? Why didn't you take a picture of something nice?' My own involvement in the school component of the project ended there, but what I found out later was that the teachers and the principal embarked upon the practice of monitoring the toilets. While I have no idea how long this practice lasted,

I can only conjecture that this local policy change (monitoring the toilets) must have made a difference to the safety and security of the girls.

Some months later, I participated in a policy discussion in New York that was sponsored by the Child Protections division of the UN. It was the photograph of the toilet which was projected onto the large screen as part of a PowerPoint presentation, that makes a very dramatic statement about sanitation and security in the lives of girls in sub-Saharan Africa. One of the experts in water and sanitation, who himself had done field work in the area, commented: 'You read about building wells and toilets in reports all the time [and you see them] but you think about them differently when you see a picture of an actual well or actual toilet. Here the fact that a child actually took the photograph speaks volumes.' A policy outcome of the session was that experts in the areas of water and sanitation and child protection realized that they needed to consider the location of the toilets not just in relation to sanitation but also in relation to issues of security. They saw that they needed to provide support to schools to monitor toilets in the context of gender-based violence.

Friday Absenteeism project (South Africa)

In this project, children from an informal settlement participated in a photovoice activity, which led to several policy changes in relation to food security and gender violence. A critical issue in the school was the fact that many of the children in the senior primary grades missed school on Fridays. The school is located about 160 kilometres inland and north of Durban, and it serves a large number of children who live in informal settlements surrounding, but not adequately served by, a cluster of small factories and light industry. The usual problems of poverty, unemployment and high rates of HIV infection and illness abound in the community and contribute to many interruptions to schooling (i.e., children miss classes).

The principal and staff at the primary school and at other schools in the area already knew why the children missed school but were not sure how to address the absenteeism – Friday was market day and many of the children in the senior primary grades were often called on to work in the market to earn money to at least provide for the basic nutritional needs of the families over the weekend. This is an important point, for although there was a school feeding scheme from Monday to Friday, no provision existed for help with food over the weekends. The principal was concerned because the children could not afford to miss one day per week of school, and this behaviour also sent a message to other children that school wasn't important.

However, finding effective strategies to address the problem remained a challenge. While there were a variety of approaches the principal and staff might have taken to address the problem (including doing nothing, given the range of curricular, administrative and social issues that confront school staff), the participation of the principal in a university module on cinematic and documentary texts was instrumental to his belief that working with the visual would yield transformative results among the learners, and possibly in the community as well (Mitchell et al., 2006a). From this understanding, he saw the potential for the young people to use photography, not only to document the problems they faced but also to identify and/or influence the development of strategies within the school, within the community, and within the government departments responsible for young people's well-being. So, through a photovoice project, he involved his sixth-grade class in analysing the problems and identifying possible solutions to this problem of school attendance and other troubles affecting the community.

The children's narratives in the photographs, posters and writing reveal a variety of issues. One issue highlighted is alcoholism among adults in the community – this is captured in a caption to a photograph: 'If we look at these people who are living in this shack, they are drinking alcohol. They are not working. The schoolchild cannot survive in this condition.' Other issues identified by the children included high levels of unemployment, the need for housing, the lack of clean water and sanitation, and the danger to children of even coming to school because they have to cross a wide highway that has no bridge over it. Most importantly, the photographs draw attention to the effects of poverty, and they provide visual evidence of why children as young as 11 or 12 must supplement the family income. Poverty leads to some children having to miss school to take care of younger siblings. In their caption to one of the photographs, the students note: 'This photo shows us the rate of children who are absent from schools. These children are absent because they have to look after their baby sister or brother while their parents are working.' The photographs taken in the market not only show scenes of the adults who run the market trying to make a living but also show the children's peers at work and not at school. The children also took pictures of learners from nearby schools, demonstrating that Friday absenteeism was a widespread problem in the district. One particular photograph is of a boy who was working in the market to raise money for a school trip to Durban, which he could not otherwise afford. The caption reads 'He absented himself from school because they had a trip to Durban. He decided to look for a part-time job because he needs the money. He has no parents.'

The photographs and captions also reflect upon the conditions of the school itself. For example, one of the girls working in the market spoke about issues of safety and security in her classroom. Her teacher, she indicated, had been making sexual advances towards her. Being away from school on Fridays was an escape from this unwanted attention. The engagement of the children extended from the preliminary discussions about school attendance, through to two photography field trips during school hours: one to their own community in the informal settlement and the other to the market. When they returned to the classroom, they worked in small groups to create posters of their work, and it was these photo-posters that were eventually presented to stakeholders in the community.

The insider data produced by the children in the project had implications for policy development at the school and community level. For example, from the data, the principal instituted disciplinary action against the teacher who allegedly was sexually harassing a female learner. He also raised the issue of absenteeism with other principals in the district and planned for a community-based stakeholders' forum, at which the children were to present their posters. From this work, and because the school was registered as a Section 21 (not-for-profit) company, he was able to approach donors and corporate funders and attract financial support for a feeding scheme for the weekends as well as during the week. Clearly, the follow-up intervention does not solve the issues of unemployment and poverty, and whenever I talk about such 'happy results' at a conference or with my students, I think of how much this sounds like a band-aid solution. However, at the level of a school taking action from the ground up and from the perspective of children who received some food and attention that they would not otherwise have received, it is still, in my opinion, worth regarding as a success story for the visual.

Here are the Pictures but is Anyone Looking?

On the technicalities and politics of display

One of the challenges in visual research, including the two projects just discussed, is reaching audiences, particularly those who are deemed to be the people who can do something, ranging from local policy makers and other community members through to national or global audiences. In the case of the *Feeling Safe/Feeling Not so Safe* project, the possibility for action started at the level of the principal and teachers, who saw the photographs and decide to do something, and although it was somewhat accidental (in that no formal presentation took place), something happened. At the level of the UN, the interaction was more strategic: here was an audience who should see the pictures, and it was important (for me) to use the opportunity and technology to do this. I showed the photo of the toilet in a PowerPoint presentation on a big screen because just passing around a small snap-shot at a conference of 50 or more people would not have had the same impact.

I am always interested in what others involved in working with the visual in community research do with participant-produced photos, drawings and videos. What is the best way of making public the productions that participants decide others should see? What do visual researchers need to know about the use of various forms of display (exhibitions, banners, websites, PowerPoint presentations, books and so on)? When I started working with visual data, I don't think I had any idea that I would spend so much time trying to work out the technicalities of display and over the years have come to have a great deal of appreciation for good working relationships with carpenters, personnel in print shops, and maintenance staff. From seeking out the type of adhesive that will keep up a photo exhibit for a whole evening to locating mobile chart stands, to scrutinizing what a clothesline can be attached to in order to exhibit a set of drawings or photos, to tracking down a generator to screen a locally made video – these can be central to the 'making public' process. This work is often far removed from more conventional display areas such as museums, libraries or art galleries. It has more typically been displayed outside the principal's office in a school, at a local petrol station, or on a chicken-wire fence. What follows are some key elements and consideration of display that I have drawn from my own previous work or from that of various researchers with whom I have been associated.

In the right place

In the first chapter of this book, I make reference to Ardra Cole and Maura McIntyre's (2006) *Living and Dying with Dignity* exhibition that included a vast clothesline of diapers (from baby size to adult size) strung across the foyer of the Canadian Broadcasting Corporation building in downtown Toronto, Canada. The foyer is a very public site and one that thousands of people pass through every day. In other public exhibitions, the focus is on the relevant ministry or government office. For example, Jen Thompson (2009) in her intergenerational photovoice project of environmental concerns in Sierra Leone, wanted the Ministry of Agriculture to see for themselves the issues, so she arranged to set up an exhibition in Freetown in a government office. Cost was important but so was the need to create an exhibition that was not intrusive and did not necessitate structural changes to the environment. Her solution was to mount a clothesline and clip the photographs to the line.

Figure 10.1   Clothesline display of environmental issues at Ministry of Agriculture (Sierra Leone)

For another exhibition, which we hoped would provide an opportunity to showcase young rural South Africans' photos of stigma to their families, our team was told that if the exhibition took place at the school, no one would come. As a result of the devastating effects of HIV and AIDS, many of the young photographers were being raised by grandparents or other family members who were unlikely to come to the school. Instead, the principal told us to 'set up the exhibition in the middle of the village on Pensioners' Day'. Our team had to consider what that might look like and how to anticipate the effect of the weather, location, stability and mobility.

Simple and local

In their work with the Durban South Photography Project, Du Toit and colleagues (2007) engaged community members in addressing through photography (their own and family photography) the environmental and related issues in the Wentworth and Merebank communities as a result of industrial pollution. Not unlike Wendy Ewald (1985), the researchers developed a series of photography and literacy workshops for first-time photographers and set up the participants' local exhibitions. Noting the importance of the local, they write:

> From the start, the project was planned as incorporating a programme of exhibitions integrated with the process of producing photographs, as opposed to culminating in one exhibition held away from where the pictures were taken. Instead, we held three workshops-cum-exhibitions in Wentworth and Merebank in the first two years, always in the municipal library, chosen as an accessible venue frequented by many people from the area. … An important aspect of the exhibitions was also to invite comments from viewers. Our first effort to do so using a conventional visitors' book was unsuccessful. From 2003, we placed large sheets of paper in the venue, asking various questions in order to invite comments and criticism. (Du Toit et al., 2007: 270–1)

In Zainul Sajan Virgi's photovoice work with a group of girls in a project on abject intergenerational hardship in Mozambique, it was critical that the girls themselves appreciated what their pictures looked like 'on display' (Sajan Virgi and Mitchell, in press). Like Thompson, Sajan Virgi used a clothesline but in a more modest way because the exhibit had to be set up and taken down within a couple of hours on the school grounds (see Figure 10.2 on the next page).

Mobility

A couple of years ago we set up an exhibition at McGill University that showcased photos created by primary school girls in Montreal as well as photos produced by girls in South Africa, Rwanda and Swaziland. The Montreal schoolgirls attended and participated in setting up the exhibition as the final part of their photovoice project. All of the photos had been taken in school settings, and our initial idea had been to use the kind of wire fencing that seems to surround schools around

Figure 10.2   Clothesline display at school (Mozambique)

Figure 10.3   Use of chicken wire to mount exhibition (Montreal, Canada)

the world. However, the exhibition could only be set up for one day and had to be relocated to another site after the interactive session with local girls. Our solution was to use chicken wire, which is light and mobile.

Authenticity

Something that I have found interesting is the response of various audiences to photovoice projects that include captions that are in the handwriting of

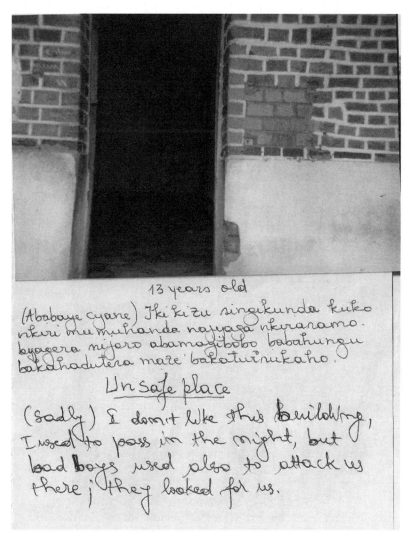

Figure 10.4 Handwritten captions

participants or transcribers/translators versus those that include captions that are typewritten. I have watched how audiences look at the images and, while my findings may not be very scientific, it has seemed to me that viewers interact more with the captions that are handwritten. Notwithstanding the fact that handwriting perhaps demands more of the viewer's attention, there seems to be more engagement with the visual and written texts.

Ownership

But display is not just about reaching communities and policy makers, it is also part of the participatory process itself. A group of young people who have spent several weeks on a photo project in which they have made decisions about all aspects of the process should also, as much as possible, have some say about who should see the photos, drawings or video and how and where. In these decisions, there is a need to have some consideration of audience and the appropriateness of display. A very formal 'hanging' of photos mounted and framed by wood and glass may be appropriate for a gallery but not for a community centre in a rural area where the majority of the audience will not have

Figure 10.5 Individual poster-size exhibitions

frames with glass in their homes, and where the glass could actually be danger-ous. Cost is also a critical feature, and the technical aspects of display should not overtake the project.

Large personal posters produced by participants that include their images and captions is a way to address the possibility that one large exhibition may take away from individual contributions. Fumane Khanare (2009), in her work related to HIV and AIDS and involving youth in rural South Africa, found that poster-size 'exhibits' were a way to maintain ownership, particularly because participants were going to speak about the photos they had produced in front of an audience. As I have noted elsewhere (Mitchell and Reid-Walsh, 2002), there is something about being able to hang on to one's own photos in the process of discussing them. These poster displays meant that the individual photographers physically retained ownership.

In another photovoice project, the photos were simply clipped on to a wire strung across the room and at eye level. In a photo workshop, each participant was able to select (and hold) the photo he or she wanted to present to the larger group and then clip it back onto the wire when finished. In both of these examples, the importance of the materiality of the photo-as-object is acknowledged, as is the ownership factor.

A third type of ownership can be seen in the use of small photo albums, or what I call the *album project*. In Chapter 3, there is an account of a small album, produced by Tao, dealing with the political and social changes in China as read through the lens of dress. Her album is an example of the album project, which has been under way since 2004 and was first developed through a course on cinematic and docu-mentary texts at the University of KwaZulu-Natal in South Africa. The idea behind the album project is the construction of a personal documentary, either through using a photovoice approach or working with already existing family photographs. The process, as described elsewhere (Knowles and Cole, 2008; Mitchell and Allnutt, 2008; Mitchell et al., 2009), follows a few simple steps:

1 Form a personal collection of photos by selecting seven or eight photos that fit a particular theme or narrative.
2 Work with the images, deciding on the order and the overall thematic area.
3 Create a title and a short curatorial statement of 200 words or so that will fit into the plastic sleeve.
4 Compose short captions for the photos that will fit into the plastic sleeves opposite them.

The album can include other sections such as a dedication or 'about the author', and these should also be contained within the plastic sleeves of the album. Ideally, participants will have a chance to present their albums to an audience (offering, for example, the back story to their documentary), and of course the material artefact of the album can be displayed to other audiences.

Figure 10.6 The album project

Aesthetics

But beyond these examples taken from studies with other researchers with whom I have worked, Wendy Ewald, in her various projects with children as photographers, offers approaches to display that speak directly to the aesthetics of display. And while there are many other entry points for discussion related to aesthetics in participatory visual research, one of the most obvious areas relates to audience and display. One of her projects, the Peace and Harmony: Carver Portraits Project (Ewald, 2006), involved the production of huge larger-than-life banners containing portrait photos of the children in the project. While most of the banners were displayed on various public buildings in the community, at least one of them was displayed on a house. As Hyde (2005) writes, 'The 12 installation sites juxtapose portraits of children – their faces and the backs of their heads – with ordinary objects chosen by the children (2005: 183). She goes on to note: 'The images stand alone [in the various sites] as powerful testimonies to the children's lives. But given their massive size, their symbolically rich location, and their public accessibility, the banners become even more compelling.' The design of the display intentionally sets out to alter the course of how people see and interact with the community: 'She [Ewald] designed the installation as a circuitous path that takes viewers through the community to each site – those Ewald chose and those selected by the participating children who walk through the neighbourhood everyday on their way to and from school' (2005: 188). The way Ewald presents this work changes the meaning of the portraits themselves as well as their impact. 'By presenting the work within the public spaces of her collaborators' lives instead of within the more exclusive halls of a museum or gallery, Ewald expands and diversifies her audience and creates the potential for meaningful dialogue' (Hyde, 2005: 189). It is worth noting, as Hyde does, that a year after the banners were first installed, the community was still talking about them. Furthermore, there was a discussion about moving the banners into a community centre eventually so that they could be viewed beyond the life of the project.

Clearly, this discussion of aesthetics goes beyond policy and extends to the consideration of the impact of the work on a variety of audiences (and the producers themselves). One aspect of this I described earlier is the critical one of ensuring that the visual products are actually viewed by different audiences (local communities, governments and funders). When the producers are the ones who choose the images for display (in videos or in exhibitions of drawings and photos), there is already a selection process that reflects the aesthetic of the participants. Which photos will convey the message? Which scenes from the video footage will have an impact? The longer I have worked in the area of participatory visual work, the more I have come to regard the significance of the ways in which producers themselves cast their own critical (and appreciative) eyes over the work. Chapter 8 on 'looking' examines one aspect of this, and photography, in particular, is very democratic in relation to aesthetics. In a photovoice project involving eighth- and ninth-grade students in and around the town of Jimma in rural Ethiopia, the photographers explored environmental issues related to 'growing up in the land of coffee'. Notwithstanding the fact that the areas they were photographing are to my mind (as an outsider) visually rich, I am struck by the ways in which the photographers who live there contemplate their own work. For example, in a 'making public' PowerPoint presentation that they shared with their classmates and the rest of the school, they made numerous references to the quality of the photos. About one photo, they commented: 'This one is perhaps not the best photo, it is a little blurry, but it shows the way cutting has contributed to soil erosion.' About another, which offered a staged scene of their hands holding up a globe against the backdrop of a blue sky dotted with white fluffy clouds, they proudly exclaimed: 'I think you will agree that this is truly a beautiful photo'. Even as they gave the presentation, they paused to savour the composition of this photo. Alongside the responses of the photographers to their work is the response of their teacher. He could not believe that his students had produced such work, but perhaps it was the case that he, along with his students, was seeing this rural community represented in visual images for the first time. Indeed, the fact that participatory visual projects tend to capture images of scenes seldom ever seen within the public domain (e.g., never portrayed in tourist brochures and official photos) already contributes, I would argue, to a local aesthetic. Some images taken during these projects are not beautiful in the sense of travel or landscape photography. Pictures of unsafe toilets would be one example. Other images, as these students pointed out, were meant to be beautiful *and* to convey a message. Both categories of photos, if they were taken by outsiders, might fall into what Lutz and Collins (1993) describe as an exoticising of local culture. When these scenes are taken by insiders, they may carry a different aesthetic.

How should we account for – or build in – an aesthetic in non-art photography that is produced *by* and often *for* non-professional audiences? Elsewhere, Katie MacEntee and I (MacEntee and Mitchell, in press) raise a number of other questions that could serve to frame the idea of a 'participant aesthetic'. How does a consideration of aesthetics contribute to the 'reach' of the work? What is the potential of the audience to contribute to an analysis of art produced as part of participatory visual research? How might documenting the analysis of the audience help inform our understanding of the role of participatory methods in social change? Will including audience perspectives encourage viewers to engage differently in the work? An essay by Yoshiaki Kai (2010) helps to contextualize these questions by raising the possibility that snapshots and other vernacular photography cease to be snapshots when they become part of public display. While Kai is speaking specifically of display in curated exhibitions in galleries and museums, the examples just discussed of public display in local settings might be seen as performing a similar function. Kai refers specifically to the genre of photos (both from art photography and vernacular photography) where the shadow of the photographer is present, and draws on Geoffrey Batchen's curated exhibition 'Suspending Time' (Batchen, 2010), which is made up of photos by professional photographers who intentionally included the presence of the photographer's shadow, alongside an extensive collection of vernacular photographs/family photos in which we see the shadow of the photographer (more likely unintentional, in this case). As noted in Chapter 8, shadows of the photographer frequently appear in images produced in photovoice projects, and like Batchen, who put out a call to various colleagues for examples of vernacular photography that included shadows and mirror images for the Suspending Time exhibition, I was able to collect a number of examples, including some that could not be used because they might be incriminating. Kai refers to shadows in the art photography in Jeffrey Fraenkel's (2007) *The Book of Shadows* and in Lee Friedlander's (1970) *Self Portrait* as instances of what can be described as a 'snapshot aesthetic' (Kai, 2010: 170), but at the same time he wonders about the status of a photo that includes the shadow of the photographer – his grandfather, he thinks – in his family album. He links this to Roland Barthes' notion in *Camera Lucida* (Barthes, 1981) of punctum, the accidental details of the photo. Kai writes:

> …it seems unlikely to me, as far as I can remember, that my grandfather, the putative maker of this snapshot, had the inventiveness to use his own shadow as a visual sign in order to show his connectedness to his family or for whatever creative reason. But staring at this tiny, rather boring snapshot, I come to think that I cannot really tell the answer after all. (Kai, 2010: 187)

In considering the aesthetics of display, there are other concerns that may be specific to the particular visual mode. Within participatory video, for example, some of the work may fall into more conventional documentary style. In much of my experience with participatory video in Southern and Eastern Africa, however, participants have chosen to work in a fictional (and often melodramatic) mode – more in line with soap operas that carry social messages. It is a genre with its own aesthetic (see, for example, the work of Nuttall and Michaels, 2001) and one that fits within the broader area of Entertainment Education. Its purpose is to entertain and, at the same time, to convey messages about health issues such as voluntary counseling and testing or civic engagement messages such as voting in municipal elections. The extent, then, to which audiences get the message and are entertained is critical. Moreover, as highlighted in Chapter 5 on community video, much of this work, for reasons of safety and security, transportation, and cost is often shot on school sites, where staging is necessary. The aesthetic of this work has to be appreciated in a way that doesn't focus solely on a need for realistic settings.

The use of different genres also carries over into photovoice. In the project with Ethiopian young people noted previously, many of their poster board displays of photos and captions were put together in ways that were meant to engage the viewer interactively. 'How do you think it feels to be poor and alone?' one group writes, alongside a photo of a herder boy and the cows he is responsible for. 'How would you like to be alone carrying this water jug everyday?' is the caption alongside a photo of a girl who is fetching water. Through the photos and these interrogative captions these young photographers force the viewer to consider issues of gender in coffee production. In another poster board exhibit, the photos are presented in a more straightforward documentary so that the viewer sees all of the key phases of coffee production, from planting and harvesting to the social aspects of a coffee ceremony and the transportation of coffee to distance markets. Importantly, then, it is the series of 10 or so photos taken together that create a narrative. What is critical is an aesthetic for reading these images as a photo essay or photo documentary rather than as individual photos.

Katie MacEntee, in her work with young people and collage in addressing HIV & AIDS, draws attention to several aesthetic features that might be applied to community-produced artistic work (and that operate across various modes and genres). Drawing on the work of Eisner (1997), Denzin (2000), Ellis (2000), and Richardson (2000), she identifies and applies a set of four criteria to an analysis of the collages:

- **Persuasiveness**: 'addressing the sincerity or genuineness of the creative product' (in Raht et al., 2009: 230).
- **Being evocative**: 'drawing forth emotion, meaning, and understanding' (in Raht et al., 2009: 231)
- **Action oriented**: 'Judging the creative work's action orientation attempts to uncover how the creative process inspired learners to take action in their own lives and to inspire action in their communities' (in Raht et al., 2009: 232)
- **Reflexivity**: 'Becoming more self-aware as a result of producing or interacting with the creative artifact and also considering the ethical implications of the work' (in Raht et al., 2009: 233)

These are criteria that may be challenging to operationalize (or evaluate), particularly when it comes to funders, but they are all qualities that reflect the overarching goals of participatory visual research, and at the same time, most are qualities that complement other work within artistic communities.

Local Curation

Kathleen Hyde's (2005) description of Wendy Ewald's banner installation suggests a great deal of intentionality and planning. I would like to offer an account that is somewhat the antithesis – to suggest that one should abandon intentionality and planning but more to highlight some unexpected outcomes in relation to the local as a result of hurrying to set up an exhibition of a community photography project in Kigali in time for a conference that was to take place the next day. The photos had all been taken in a local market by the group-in-training (university students from Rwanda and some visiting academics from Tanzania, South Africa, DRC and Ethiopia – all interested in participatory visual methodologies) and to address the prompt *Challenges and solutions to the social and economic empowerment of women*. The group had completed the picture taking, caption writing and selection process (of choosing a set of photos to enlarge) but were not available to actually set up the display. With the photographs back from a print shop and ready for display, I found myself simply trying to get the photos hung – and with more attention to varying the portrait and landscape formats than anything else. The building supervisor of the college where the conference was going to take place had managed to locate portable display screens, and he had come to watch me for a few minutes as I randomly placed the photos until it was clear to him that I had no real conceptual sense of how the images should go. 'No, you mustn't hang this photo of someone working in textiles next to the photo of selling vegetables. Women in textiles and women in food marketing – they are not the same thing. Here, hang this one of the woman selling grain next to the vegetables'. At that point, he simply took over, and although my attempt to vary the size and shape of the photos had been thwarted, the photos were now grouped in a way that made some sense to him and, indeed, he was right that even in the market, the various types of trade are separated. My point here is not only that the building supervisor was right and I was wrong, or that there is only one way to organize a display, but also that local analysis and local participation greatly contributes to the exhibition process.

Mining Multimedia

The preceding discussions may suggest a unidimensionality to display. It may appear a matter of choosing clotheslines, banners, chicken wire or mobile display boards. However, it is the multi-audience dimensionality of visual research that is so important. The same set of images, regardless of whether they are drawings or photos or digital stories, may reach different audiences through different formats. The very simple schoolyard clothesline format was appropriate in Sajan Virgi and Mitchell's (in press) work with the girls in Mozambique, but would need to be refined for a government audience. Thompson in her work in Sierra Leone used an LCD projector, laptop, generator and screen outdoors to show the photo images in the local setting. That way, everyone in the village was able to see the photos and on a large screen. The simple wire and clip format was more appropriate for officials from the Ministry of Agriculture. The exhibit could stay up over a period of time so that officials and visitors could view the photos over the course of a week or more. As Thompson observed, it meant that politicians who had not managed to visit their local riding because of time constraints and responsibilities were still able to know what was going on. And then there is the possibility of transformation of some of these exhibits into photo books. Two examples of this approach include *Visual Voices: 100 Photographs of Village China by the Women of Yunman Province* (Wu et al., 1995) – a book which draws on the photovoice project set up by Caroline Wang – and *Voices and Images: Mayan Ixil Women of Chajul*, which presents the images of women in Guatemala. Led by Brinton Lykes, the Mayan women took photos to tell the story of the aftermath of the war and its impact on their lives. What is obvious in this work is the participation of the women themselves in 'producing' the book exhibit. As Lykes explains: 'They pored over thousands of photographs and hours of interviews to create the text you have before you' (2004: 20) (see also Lykes, 2001a; Lykes and Coquillon, 2006). In another photo project by Olivier and colleagues (2009) in the Eastern Cape in South Africa, local exhibitions by women teachers became part of a low cost, widely accessible book titled *Picturing Hope*.

In Whose Interest?

Starting off with a consideration of ethics and including many references to ethical concerns throughout, this book would not be complete without a discussion of ethical issues related to display. The concerns are not only about whose pictures are being shown or whether particular photo-subjects might be recognized but in some cases about the rights of the community itself to decide what can be shown and to whom and for what reason. One outcome of a rural project involving trainee teachers was the possibility of mounting an exhibition of their photographs from their practical experience for a national conference in South Africa. The photos highlighted how the pre-service teachers were seeing issues of poverty, HIV and AIDS, and gender violence – touching on hope and transformation.

The exhibition (aptly titled, as it turned out, *Things Fall Apart ... And Come Together Again*) was to be curated by the pre-service teachers in negotiation with the two rural schools where they had been teaching. It was the 'making public' of the images that served to highlight some of the tensions of the school–university partnership. Prior to preparing the photos for mounting, several of the pre-service teachers returned to the schools to discuss with the principals the use of the particular photos that they wanted to include in the exhibition. In one school, the principal immediately agreed and signed the appropriate documents. In another, however, the principal was not at all certain that he wanted images of his school displayed publicly. Moreover, he commented that he found it hard to see any benefit to the school. His concern highlighted the differing agendas of the university (preparing new teachers and doing research) and the school (ensuring education for learners and dealing with challenges such as high levels of poverty and child-headed households as a result of HIV and AIDS). The principal was also concerned about who would see the photos. Would the exhibition bring any censure to the school? How would parents and other community members react to the idea that images of their local school were being shown in public? A lack of confidence and trust was evident when he asked the question, 'How does research [through photos] help us?'.

As I describe elsewhere (Mitchell et al., 2010), at the same time as the pre-service teachers were seeking permission to use the photos for the exhibition, the coordinator of the project, who was keen to assist, had occasion to visit the school (headed by the principal mentioned above) in order to set up a focus group with community members as part of the overall evaluation of the project. Coincidentally, the principal was also trying to set up a community event at the school. The coordinator happened to mention to the principal that he would be happy to bring along a portable public address system – something that could easily be borrowed from the Media Centre of the university. In the meantime, the pre-service teachers had decided to mount the exhibition without the photos from that particular school. Suddenly, however, the principal contacted the coordinator directly and informed him that the school and the parents had given consent to use the photographs in the exhibition. It became evident that the provision of the audio system for the community event served as an opportunity to enhance mutual trust between the school and university and gave a clear message to the school community that the 'partners' were there to help each other. For us, the episode was a powerful reminder of the ethical complexities associated with the taking of photographs and their use for a variety of audiences. It was also a reminder of the role of photographs in helping to make visible the social challenges and complexities that school communities face and that teacher education programmes need to take into account – as was evident in the resulting exhibition.

Display and Video

Reaching audiences through video may sometimes be more difficult than through photo exhibitions, even though on the surface at least it should be easier: no photos to mount, no concern about whether the adhesive will hold, no negotiation of wall space. As noted in the previous chapter, it may well be that becoming a filmmaker is a key component of working in the area of the visual. In that chapter I offer a description of the composite video, which can serve as an analytic tool in the production phase (What are the important behind-the-scenes shots?

What is the story being told?) as well as a visual text, not unlike the photo exhibits described above, constructed to represent the interests and purposes of the participants and with the idea of reaching other audiences: funders, a government agency, or the broader community. Many of the same issues related to location discussed in the preceding sections apply to video screenings, particularly in terms of ensuring that communities themselves have access, and again, the use of community halls and other local venues are critical, even though it might mean renting a generator where there is limited or no access to electricity and setting up outdoor screenings to accommodate large numbers (Levine, 2009).

Screenings for government officials and other policy makers may not be so easy to organize, although one solution is to simply invite the various stakeholders to community screenings so that they can see for themselves the impact of this work at a local level. As researchers, we might need to get ourselves onto a conference programme or invited to present at a meeting of stakeholders or policy makers – and there, issues of time and setting are important. The sheer plethora of DVDs along with easy access to YouTube often makes it harder to get someone to actually sit down and view the text in an uninterrupted way – something that may not be guaranteed on a computer screen. At the same time, because of YouTube and Facebook, it is possible that expecting a government official or individual community members to view a video might be 'just what one does'; increasingly, there is a culture of online viewing.

Finally, the issues of ownership and authenticity raised in previous sections above are equally relevant to the discussion of video. As researchers, do we strive for technical sophistication, which may mean that the input of the participants is sidelined in the pursuit of quality, or do we stick with what community participants have produced, even though the quality may mean that sometimes it will be difficult to get the attention or hold the attention of audiences beyond the most immediate community or group?

Image and Imagination: The Future of Display in Participatory Research

Although the politics and technicalities of display in visual research could be the subject of a whole book, it seemed appropriate to speak about display in a chapter on reaching community and policy makers as a starting point for what could become a much more developed area. Indeed, as the examples above suggest, visual research that seeks to influence change needs to include work on display, an area that is currently under-studied and indeed often ignored. In the same way that we expect to see references to how researchers have handled recruitment or ethical issues or tensions within the process of participation, we might ask more about display itself, including the study of display with particular audiences, work in different sites, and multidimensional aspects of working with the same set of images. One of the few up-close studies of curation and exhibition – outside of more conventional museum study and other artistic studies – is Kathryn Church's

(2008) in-depth chapter 'Exhibition as Inquiry: Travels of an Accidental Curator', in which she describes the setting up and curating of an exhibition that featured her mother's work as a dressmaker of wedding dresses, Fabrications: Stitching Ourselves Together. Writing as a sociologist working in arts-based research and as an accidental curator, Church argues for making the 'doing' of this work more visible and for the work to be treated as inquiry in and of itself. She concludes:

> In this chapter, I have made a case for taking objects seriously, encountering them directly, proceeding object by object to unfold a study, tracking back and forth in the dialogic space between objects and their makers/users, and working reflexively with our limitations, confusions and discoveries. ... As a novice creative researcher in a three-dimensional medium, I was thrown off of what I knew, invariably falling on strange ground, seeing afresh or asker. At this point in the history of arts-informed research, many of us are in this position. As we acquire the skills we need to produce artistically 'credible' work, I want to argue that our liminality is illuminating. (2008: 433)

Not every display of community produced work is at the level of the community. Sometimes it is necessary to take the visual work to other levels, and this may not always involve the community directly. As noted in the earlier example of 'feeling safe and feeling not so safe', policy dialogue took place when I incorporated community-produced photos into a PowerPoint presentation made to a UN group in New York. Although researchers ask permission to show images in their publications, how is this understood by participants? Do the girls living in Swaziland who produced the images of the toilets have an understanding of what it means to have these images projected onto a movie screen as part of a PowerPoint presentation? What is the researcher's responsibility to incorporate a discussion of the aesthetics into the presentation itself? In the case of the photos of the toilets, the girls received somewhat negative reactions from their teachers: 'Why didn't you take a picture of something beautiful?' When the images were presented in New York, however, they received a different reaction – one of both shock and provocation – but, ultimately, action. With the blurring of boundaries between academic and public policy forums, there is a need to explore display further under the umbrella concern of how best to represent community-based work outside of local communities.

We might think of an emerging scholarship of display that fits under the broader issue of display-as-inquiry, bringing together, as it inevitably would, technical issues and participatory processes and policy dialogue.

On a Final Note

For months during the writing of this book – and especially thinking about the last chapter – I carried around Susan Sontag's (2003) book *Regarding the Pain of Others*, published the year before she died. I somehow could not get out of my mind her analysis of images, usually public images, and what she regarded as the numbed response we have to images of horror. One of the paragraphs in that book that struck me as being particularly relevant to this last chapter is the one in which she writes: 'Harrowing photographs do not inevitably lose their power to shock. But they are not much help if the task is to understand. Narratives can make us understand. Photographs do something else: they haunt us' (2003: 80). I began to realize that at least some of the photographs and other images that I had selected for this book were ones that I myself had found haunting: the image of the closed door in the video *Rape* and the screams of the girl coming from behind it (Chapter 5), the hanging boy (Chapter 6), the drawing of the drowned baby (Chapter 7), and the photograph of the toilet discussed earlier in this chapter. I keep returning to these images, not because I am too lazy to find new pictures 'to make a point' but rather because there are images that community photographers, filmmakers and artists have produced that simply stay with me. I don't think I have made up theories to go with these images. Rather, they have compelled me to dig deeper into what the images might mean, or their significance to the people who have produced them. Not all the images that haunt me are images of pain. For example, one image of a community health care worker in a rural area who is holding up a picture of the clinic where she works and saying 'This is our place', moves me, especially every time I hear her say this in a video production on work with visual images (*Our Photos, Our Videos, Our Stories*). In that same video, a local teacher, Thembinkosi, talks about an album he produced from a series of family photographs dealing with the AIDS-related death of his sister. In the video, he curates his album:

> Photo 1: Here I am as a baby. Mainly my history consists of certain memories because I was born to an unmarried couple. My father did not take care of us. He did not take care of my mother. So we grew up under very challenging and threatening conditions.

> Photo 2: Here I included my photo from my first graduation. ... This is my mom and this is my gran. If you go through the story – here, in the last sentence – my mother failed to address the guests on the evening. Instead, she cried. I was crying for the whole time in the few days before the graduation because I didn't really know that I was actually reaching the end of the process of studying, and no one predicted the outcome. We never thought that at the end of the day there would be such a wonderful history. And today I am a teacher.

> Photo 3: For the very first time, I wanted to tell a story about my late sister. She died in 2002. When I fetched the medical report from the hospital, they stated that the cause of death was streptococcal meningitis, which later I discovered that it's associated with HIV/AIDS.

> Photo 4: My sister's son – he's age 11 now, and he's very close to my heart. I'm always worried because he never spoke about his late mother, and I keep on wondering what's going on in his life. What does he think about his mother? Obviously, he misses her, but I just need that one thing brought up in order to talk about it.

Photo 5: My mother, she took the album and went through it until she fell asleep with the album – holding it like this [demonstrates the way his mother is clutching the album to her chest]. And in a way it was, in a way I was touched, and I said to myself 'Oh, for the very first time I managed to deliver a message,' because of its history of my family, it's a shared history but we never had a chance to discuss it, to revise, to look back and talk about the future, let alone the challenges within my household. (from Mitchell et al., 2009)

Perhaps it is because I have viewed this video so many times and with so many audiences that it continues to haunt me, or perhaps it is because the responses of audiences to this scene in the video reinforce the moving quality of Thembinkosi's words and pictures.

These examples may seem like a very self-indulgent way to end a book called *Doing Visual Research*. It is important, however, to not lose sight of why we do the work we do. If we think that change is always about someone else, or about some division of policy-making *out there*, we fail to recognize that all of us who engage in research, visual or otherwise, are already in positions to affect some change or some social action somewhere. We can do this most effectively when we attend to the details of both production and display. Let us, then, be haunted by images, and work with communities in ways that ensure that others are similarly haunted.

References

Allen, D. (2009) *Living with Kidney Failure* (Personal Communication). Montreal, Canada: McGill University Department of Integrated Studies in Education.

Allen, D. and Hutchinson, T. (2009) 'Using PAR or "abusing its good name"?: The challenges and surprises of photovoice and film in a study of chronic illness', *International Journal of Qualitative Methods*, 8: 1–128.

Allnutt, S. (2008) *I Know My Place*. Unpublished doctoral dissertation, McGill University.

Allnutt, S. (2009) *Knowing My Place: Learning Through Memory and Photography*. Unpublished thesis, McGill University.

Alzheimers Still Life 1. At www.utoronto.ca/CAIR/projects.html#alz, accessed 29 April 2008.

Bagley, C. and Cancienne, M. (eds) (2002) *Dancing the Data*. New York, NY: Peter Lang.

Bagnoli, A. (2008) 'Anonymizing visual data', in NCRM Working paper, *Visual Ethics: Ethical Issues in Visual Research*, at http://eprints.ncrm.ac.uk/421/, accessed 3 September 2010.

Banks, M. (2001) *Visual Methods in Social Research*. London: Sage.

Barnes, D., Taylor-Brown, S. and Wiener, L. (1997) 'I didn't leave y'all on purpose: HIV-infected mothers' videotaped legacies for their children', *Qualitative Sociology*, 20(1): 7–32.

Barnett, T. and Whiteside, A. (2003) *AIDS in the Twenty-first Century: Disease and Globalization*. Basingstoke: Palgrave Macmillan.

Barone, T. (2001) 'Science, art, and the predispositions of educational researchers', *Educational Researcher*, 30(7): 24–8.

Barthes, R. (1981) *Camera Lucida: Reflections on Photography* (Trans. Richard Howard). New York, NY: Hill and Wang.

Batchen, G. (2004) *Forget Me Not: Photography and Remembrance*. New York, NY: Princeton Architectural Press.

Batchen, G. (2010) *Suspending time: Life–photography–death* [Curated exhibition]. Shizuoka, Japan: Izu Photo Museum.

Bell, B. (2007) 'Private writing in public spaces: Girls' blogs and shifting boundaries', in S. Weber and S. Dixon (eds), *Growing Up Online: Young People and Digital Technologies*. New York: Palgrave Macmillan. pp. 95–111.

Bell, S. (2002) 'Photo images: Jo Spence's narratives of living with illness', *Health*, 6(1): 5–30.

Berger, J. (1972) *Ways of Seeing*. Harmondsworth, England: Penguin Books.

Best, A. (2000) *Prom Night: Youth, School and Popular Culture*. New York: Routledge.

Bhana, D., de Lange, N. and Mitchell, C. (2009) 'Male teachers talk about gender violence: "Zulu men demand respect"', *Educational Review*, 61(1): 49–62.

Bloustien, G. (2003) *Girl Making: A Cross-cultural Ethnography on the Processes of Growing Up Female*. Oxford: Berghahn Books.

Borges, P. (2008) www.philborges.com/we/women-empowered.html, accessed 4 September 2010.

Born into Brothels: Calcutta's Red Light Kids (2004) [Documentary film]. Z. Briski (Director) and R. Kaufman (Director). USA: Red Light Films.

British Sociological Association (2006) 'Visual Sociology Group's Statement of Ethical Practice', retrieved from British Sociological Association website at www.visualsociology.org.uk/about/ethical_statement.php

Brown, B. (1998) 'How to do things with things (a toy story)', *Critical Inquiry*, 24(4): 935–64.

Brown, B. (ed.) (2004) *Things*. Chicago: University of Chicago Press.

Brown, L. and Gilligan, C. (1993) 'Meeting at the crossroads: Women's psychology and girls' development', *Feminism & Psychology*, 3(1): 11–35.

Buckingham, D. (2008) *Youth, Identity, and Digital Media*. Cambridge, MA: MIT Press.

Burt, S. and Code, L. (eds) (1995) *Changing Methods: Feminists Transforming Practice*. Peterborough, ON: Broadview Press.

Butler, J. (1990) *Gender Trouble*. New York: Routledge.

Campbell, C. (2003) *Letting Them Die: Why HIV/AIDS Intervention Programmes Fail*. Bloomington: Indiana University Press.

Candlin, F. and Guins, R. (2009) *The Object Reader*. New York: Routledge.

Carson, F. and Pajaczkowska, C. (2000) *Feminist Visual Culture*. Edinburgh: Edinburgh University Press.

Chalfen, R. (1987) *Snapshot Versions of Life*. Bowling Green, OH: Bowling Green State University Popular Press.

Chalfen, R. (2002) 'Snapshots "r" us: the evidentiary problematic of home media', *Visual Studies*, 17(2): 141–9.

Chaplin, E. (2006) 'The convention of captioning: WG Sebald and the release of the captive image', *Visual Studies*, 21(1): 42–53.

Chege, F. (2006) '"He put his hands between girls' thighs": Using student teachers' memories to tackle gender violence', in F. Leach and C. Mitchell (eds), *Combating Gender Violence in and Around Schools*. Stoke on Trent, UK: Trentham Books. pp. 189–98.

Church, K. (2008) 'Exhibiting as inquiry: Travels of an accidental curator', in G. Knowles and A. Cole (eds), *Handbook of the Arts in Qualitative Research: Perspectives, Methodologies, Examples and Issues*. London: Sage. pp. 421–34.

Citron, M. (1999) *Home Movies and Other Necessary Fictions*. Minneapolis: University of Minnesota Press.

Clacherty, G. (2005) *Refugee and Returnee Children in Southern Africa: Perceptions and Experiences of Children*. Pretoria: UNHCR.

Clark, A. (2008) 'Anonymising research data', Real Life Methods Working Paper, available at www.ac.uk/research/outputs/publications

Clifford, J. and Marcus, G. (1986) *Writing Culture: The Poetics and Politics of Ethnography*. Berkeley: University of California Press.

Cohen, L. (2007) 'Transana: Qualitative analysis for audio and visual data', in N. de Lange, C. Mitchell and J. Stuart (eds), *Putting People in the Picture: Visual Methodologies for Social Change*. Rotterdam: Sense. pp. 173–84.

Cole, A. and McIntyre, M. (2004) 'Research as aesthetic contemplation: The role of the audience in research interpretation', *Educational Insights*, 9(1).

Cole, A. and McIntyre, M. (2006) *Living and Dying with Dignity: The Alzheimer's Project*. Halifax, NS: Backalong Books.

Cole, A. and McIntyre, M. (2008) 'Installation art-as-research', in G. Knowles and A. Cole (eds), *Handbook of the Arts in Qualitative Research: Perspectives, Methodologies, Examples and Issues*. Thousand Oaks, CA: Sage. pp. 287–98.

Commitments, The (1991) [Film]. A. Parker (Director), L. Myles and R. Randall-Cutler. United States: Twentieth Century Fox.

Crawford, J, Kippax, S., Onyx, J., Gault, U. and Benton, P. (1992) *Emotion and Gender: Constructing Meaning from Memory*. London: Sage.

Daston, L. (2007) *Things that Talk: Object Lessons from Art and Science*, New York Zone Books.

Davidov, V. (2004) 'Representing representations: The ethics of filming at Ground Zero', *Visual Studies*, 19(2): 162–9.

De Lange, N., Mitchell, C., Moletsane, R., Stuart, J., Buthelezi, T. and Taylor, M. (2006) 'Seeing with the body: Educators' representations of HIV and AIDS', *Journal of Education*, 38(1): 44–66.

De Lange, N., Mitchell, C. and Stuart, J. (eds) (2007) *Putting People in the Picture: Visual Methodologies for Social Change*. Rotterdam: Sense.

De Lange, N., Mnisi, T., Mitchell, C. and Park, E. (2010) 'Giving life to data: University–community partnerships in addressing HIV and AIDS through building digital archives', *E-learning and Digital Media*, 7(2).

De Lange, N., Smith, A. and Stuart, J. (in press) 'Learning together: Teachers and community health care workers draw each other', in L. Theron, C. Mitchell, A. Smith and J. Steward (eds), *Picturing Research: Drawing as Visual Methodology*. Rotterdam: Sense.

Denver, J. (1975) 'Calypso', *Windsong* (Vinyl LP). New York, NY: RCA Victor Records.

Denzin, N. (1997) 'Performance texts', in W. G. Tierney and Y. S. Lincoln (eds), *Representation and the Text: Re-framing the Narrative Voice*. Albany: State University of New York Press. pp. 179–217.

Denzin, N.K. (2000) 'Aesthetics and the practices of qualitative inquiry', *Qualitative Inquiry*, 6(2): 256–265.

Denzin, N.K. (2003) 'The cinematic society and the reflexive interview', in J. Gubrium and J. Holstein (eds), *Postmodern Interviewing*. Thousand Oaks, CA: Sage Publications. pp. 141–56.

Doyon, P. (2009) *Girls Don't Do Wires: An Exploration of Adolescent Girls' Media Production*. Unpublished doctoral dissertation, McGill University.

Druick, Z. (1998) '"Ambiguous identities" and the representation of everyday life: Notes towards a new history of production policies at the NFB of Canada', *Canadian Issues*, 10.

Du Toit, M. (2006) *On the Ethics and Aesthetics of Display*. Centre for Visual Methodologies for Social Change Seminar, Durban, South Africa, May.

Du Toit, M. and Gordon, J. (2007) 'The means to turn the key: The South Durban Photography Project's workshops for first time photographers, 2002–2005', in N. de Lange, C. Mitchell and J. Stuart (eds), *Putting People in the Picture: Visual Methodologies for Social Change*. Rotterdam: Sense. pp. 257–73.

Dublin Core Metadata Initiative (2008) Available at www.dublincore.org/

Dyson, L. and Leggett, M. (2006) *Towards a Metadesign Approach for Building Indigenous Multimedia Cultural Archives*. Paper presented at the 12 ANZSYS Conference, December, retrieved from www.staff.it.uts.edu.au/~laurel/Publications

Ebersohn, L. and Eloff, I. (2007) 'Lessons from postgraduate studies employing photographic methodology', in N. de Lange, C. Mitchell and J. Stuart (eds), *Putting People in the Picture: Visual Methodologies for Social Change*. Rotterdam: Sense. pp. 203–18.

Edwards, E. (2002) 'Material beings: Objecthood and ethnographic photographs', *Visual Studies*, 17(1): 67–75.

Edwards, E. and Hart, J. (2004) *Photographs Objects Histories: On the Materiality of Images*. London: Routledge.

Egeland, J. (2005) 'Foreword', in J. Ward, *Broken Bodies, Broken Dreams: Violence Against Women Exposed*. New York: OCHA/IRIN.

Eisner, E. (1995) 'What artistically crafted research can help us to understand about schools', *Educational Theory*, 45(1): 1–6.

Eisner, E.W. (1997) 'The promise and perils of alternative forms of data representation', *Educational Researcher*, 26(6): 4–10.

Ellis, C. (2000) 'Creating criteria: An ethnographic short story', *Qualitative Inquiry*, 6(2): 273–77.

Ely, M., Anzul, M., Friedman, T., Garner, D. and McCormack Steinmetz, A. (1991) *Doing Qualitative Research: Circles within Circles*. London: RoutledgeFalmer.

Ewald, W. (1985) *Portraits and Dreams: Photographs and Stories by Children of the Appalachians*. New York: Writers & Readers.

Ewald, W. (1992) *Magic Eyes: Scenes from an Andean Girlhood*. Seattle, WA: Bay Press.

Ewald, W. (1996) *I Dreamed I Had a Girl in my Pocket: The Story of an Indian Village*. New York, NY: W.W. Norton.

Ewald, W. (2000) *Secret Games: Collaborative Works with Children, 1969–1999*. Zurich, Switzerland: Scalo.

Ewald, W. (2006) *In Peace and Harmony: Carver Portraits*. Richmond, VA: Visual Arts Center of Richmond.

Ewald, W. and Lightfoot, A. (2001) *I Wanna Take me a Picture: Teaching Photography and Writing to Children*. Boston: Beacon Press.

Fire+Hope (2004) [Documentary] C. Mitchell (Producer) and S. Walsh (Director). Canada.

Fischer, M. and Zeitlyn, D. (2003) 'Visual Anthropology in the Digital Mirror: Computer-assisted Visual Anthropology'. Canterbury: Centre for Social Anthropology and Computing, http:// lucy.ukc.ac.uk/dz/layers_nggwun.html

Fiske, J. (1987) 'British cultural studies and television', in R.C. Allen (ed.), *Channels of Discourse: Television and Contemporary Criticism*. London: Methuen. pp. 284–326.

Fiske, J. (1991) *Understanding Popular Culture*. Boston, MA: Unwin.

Flicker, S., Larkin, J., Smilie-Adjarkwa, C., Resoutle, J.P., Barlow, K., Dagnino, M. and Mitchell, C. (2007a) 'It's hard to change something when you don't know where to start: Unpacking HIV vulnerability with Aboriginal youth in Canada', *Pimatisiwin: A Journal of Indigenous and Aboriginal Communities*, 5(2): 174–200.

Flicker, S., Travers, R., Guta, A., McDonald, S. and Meagher, A. (2007b) 'Ethical dilemmas in community-based participatory research: Recommendations for institutional research boards', *Journal of Urban Health*, 84(4): 478–93.

Ford, N., Odallo, D. and Chorlton, R. (2003) 'Communication for a human rights perspective: Responding to the HIV/AIDS pandemic in Eastern and Southern Africa', *Journal of Health Communication*, 8(6): 519–612.

Fraenkel, J. (2007) *The Book of Shadows*. San Francisco, CA: Fraenkel Gallery.

Friedlander, L. (1970) *Self Portrait*. New York, NY: Haywire Press.

Geertz, C. (1973) *The Interpretation of Cultures: Selected Essays*. New York: Basic Books.

Geist, A. and Carroll, P. (2002) *They Still Draw Pictures. Children's Art in Wartime from the Spanish Civil War to Kosovo*. Champaign, IL: University of Illinois.

Gitlin, A. (1994) *Power and Method: Political Activism and Educational Research*. New York: Routledge.

Glenn, J. and Hayes, C. (eds) (2007) *Taking Things Seriously: 75 Objects with Unexpected Significance*. New York: Princeton Architectural Press.

Goldstein, T. (2000) 'Hong Kong, Canada: Performed ethnography for anti-racist teacher education', *Teaching Education*, 11(3): 311–26.

Gray, R. (2000) 'Graduate school never prepared me for this: Reflections on the challenges of research based theatre', *Reflective Practice*, 1(3): 377–90.

Gray, R. and Sinding, C. (2002) *Standing Ovation: Performing Social Science Research about Cancer*. Walnut Creek, CA: AltaMira.

Gray, R., Fitch, M., Davis, C. and Phillips, C. (2000) 'Challenges of participatory research: Reflections on a study with breast cancer self-help groups', *Health Expectations*, 3(4): 243–52.

Gray, R., Ivonoffski, V. and Sinding, C. (2001a) 'Making a mess and spreading it around: Articulation of an approach to research-based theatre', in A. Bochrer and C. Ellis (eds), *Ethnographically Speaking: Autoethnography, Literature, and Aesthetics*. Walnut Creek, CA: Altamira. pp. 57–75.

Gray, R., Sinding, C. and Fitch, M. (2001b) 'Navigating the social context of metastatic breast cancer: Reflections on a project linking research to drama', *Health*, 5(2): 233–48.

Griffin, G. (2000) *Representations of HIV and AIDS: Visibility Blue/s*. Manchester: Manchester University Press.

Gross, L., Katz, J. and Ruby, J. (2003) 'Introduction: Image ethics in the digital age', in L. Gross, J.S. Katz and J. Ruby (eds), *Image Ethics in the Digital Age*. Minneapolis: University of Minnesota Press. pp. vii–xxv.

Grover, J. Z. (1994) 'OI: Opportunistic identification, open identification, in PWA portraiture', in C. Squires (ed.) *Over Exposed: Essays an Contemporary Photography*. New York: The New Press. pp. 105–122.

Gubrium, A. (2009) 'Digital storytelling: An emergent method for health promotion research and practice', *Health Promotion and Practice*, 10(2): 186–91.

Hampl, P. (1996) 'Memory and imagination', in J. McConkey (ed.), *The Anatomy of Memory*. New York: Oxford University Press. pp. 201–11.

Harper, D. (2001) *Changing Works: Visions of a Lost Agriculture*. Chicago, IL: University of Chicago Press.

Harper, D. (2002) 'Talking about pictures: A case for photo elicitation', *Visual Studies*, 17(1): 13–26.

Harris, B. (1999) 'Photography in colonial discourse: The making of "the other" in Southern Africa, c. 1850–1950', in W. Hartmann, J. Silvester and P. Hayes (eds), *The Colonizing Camera: Photographs in the Making of Namibian History*. Athens: Ohio University Press. pp. 20–4.

Harris, B. (2002) 'Photographic visions and narrative inquiry', *Narrative Inquiry*, 12(1): 87–111.

Hartley, J. (1999) *Uses of Television*. London: Routledge.

Haug, F. (1999) *Female Sexualization: A Collective Work of Memory*. London: Verso Books.

Heath, S., Charles, V., Crow, G. and Wiles, R. (2007) 'Informed consent, gatekeepers and go-betweens: Negotiating consent in child-and youth-orientated institutions', *British Educational Research Journal*, 33(3): 403–17.

Heider, K. (2006) *Ethnographic Film*. Austin, TX: University of Texas Press.

Henderson, P. (2003) *Annotated Bibliography on Childhood with Emphasis on Africa: General Findings and Recommendations*. Dakar: CODESRIA.

Higonnet, A. (1998) *Pictures of Innocence: The History and Crisis of Ideal Childhood*. London: Thames & Hudson.

Hodder, I. (1998) 'The interpretation of documents and material culture', in N. K. Denzin and Y.S. Lincoln (eds), *Collecting and Interpreting Qualitative Materials*. Thousand Oaks, CA: Sage. pp. 155–72.

Holland, J., Ramazanoglu, C., Sharpe, S. and Thomson, R. (1997) 'Feminist methodology and young people's sexuality,' in R. Parker and P. Aggleton (eds) *Culture, Society and Sexuality*. London: Taylor & Francis. pp. 457–473.

hooks, b. (1994) 'In our glory: Photography and black life', in D. Willis (ed.), *Picturing Us: African American Identity in Photography*. New York: The New Press. pp. 43–55.

HRW (Human Rights Watch) (2001) *Scared at School: Sexual Violence Against Girls in South African Schools*. US: HRW.

Hubbard, J. (1994) *Shooting Back from the Reservation: A Photographic View of Life by Native American Youth*. New York: New Press.

Hughes, L. (2004) *Digitizing Collections: Strategic Issues for the Information Manager*. London: Facet.

Hurdley, R. (2006) 'Dismantling mantelpieces: narrating identities and materialising culture in the home', *Sociology*, 40(4): 717–33.

Huvila, I. (2008) 'Participatory archive: Towards decentralised curation, radical user orientation, and broader contextualisation of records management', *Archival Science*, 8: 15–36.

Hyde, K. (2005) 'Portraits and collaborations: A reflection on the work of Wendy Ewald', *Visual Studies*, 20(2): 172–90.

Iliffe, J. (2006) *The African Aids Epidemic: A History*. Oxford: James Currey.

Jenkins, H. (2006) *Convergence Culture: Where Old and New Media Collide*. New York: New York University Press.

Jenson, J. (2010) Raising the bar on 'voice' in a troubled community: students' media projects. DIY citizenship, critical making and social media conference. University of Toronto, November 11–14.

Jewkes, R., Levin, J., Mbananga, N. and Bradshaw, D. (2002) 'Rape of girls in South Africa', *Lancet*, 359(26): 319–20.

John, E. (1973) 'Funeral for a Friend/Love Lies Bleeding', *Goodbye Yellow Brick Road* [CD]. France: MCA Records.

Kai, Y. (2010) 'The shadows of snapshots'. In G. Batchen, *Suspending time: Life–photography–death* [exhibition catalogue]. *Shizuoka*, Japan: Izu Photo Museum.

Karlsson, J. (2007) 'The novice visual researcher', in N. de Lange, C. Mitchell and J. Stuart (eds), *Putting People in the Picture: Visual Methodologies for Social Change*. Rotterdam: Sense. pp. 185–202.

Kearney, M. (2006) *Girls Make Media*. New York: Routledge.

Khanare, F. (2009) *School Management Team's (SMT) Response to Psychosocial Aspects of Orphans and Vulnerable Children in the Context of HIV/AIDS: A Study of Senior Secondary Schools at Vulindlela District in KwaZulu-Natal*. Unpublished MEd dissertation, Durban: University of KwaZulu-Natal.

Knight, J. (2001) 'Video', in F. Carson and C. Pajaczkowska (eds), *Feminist Visual Culture*. Edinburgh: University of Edinburgh Press. pp. 249–64.

Knowles, J. and Cole, A. (2008) *Handbook of the Arts in Qualitative Research: Perspectives, Methodologies, Examples, and Issues*. Thousand Oaks, CA: Sage.

Kretzmann, J. and McKnight, J. (1993) *Building Communities from the Inside Out*. Chicago, IL: ACTA.

Küchler, S. and Miller, D. (2005) *Clothing as Material Culture*. Oxford: Berg Publishers.

Kuhn, A. (1995) *Family Secrets: Acts of Memory and Imagination*. London: Verso Books.

Kuhn, A. (1996) 'Remembrance', in L. Heron and V. Williams (eds), *Illuminations: Women Writing on Photography from the 1850s to the Present*. Durham, NC: Duke University Press. pp. 146–61.

Langford, M. (2001) *Suspended Conversations: The Afterlife of Memory in Photographic Albums*. Montreal: McGill-Queen's University Press.

Lankshear, C. and Knobel, M. (2006) *New Literacies*. London: Open University Press.

Larkin, J., Lombardo, C., Walker, L., Bahreini, R., Tharao, W., Mitchell, C. and Dubazane, N. (2007) 'Taking it global Xpress: Youth, photovoice and HIV/AIDS', in N. de Lange, C. Mitchell and J. Stuart (eds), *Putting People in the Picture: Visual Methodologies for Social Change*. Rotterdam: Sense. pp. 31–43.

Leach, F. (2006) 'Researching gender violence in schools: Methodological and ethical considerations', *World Development*, 34(6): 1129–47.

Lee, R. (1993) *Doing Research on Sensitive Topics*. London: Sage.

Levine, S. (2009) 'Steps for the future: HIV/AIDS, media activism and applied visual anthropology in Southern Africa', in S. Pink (ed.), *Visual Interventions: Applied Visual Anthropology*. New York, NY: Berghahn Books. pp. 71–89.

Life Lines (2008) At www.utoronto.ca/CAIR/projects.html#alz, accessed 29 April 2008.

Linden, J. and Green, A. (2006) 'Don't leave data in the dark: Issues in digitizing print statistical publications', *D-Lib Magazine*, 12(1), retrieved 2 April 2008.

Lister, M. and Wells, L. (2001) 'Seeing beyond belief: Cultural studies as an approach to analysing the visual', in T. van Leeuwen and C. Jewitt (eds), *Handbook of Visual Analysis*. London: Sage. pp. 61–91.

Loizos, P. (2000) 'Video, film and photographs as research documents', in M.W. Bauer and G. Gaskell (eds), *Qualitative Researching with Text, Image and Sound: A Practical Handbook*. London: Sage. pp. 93–107.

Lutz, C. and Collins, J. (1993) *Reading National Geographic*. Chicago: University of Chicago Press.

Lykes, M. (1989) 'Dialogue with Guatemalan Indian women: Critical perspectives on constructing collaborative research', in R. K. Unger (ed.), *Representations: Social Constructions of Gender*. Amityville, NY: Baywood. pp. 167–85.

Lykes, M. (1997) 'Activist participatory research among the Maya of Guatamela: Constructing meanings from situated knowledge', *Journal of Social Issues*, 53(4): 725–46.

Lykes, M. (in collaboration with Mateo, A., Anay, J., Caba, A., Ruiz, U. and Willaims, J.) (1999) 'Telling stories – rethinking lives: Community education, women's development and social change among the Maya Ixil', *International Journal of Leadership in Education*, 2(3): 207–27.

Lykes, M.B. (2001a) 'Activist participatory research and the arts with rural Mayan women. Interculturality and situated meaning making', in D.L. Tolman and M. Brydon Miller (eds), *From Subject to Subjectivities: A Handbook of Interpretive and Participatory Methods*. New York: New York University Press. pp. 183–99.

Lykes, M.B. (2001b) 'Creative arts and photography in participatory action research in Guatemala', in P. Reason and H. Bradbury (eds), *Handbook of Action Research: Participative Inquiry and Practice*. Thousand Oaks, CA: Sage. pp. 363–71.

Lykes, M. B. and Coquillon, E. (2006) 'Participatory and action research and feminisms: Towards transformative praxis', in S. Hesse-Biber (ed.), *Handbook of Feminist Research: Theory and Praxis*. Thousand Oaks, CA: Sage. pp. 297–326.

Magic Flute, The (1975) [Film]. E. Shikaneder (Libretto) and I. Bergman (Screenplay). Sweden: Sweriges Radio.

MacEntee, K. and Mitchell, C. (in press) 'Lost in translation', in L. Theron, C. Mitchell, A. Smith, and J. Stuart (eds), *Picturing Research: Drawing As Visual Methodology*. Rotterdam, The Netherlands: Sense.

Mak, M. (2006) 'Unwanted images: Tackling gender-based violence in South African school through youth artwork', in F. Leach and C. Mitchell (eds), *Combating Gender Violence in and Around Schools*. London: Trentham Books. pp. 113–23.

Mak, M., Mitchell, C. and Stuart, J. (2005) *Our Photos, Our Videos, Our Stories* [Documentary]. Montreal, Canada: Taffeta Production.

Marchessault, J. (1995) 'Reflections on the dispossessed video and the "Challenge for Change" experiment', *Screen*, 36(2): 131–46.

Martin, M. (2004) 'HIV/AIDS in South Africa: Can the visual arts make a difference', in K.D. Kauffman and D.L. Lindauer (eds), *AIDS and South Africa: The Social Expression of a Pandemic*. New York: Palgrave Macmillan. pp. 120–35.

Mavor, C. (1997) 'Collecting loss', *Cultural Studies*, 11(1): 111–37.

McKee N., Bertrand J. and Becker-Benton, A. (2004) *Strategic Communication in the HIV/AIDS Epidemic*. New Delhi: Sage.

Mendel, G. (2001) *A Broken Landscape: HIV and AIDS in Africa*. London: Network Photographers.

Miller, D. (ed.) (1998) *Material Cultures: Why some Things Matter*. London: UCL Press.

Miller, J. (2007) 'Capturing the visual traces of historical change: The Internet Mission Photography Archive', in G. C. Stanczak (ed.), *Visual Research Methods: Image, Society and Representation*. London: Sage. pp. 83–120.

Milne, E.-J. (2010) *Saying 'No' to Participatory Video*. Paper presented to the Canadian Society for Studies in Education Conference, Montreal, June.

Mitchell, C. (1996) *(Dis)posable Texts, Immoveable Furniture and Reconstructing the Family Album*. Paper presented at the annual meeting of the Association of Bibliotherapy and Applied Literature Conference, Learned Societies. Brock University, St. Catharine's, Ontario, May.

Mitchell, C. (2004) 'Was it something I wore?', in S. Weber and C. Mitchell (eds), *Not Just Any Dress: Narratives of Memory, Body and Identity*. New York: Peter Lang. pp. 83–88.

Mitchell, C. (2005) 'Mapping a southern Africa girlhood in the age of AIDS', in L. Chisholm (ed.), *Gender Equity in South African Education*. Pretoria: HSRC Press. pp. 92–112.

Mitchell, C. (2006a) 'Taking pictures and taking action in visual arts-based methodologies in research as social change', in T. Marcus and J. Hofmaener (eds), *Shifting Boundaries of Knowledge*. Pietermaritzburg: UKZN Press. pp. 227–241.

Mitchell, C. (2006b) 'In my life: Youth stories and poems on HIV/AIDS: Towards a new literacy in the age of AIDS', *Changing English*, 13(3): 355–68.

Mitchell, C. (2009a) *Dress-Fitting. Was it Something I Wore?* Symposium, Durban, South Africa, August.

Mitchell, C. (2009b) *What Can a Girl do with a Camera? Girls, Media and Hypersexualization*. YWCA, Montreal, May.

Mitchell, C. (2009c) What difference does this make? Participatory visual methodologies in the age of AIDS. Key-note address, First International Visual Methodologies Conference, University of Leeds, September.

Mitchell, C. (2009d) 'Geographies of danger: School toilets in sub-Saharan Africa', in O. Gershenson and B. Penner (eds), *Ladies and Gents*. Philadelphia, PA: Temple University Press. pp. 62–74.

Mitchell, C. (2010) 'Researching things, objects and gendered consumption in childhood studies', in D. Buckingham and V. Tingstad (eds), *Childhood and Consumer Culture*. London: Palgrave. pp. 94–110.

Mitchell, C. and Allnutt, S. (2008) 'Photographs and/as social documentary', in G. Knowles and A. Cole (eds), *Handbook of the Arts in Qualitative Research: Perspectives, Methodologies, Examples and Issues*. London: Sage. pp. 251–64.

Mitchell, C. and De Lange, N. (in press) 'Community based video and social action in rural South Africa', in L. Pauwels and E. Margolis (eds), *Handbook on Visual Methods*. London: SAGE.

Mitchell, C. and Kanganyara, P. (2005) *Through the Eyes of Children and Young People*. Kigali: UNICEF.

Mitchell, C. and Mothobi-Tapela, I. (2004) *No Turning Back: Youth and Sexual Violence In and Around Schools in Swaziland and Zimbabwe*. EASARO UNICEF.

Mitchell, C. and Reid-Walsh, J. (2002) *Researching Children's Popular Culture: The Cultural Spaces of Childhood*. London and New York: Routledge.

Mitchell, C. and Smith, A. (2003) 'Sick of AIDS: Literacy and the meaning of life for South African youth', *Culture, Health & Sexuality*, 5(6): 513–22.

Mitchell, C. and Umurungi, J. (2007) 'What happens to girls who are raped in Rwanda', *Children First*, 11(65): 13–18.

Mitchell, C. and Weber, S. (1999) *Reinventing Ourselves as Teachers: Beyond Nostalgia*. London: Falmer Press.

Mitchell, C. and Weber, S. (2000) Prom Night was the First and Last Time I Felt Normal. Paper presented at the annual conference of the Popular Culture Association, New Orleans, Louisiana, 19–22 April.

Mitchell, C., Kusner, C. and Charbonneau-Gowdy, P. (2004a) 'Seeing for ourselves: When classroom teachers make documentary films', *Changing English*, 11: 279–89.

Mitchell, C., Walsh, S. and Larkin, J. (2004b) 'Visualizing the politics of innocence in the age of AIDS', *Sex Education*, 4(1): 35–47.

Mitchell, C., de Lange, N., Moletsane, L., Stuart, J. and Buthelezi, T. (2005a) 'The face of HIV and AIDS in rural South Africa: A case for photo-voice', *Qualitative Research in Psychology*, 3: 257–70.

Mitchell, C., Moletsane, R., Stuart, J., Buthelezi, T. and de Lange, N. (2005b) 'Taking pictures/taking action! Using photo-voice techniques with children', *ChildrenFIRST*, 9(60): 27–30.

Mitchell, C., Stuart, J., Moletsane, R. and Nkwanyana, C.B. (2006a) 'Why we don't go to school on Fridays: Youth participation and HIV and AIDS', *McGill Journal of Education*, 41: 267–82.

Mitchell, C., Walsh, S. and Moletsane, R. (2006b) 'Speaking for ourselves: A case for visual arts-based and other participatory methodologies in working with young people to address sexual violence', in F. Leach and C. Mitchell (eds), *Combating Gender Violence in and Around Schools*. London: Trentham Books. pp. 103–11.

Mitchell, C., de Lange, N. and Xuan Thuy, N. (2008) 'Let's not leave this problem: Exploring inclusive education in rural South Africa', *Prospects*, 38(1): 99–112.

Mitchell, C., Weber, S. and Pithouse, K. (2009) 'Facing the public: Using photography for self-study and social action', in D. Tidwell, M. Heston and L. Fitzgerald (eds), *Research Methods for the Self-study of Practice*. New York: Springer-Verlag. pp. 119–34.

Mitchell, C., Pascarella, J., De Lange, N. and Stuart, J. (2010) 'We wanted other people to learn from us': Girls blogging in rural South Africa in the age of AIDS', in S. Mazzarella (ed.), *Girl Wide Web 2.0: Revisiting Girls, the Internet and the Negotiation of Identity*. New York: Peter Lang.

Mitchell, C., de Lange, N. and Moletsane, L. (in press) 'Before the cameras roll', in L. Theron, C. Mitchell, A. Smith and J. Stuart (eds), *Picturing Research: Drawing as Visual Methodology*. Rotterdam: Sense.

Mitchell, W. (2005) *What do Pictures Want?: The Lives and Loves of Images*. Chicago: University of Chicago Press.

Mizen, P. (2005) 'A little light work? Children's images of their labour', *Visual Studies*, 20(2): 124–39.

Mnisi, T. (2010) *Beyond Visual Data: How Educators use Metadata to Help Learners Understand Issues on HIV and AIDS Stigma*. Unpublished MEd dissertation. Durban: University of KwaZulu-Natal.

Moletsane, R. (2006) 'Many are called, few will remain: HIV/AIDS and the matric in the South African school system', in V. Reddy (ed.), *Marking Matric. Colloquium Proceedings*. Cape Town: HSRC Press. pp. 201–12.

Moletsane, R. and Mitchell, C. (2007) 'On working with a single photograph', in N. de Lange, C. Mitchell and J. Stuart (eds), *Putting People in the Picture: Visual Methodologies for Social Change*. Rotterdam: Sense. pp. 131–40.

Moletsane, R., de Lange, N., Mitchell, C., Stuart, J., Buthelezi, T. and Taylor, M. (2007) 'Photo-voice as a tool for analysis and activism in response to HIV and AIDS stigmatisation in a rural KwaZulu-Natal school', *Journal of Child & Adolescent Mental Health*, 19(1): 19–28.

Moletsane, R., Mitchell, C., Smith, A. and Chisolm, L. (2008) *Methodologies for Mapping a Southern African Girlhood in the Age of Aids*. Amsterdam: Sense.

Moletsane, R., Mitchell, C., de Lange, N., Stuart, J., Buthelezi, T. and Taylor, M. (2009) 'What can a woman do with a camera? Turning the female gaze on poverty and HIV and AIDS in rural South Africa', *International Journal of Qualitative Studies in Education*, 22(3): 315–31.

Mulvey, L. (1989) *Visual and Other Pleasures*. Basingstoke: Palgrave Macmillan.

Nolen, S. (2007) 'Where have all the Swazis gone?', *The Globe and Mail*, 22 December: A14.

Nuttall, S. (2009) *Entanglement: Literary and Cultural Reflections on Post-apartheid*. Johannesburg: Wits University Press.

Nuttall, S. and Michaels, C.-A. (2001) *Senses of Culture: South African Cultural Studies*. Cape Town, South Africa: Oxford University Press.

Oliver, K. (2009) *Storyboards: An Unauthorized Biography*. Retrieved from www.eventdv.net/Articles/News/Feature/Storyboards-...-An-Unauthorized-Biography-37787.htm

Olivier, T., Wood, L. and de Lange, N. (2009) *Picturing Hope in the Face of Poverty, As Seen Through the Eyes of Teachers*. Cape Town, South Africa: Juta.

Packard, J. (2008) 'I'm gonna show you what it's really like out here: The power and limitation of participatory visual methods', *Visual Studies*, 23(1): 63–77.

Paley, N. (1995) *Finding Art's Place: Experiments in Contemporary Education and Culture*. London: Routledge.

Park, E., Mitchell, C. and de Lange, N. (2007) 'Working with digital archives: Photovoice and meta-analysis in the context of HIV and AIDS', in N. de Lange, C. Mitchell and J. Stuart (eds), *Putting People in the Picture: Visual Methodologies for Social Change*. Rotterdam: Sense. pp. 163–72.

Park, E., Mitchell, C. and de Lange, N. (2008a) 'Social uses of digitisation within the context of HIV/AIDS: Metadata as engagement', *Online Information Review*, 32(6): 716–25.

Park, E., Mitchell, C. and de Lange, N. (2008b) *Working with Digital Archives: Giving Life (to Data) to Save Lives (in the Age of AIDS)*. Paper presented at American Educational Research Association Annual Meeting, New York, April 13–17.

Pauli, L. (2006) *Acting the Part: Photography as Theatre*. London: Merrell.

Pauwels, L. (2002) 'The video- and multimedia-article as a mode of scholarly communication: Toward scientifically informed expression and aesthetics', *Visual Studies*, 17(2): 150–9.

Pauwels, L. (2006) 'Representing moving cultures: Expression, multivocality and reflexivity in anthropological and sociological filmmaking', in L. Pauwels (ed.), *Visual Cultures of Science*. Lebanon, NH: Dartmouth College Press. pp. 120–52.

Pearce-Moses, R. (2005) *A Glossary of Archival and Records Terminology*. Chicago, IL: Society of American Archivists.

Pink, S. (2001) *Doing Visual Ethnography*. Thousand Oaks, CA: Sage.

Pink, S. (2004) *Home Truths: Gender, Domestic Objects and Everyday Life*. New York, NY: Berg.

Pink, S. (2007) *Visual Interventions: Applied Visual Anthropology*. New York: Berghahn Books.

Pithouse, K. and Mitchell, C. (2007) 'Looking into change: Studying participant engagement in photovoice projects', in N. de Lange, C. Mitchell and J. Stuart (eds), *Putting People in the Picture: Visual Methodologies for Social Change*. Rotterdam: Sense. pp. 141–51.

Pointon, M. (1999) Materializing mourning: Hair, jewellery and the body', in M. Kwint, C. Breward and J. Aynsle (eds), *Material Memories: Evocation and Design (Materializing Culture)*. Oxford: Berg. pp. 39–57.

Prosser, J. (1998) *Image-based Research: A Sourcebook for Qualitative Researchers*. London: Routledge.

Prosser, J. (2000) 'The moral maze of image ethics', in H. Simons and R. Usher (eds), *Situated Ethics in Educational Research*. London: RoutledgeFalmer. pp. 116–32.

Prosser, J. (2007) 'Visual mediation of critical illness: An autobiographical account of nearly dying and nearly living', *Visual Studies*, 22: 185–99.

Prosser, J. (2010) *Ethical Issues in Visual Research*. Presentation to UKZN Ethics Committee and Faculty Seminar at the University of KwaZulu-Natal, March.

Prosser, J. and Burke, C. (2008) 'Image-based educational research', in J. G. Knowles and A. Cole (eds), *Handbook on the Arts in Qualitative Research*. London: Sage. pp. 407–20.

Raht, D., Smith, J. and Macentee, K. (2009) 'Engaging youth in addressing HIV&AIDS: Teaching and HIV and AIDS in the South African classroom', in C. Mitchell and K. Pithouse (eds), *Teaching and HIV&AIDS*. Johannesburg: Macmillan. pp. 219–36.

Renold, E., Holland, S., Ross, N. and Hillman, A. (2008) '"Becoming participant": Problematizing "informed consent" in participatory research with young people in care', *Qualitative Social Work*, 7(4): 427–47.

Rhodes, C. (2000) *Outsider Art: Spontaneous Alternatives*. London: Thames & Hudson.

Richardson, L. (2000) 'Evaluating ethnography', *Qualitative Inquiry*, 6(3), 253–55.

Riggins, S. (1994) 'Fieldwork in the living room: An autoethnographic essay', in S. H. Riggins (ed.), *The Socialness of Things: Essays on the Socio-Semiotics of Objects*. Berlin: Moutin de Gruyter. pp. 101–47.

Rist, R. (2003) 'Influencing the policy process with qualitative research', *Collecting and Interpreting Qualitative Materials*, 2: 619–44.

Rohde, R. (1998) 'How we see each other: Subjectivity, photography and ethnographic revision', in W. Hartmann, J. Silvester and P. Hayes (eds), *The Colonising Camera: Photographs in the Making of Namibian History*. Athens: Ohio University Press.

Rose, G. (2001) *Visual Methodologies: An Introduction to the Interpretation of Visual Materials*. London: Sage.

Rouch, J. and Feld, S. (2003) *Cine-ethnography*. Minneapolis: University of Minnesota Press.

Ruby, J. (1995) *Secure the Shadow: Death and Photography in America*. Cambridge, MA: MIT Press.

Ruby, J. (2000a) 'The ethics of image-making; or, "They're going to put me in the movies, going to make a big star out of me"', in *Picturing Culture: Explorations of Film and Anthropology*. Chicago: University of Chicago Press. pp. 137–50.

Ruby, J. (2000b) *Picturing Culture: Explorations of Film and Anthropology*. Chicago: University of Chicago Press.

Sajan Virgi, Z. and Mitchell, C. (in press) 'Picturing policy in addressing water and sanitation: The voices of girls living in abject intergenerational hardship in Mozambique', *International Education*.

Sarup, M. (1993) *An Introductory Guide to Post-structuralism and Post-modernism*. Athens: University of Georgia Press.

Sathiparsad, R. (2008) 'Developing alternative masculinities as a strategy to address gender-based violence', *International Social Work*, 51(3): 348–59.

Schratz, M. and Walker, R. (1995) *Research as Social Change: New Opportunities for Qualitative Research*. London: Routledge.

Schoeman, R. (2000) *Accelerated Response for Psychosocial Support for Children Affected with Aids in Southern Africa*, available at www.harare.unesco.org/hivaids/webfiles/Electronic%20 Versions/Concept%20Paper.doc, accessed 25 August 2010

Sekula, A. (1986) 'The body and the archive', *October*, 39: 3–64.

Sekula, A. (2003) 'Reading an archive: Photography between labour and capital', in L. Wells (ed.), *The Photography Reader*. London: Routledge. pp. 443–53.

Seshradi, S. and Chandran, V. (2006) 'Reframing masculinities: Using films with adolescent boys', in F. Leach and C. Mitchell (eds), *Combating Gender Violence In and Around Schools*. Staffordshire: Trentham. pp. 135–142.

Shilton, K. and Srinivasan, R. (2008) 'Participatory appraisal and arrangement for multicultural archival collections', *Archivaria*, 63: 87–102.

Sime, D. (2008) 'Ethical and methodological issues in engaging young people living in poverty', *Children's Geographies*, 6(1): 63–78.

Smart, R. (2003) *Policies for Orphans and Vulnerable Children: A Framework for Moving Ahead* [Report]. Washington, DC: Policy Project/USAID.

Smith, L. (1998) *The Politics of Focus: Women, Children, and Nineteenth-century Photography*. Manchester: Manchester University Press.

Smith, L. (1999) *Decolonizing Methodologies: Research and Indigenous Peoples*. London: Zed Books.

Sontag, S. (1977) *On Photography*. New York: Doubleday.

Sontag, S. (2003) *Regarding the Pain of Others*. New York: Farrar, Straus and Giroux.

Spence, J. (1986) *Putting Myself in the Picture: A Political, Personal and Photographic Autobiography*. London: Camden Press.

Spence, J. (1995) *Cultural Sniping. The Art of Transgression*. London: Routledge.

Spence, J. and Martin, R. (1988) 'Photo-therapy: Psychic realism as a healing art?', *Ten-8*, 30: 2–17.

Spence, J. and Solomon, J. (1995) *What Can a Woman do With a Camera: Photography for Women*. London: Scarlet Press.

Squiers, C. (2005) *The Body at Risk: Photography of Disorder, Illness, and Healing*. Berkeley: University of California Press.

Steinberg, J. (2009) *Three Letter Plague: A Young Man's Journey Through a Great Epidemic*. London: Vintage.

Stuart, J. (2004) 'Media matters – producing a culture of compassion in the age of AIDS', *English Quarterly*, 36(2): 3–5.

Stuart, J. (2007) *From Our Frames*. Unpublished doctoral dissertation, University of KwaZulu-Natal.

Stuart, S. (2007) 'Citizen teacher: Damned if you do, damned if you don't', *University of Cincinnati Law Review*, 76: 1281–342.

Tao, R. (2005) *Listening with our Eyes: Ying's Photographic Memories and Chinese Women's Contemporary History*. Unpublished manuscript, McGill University.

Tao, R. (2009) *Using Visual Ethnography to Address Sexuality, HIV and AIDS, and Chinese Youth*. Unpublished doctoral dissertation, McGill University.

Tao, R. and Mitchell, C. (2010) 'I never knew that pictures could convey such powerful messages: Chinese students in an English department explore visual constructions of HIV and AIDS', *Changing English*, 17(2): 161–76.

Taylor, L. (2002) *The Study of Dress History*. Manchester: Manchester University Press.

Theberge, P. (2006) 'Director's foreward', in L. Pauli (ed.), *Acting the Part: Photography as Theatre*. London: Merrell. pp. 2–6.

Thompson, J. (2009) *How We See this Place: An Intergenerational Dialogue about Conservation around Tiwai Island, Sierra Leone*. Unpublished master's thesis, McGill University.

Tobin, J. (2000) *Good Guys Don't Wear Hats: Children's Talk about the Media*. New York: Teachers' College Press.

Toy Story (1995) [Film]. J. Lasseter (Director) and S. Jobs. United States: Walt Disney Studios.

Toy Story 2 (1999) [Film]. J. Lasseter (Director) and S. Jobs. United States: Walt Disney Studios.

Turkle, S. (2007) *Evocative Objects: Things We Think With*. Cambridge, MA: MIT Press.

Visser, M. (2007) *Contextualising Community Psychology in South Africa*. Pretoria: Van Schaik.

Umurungi, J., Mitchell, C., Gervais, M., Ubalijoro, E. and Kabarenzi, V. (2008) 'Photovoice as a methodological tool for working with girls on the street in Rwanda to address HIV & AIDS and gender violence', *Journal of Psychology in Africa*, 18(3).

UNAIDS (Joint United Nations Programme on HIV and AIDS) (2008) 'AIDS 2008', at www.unaids.org, accessed 21 June 2010.

Volavková, H. (1994) *I Never Saw Another Butterfly: Children's Drawings and Poems of Terezin Concentration Camp, 1942–1944*. New York, NY: Schocken Books.

Wagner, J. (1979) *Images of Information: Still Photography in the Social Sciences*. Berkeley, CA: Sage.

Walsh, S. (2007) 'Power, race and agency: "Facing the truth" through visual methodology', in N. de Lange, C. Mitchell and J. Stuart (eds), *Putting People in the Picture: Visual Methodologies for Social Change*. Rotterdam: Sense. pp. 241–55.

Walsh, S. and Mitchell, C. (2004) 'Artfully engaged; youth, gender and AIDS activism', in G. Knowles et al. (eds), *Provoked by Art*. Toronto: Backalong Books. pp. 101–202.

Wang, C. (1999) 'Photovoice: A participatory action research strategy applied to women's health', *Journal of Women's Health*, 8(2): 185–92.

Wang, C., Burris, M. and Ping, X. (1996) 'Chinese village women as visual anthropologists: A participatory approach to reaching policymakers', *Social Science & Medicine*, 42(10): 1391–400.

Ward, J. (2005) *Broken Bodies, Broken Dreams: Violence Against Women Exposed*. Nairobi, Kenya: United Nations OCHA/IRIN.

Warner, M. (2004) 'Introduction', in M. Haworth-Booth (ed.), *Things: A Spectrum of Photography, 1850–2001*. London: Jonathan Cape in association with the V&A Museum. pp. i–iii.

Waugh, T., Barker, M. B., Winton, E. (2010) *Challenge for Change: Activist Documentary at the National Film Board of Canada*. Montreal: McGill-Queen's Press.

Weber, S. (2004) 'Boxed-in by my school uniform', in S. Weber and C. Mitchell (eds), *Not Just Any Dress: Narratives of Memory Body and Identity*. London and New York: Peter Lang. pp. 61–6.

Weber, S. and Mitchell, C. (2000) *The Prom Dress: Doing Fieldwork on Curriculum and the Body*. Paper presented at the annual conference of the American Educational Research Association, New Orleans, Louisiana, 24–28 April.

Weber, S. and Mitchell, C. (2003) *Dressing for the High School Prom: Questions of Fashion and Identity*. Paper Presented at Making an Appearance: An International Conference on Fashion, Dress and Consumption, Brisbane, Australia, July.

Weber, S. and Mitchell, C. (2004) *Not Just Any Dress: Narratives of Memory, Body, and Identity*. New York: Peter Lang.

Weber, S. and Mitchell, C. (2007) 'Imaging, keyboarding, and posting identities: Young people and new media technologies', in D. Buckingham (ed.), *Youth, Identity, and Digital Media*. Cambridge, MA: MIT Press. pp. 25–48.

White, S. (ed.) (2003) *Participatory Video: Images that Transform and Empower*. London: Sage.

Wiles, R., Prosser, J., Bagnoli, A., Clark, A., Davies, K., Holland, S., and Renold, E. (2008) *Visual Ethics: Ethical Issues in Visual Research*. Southampton, UK: National Centre for Research Methods.

Wizard of Oz, The (1939) [Film]. V. Fleming (Director) and M. LeRoy (Producer). United States: MGM.

Wu, K., Burris, M., Li, V., Wang, Y., Zhan, W., Xian, Y., Yang, K. and Wang, C. (eds) (1995) *Visual Voices: 100 Photographs of Village China by the Women of Yunnan Province*. Yunnan, China: Yunnan People's Publishing.

Yang, K. (2008) 'Video-telling workshop: turning knowledge from subjugated to subversive', in B. Kožuh, R. Kahn and A. Kozlowska (eds), *The Practical Science of Society*. Grand Forks, ND: The College of Education and Human Development, University of North Dakota. pp. 175–84.

Index

absence 99–101, 102–103, 104, 105, 108, 112, 113–114, 114–115, *see also* shadow effect in photography
activism 98, 113, 115
 activist-academic, 49
 and youth, 14, 109
 see also ACT UP; Spence, Jo
ACT UP 117
aesthetics 16, 24, 41, 158, 175, 179, 190–193, 198
 snapshot aesthetics, 66–67, 135
 see also display; evaluation
agriculture *see* photovoice
albums
 album project 4, 189
 family albums 3, 4, 25, 37, 43–44, 98, 103–104, 112, 167, 192, 199–200
 see also display
Alzheimer's disease 3–4, 47
archiving (photos and drawings)
 coding 11, 65–66, 98, 116, 118, 119, 122, 124, 126, 129
 community based archives 115, 118, 120–122, 123, 124, 133
 digital archives 65, 117, 118, 124, 125, 126, 131
 Dublin Core 122
 Greenstone software 121, 122, 123
 metadata 11, 116, 118, 119, 121–122, 123, 124, 132
 participatory archiving, 117, 118, 120, 121, 124, 125, 126, 132, 133, 134
 scanned photographs 117, 120, 121, 123, 124
arts-based methodologies 8, 35, 43, 48, *see also* Centre for Visual Methodologies for Social Change
audiences
 audiencing 66, 98
 audience texts 79, 85–87, 154
 looking at audiences 148–150

audiences *cont.*
 viewer response/engagement 85, 86, 87, 154–155, 163, 166, 167, 168, 170, 185, 187–188, 192, 200

Banks, Marcus xii, 11, 119, 159, 161
Barone, Tom 12
Barthes, Roland 192
Batchen, Geoffrey 99, 192
Berger, John 11
blogs/blogging 32, 132, 154
Bloustien, Gerry 132, 143, 144, *Born into Brothels* 30
boys
 and participatory video 29, 31, 76, 85, 86, 87, 89, 90–91, 147
 and photovoice 57, 107–108, 110, 140, 145, 148
breast cancer 48, 99
Brown, Bill 35
Buckingham, David 17
Burt, Sandra
 with Lorraine Code 13

cameras
 digital 10, 17, 32, 51, 53, 54, 55, 61–62, 71, 89, 92, 133, 141–142, 150
 Fisher-Price Pixelvision video cameras 38
 Flip video cameras 10, 38, 71, 76, 77
 Kodak Brownie Instamatics 38, 115
 point-and-shoot 4, 10, 24, 51, 53, 64, 65, 141, 148, 150
 Super 8 video cameras 10, 38, 72
 video cameras 4, 7, 10, 29, 32, 38, 71, 72, 74, 76, 89, 143, 148, 164, 168, 176
 see also community video-making
Centre for Visual Methodologies for Social Change xv, xvi
Chalfen, Richard 112, 135–136
Chaplin, Elizabeth 59

Chege, Fatuma 139
Church, Kathryn 197–198
Challenge for Change programme 178–179
Cole, Ardra 46–47
 with McIntyre 3–4, 8, 47, 184
collage 4, 5, 53, 164, 168, 193
Common Man 13, 154
community health care workers 4, 21, 52, 72, 98, 101, 102, 104, 109, 119, 120, 124, 140, 168, 169, 170, 199, *see also Learning Together* project
community-based photography 51–70, 98, 136, 162, *see also* photovoice
community video-making
 audience texts 79, 85–86, 154, *see also* audiences
 brainstorming 73, 89, 91, 165
 collectivity 87, 91, 92
 constructedness 87, 89–90, 91, 92
 convergence 87, 92
 embodiment 87, 92
 No Editing Required (N-E-R) approach 73, 74, 76, 77, 84, 87, 89, 91, 164, *see also Rape*
 post-production 78–79, 168
 primary texts 4, 79–84, 154, 162
 producer texts 79, 84–85
 reflexivity 82, 85, 87, 90–91, 92, 165
 storyboarding 7, 71, 74, 75, 77, 87, 89, 90, 165
 see also participatory video
composite video
 as communication tool 161, 162, 166, 169
 as data generation tool 162
 as reflexive tool 161–162, 165, 167
 ciné-fiche 167–168, 170, 175
 defining features 162–163
 Dress Fitting 170–172
 layering 161
 Living with Kidney Failure 174–175

composite video *cont.*
  musical soundtrack 161, 163,
    165
  Our Stories 164–167
  Over the Rainbow 172–174
  reflexivity 161–162, 164
  see also participatory video
Crawford, June 44

Daston, Lorraine 35, 39
death and dying 42, 48, 64,
    99, 100, 101, 103, 104,
    109, 110, 114, 119, 168,
    199–200, *see also* absence;
    health; Living and
    Dying with Dignity: The
    Alzheimer's Project
Denzin, Norman 8, 11, 12, 16,
    171, 193
dialysis 51, 98, *see also*
    composite video–*Living
    with Kidney Failure*
digital storytelling 5, 71, 87,
    98, 163
display
  authenticity 69, 124, 138,
    187–188, 197
  chicken wire 184, 186, 187, 194
  clotheslines 3, 47, 183, 184,
    185, 194, 195
  curated albums 170
  local curation 194
  ownership 25, 66, 87, 132,
    133, 188–189, 197
  place 22, 69, 169, 184–185
  politics of 183–184, 195, 197
  posters 182, 183, 189, 193,
    see also photovoice–
    poster-narratives
  screenings 9, 14, 62, 78, 79,
    86, 141, 149–150, 162,
    168, 170, 181, 183, 197,
    198, *see also* audiences
  see also aesthetics; ethics–
    community-based research
DIY culture 71
drawing/drawings 4–5, 7, 11, 12,
    31, 53, 54, 100, 118, 120,
    125, 127–129, 130–131,
    161, 183, 188, 191, 194,
    see also archiving; ethics;
    community video-making–
    storyboarding
dress
  and China 44, 189
  and photography 100, 110
  cowgirl dress 45, 101
  'dress stories' 43, 46, 49, 170
  Not Just Any Dress 46
  Was It Something I Wore?
    48–49

dress *cont.*
  prom dresses 46, 81, 170–172
  wedding dresses 43, 198
  see also materiality–material
    culture

Edwards, Elizabeth 25
  with Hart, Janice 11, 50, 133, 141
Eisner, Elliot W. 12, 193
Ellis, Carolyn 193
Ely, Margot 93
empowerment 12, 52, 69, 73,
    74, 75, 83, 84, 98, 122,
    155, 179, 194, *see also*
    SHOWED model
engagement 4, 5, 7, 9, 11, 14,
    16, 27, 30, 32, 54, 60, 69,
    72, 78, 89, 98, 113, 131,
    133, 135, 137, 138–142,
    150, 154, 155, 159, 163,
    164, 165–166, 167, 168,
    185, 188, 193, *see also*
    archiving–participatory
    archiving; audiences;
    evaluation
Entertainment Education
    153, 193
environmental issues 52,
    57, 87, *see also* display;
    ethics; photographs–
    environmental portraits;
    photovoice
ethics 6, 32
  anonymity 12, 21, 22,
    30–31, 125
  community-based research
    16, 28, 31–32, 66, 68,
    119, 121, 125, 195–196,
    see also research ethics
    boards
  confidentiality 12, 63, 125,
  consent form 16, 23, 24,
    25–26
  'doing least harm' 15, 22, 24,
    30–31, 125
  informed consent 17–18, 23,
    31, 37, 56, 122, 175
  Media Ethics 16, 21, 23,
    32, 56
  no faces 21
  ownership of visual data
    25, 87, 132, 133, 172,
    188–189
  pedagogy 16, 27, 32
  research ethics boards 11,
    15, 132
  visual consent form 17–18
  visual ethics 7, 15–16
  visual participatory
    methodologies 12
  see also HIV and AIDS

Ethiopia xvi, 52, 54, 62, 73, 87,
    136–137, 141, 150, 170,
    191, 193, 194
evaluation 13, 153, 155, 196
  aesthetics 179, 190–193, 198
  and engagement 139, 153
  criteria 193
Ewald, Wendy 51, 66–67, 150,
    155, 185, 190–191, 194

Fire+Hope 13, 14, 79, 86, 154
Facebook 10, 14, 15, 71,
    154, 197
Fiske, John 4–5, 79, 136, 154
Fogo Project 178
Ford, Neil
  with Odallo, Dan and
    Chorlton, Rozanne 115,
    138–139, 169
funders 9, 12, 78, 87, 138, 155,
    183, 191, 193, 197

gaze 58, 81, 136, 138, 141,
    142–144, 148, 149–150,
    155, 157
gender 36, 138, 155
  and agriculture 193
  and collectivity 91
  and HIV and AIDS 19, 20,
    21, 31, 104–105, 136,
    148, 150
  and poverty 60
  and taking/looking at
    photographs 55, 102,
    139, 144–145, 147–148
  gendered gaze 142
  gendered identities 4, 89,
    90, 162
  gendered objects 41, 42,
  gendered taboos 31
  inequalities, 93
  performing gender 91
gender-based violence 30, 31, 36,
    56, 62, 80, 84, 85, 87–88,
    89, 90, 91, 93, 98, 105, 118,
    119, 122, 125–126, 131,
    147, 162, 165, 166–167,
    181, 195, *see also* Rape
girls
  and drawings 127–129
  and participatory video 9, 31,
    73, 75, 76, 80–83, 84,
    85, 86, 89, 143–144, 147
  and photovoice 19, 28, 57,
    66, 143, 145, 148, 176,
    180, 182, 185, *see also*
    Obama, Malia
graduate supervision 52, 158, 172
Gray, Ross 8, 48
Grover, Jan Zita 117, 133
Gubrium, Aline 71

hall culture 68
Hampl, Patricia 44
Harper, Douglas 159
Harris, Barbara 58, 137, 142
Hartley, John 41
Haug, Frigga 44
health *see* Alzheimer's disease;
    breast cancer; community
    health care workers;
    dialysis; HIV and AIDS;
    Spence, Jo; stigma
Higonnet, Anne 108, 110
HIV and AIDS
    and arts-based interventions
        and evaluation 31, 120,
        153, 155
    and childhood 42
    and China 151–152
    and community 169
    and drawing 54
    and ethics 26–27, 32, 56, 125
    and photography/
        community visual
        images 26, 52, 68, 105,
        107, 109, 110, 113, 119,
        133, 136, 189, 195
    and race (South Africa)
        28–30, 92
    and South Africa 170
    and Swaziland 97
    ARVs 97, 101, 107, 118
    'challenges and solutions
        in addressing HIV and
        AIDS' 24, 37, 54, 55, 58,
        84, 98, 120, 140, 148
    'face of AIDS' 102
    *Giving Life (to Data) to Save
        Lives (in the Age of AIDS)*
        118
    invisibility of AIDS 110–112,
        113
    long wave effects 119, 126
    People Living with AIDS
        (PLWA) 117
    'sick of AIDS' 108, 120
    see also ACT UP; collage;
        Fire+Hope; gender;
        gender-based violence;
        Learning Together project;
        orphans; *Our Photos,
        Our Videos, Our Stories*;
        photovoice–curatorial
        statement; SHOWED
        model; *Soft Cover*
        project; stigma; *Taking
        Action* project; *TIG
        Xpress* project; *Youth as
        Knowledge Producers*
Hodder, Ian 49
Hubbard, James 51, 150, 152
Huvila, Isto 124

Iliffe, John 119
installations 35, 190, 194, *see* Cole
    and McIntyre; *Life Lines*
interpreting visual data
    poster-narratives 59–60, 65
    working with a single
        photograph 11, 65, 139

Jenkins, Henry 10, 32, 92
Jewkes, Rachel 105

Kearney, Mary Celeste 132, 143,
    144, 156, 157
Khayelitsha (Western Cape) *see*
    South Africa
Kids with Cameras 30
Knowles, J. Gary
    with Cole, Ardra 4, 12, 163, 189
Kuchler, Susanne
    with Miller, Daniel 43
Kuhn, Annette 44, 58, 65,
    100–101, 139, 144
KwaZulu-Natal *see* South Africa

Langford, Martha 112, 144
Lankshear, Colin
    with Knobel, Michele 139
Leach, Fiona 30–31
Learning Together project 53, 54,
    55, 57–58, 58–59, 64, 121
Life Lines 3–4, 47–48
'listening guide' 157
Lister, Martin
    with Wells, Liz 12
*Living and Dying with Dignity: The
    Alzheimer's Project* 3, 184
looking at looking *see* Chapter 8
Lutz, Catherine
    with Collins, Jane Lou 142, 191
Lykes, Mary Brinton 51, 142, 195

materiality 11, 25, 50, 100, 133,
    141, 171, 189
    material culture 4, 35–36, 37,
        47, 49, 50
    see also objects
Martin, Marilyn 113, 131
Martin, Rosy 66, 67
memory work
    afterlife of children's popular
        culture 45, 101
    first draft 44–45
    future-oriented remembering
        112
    nostalgia 43, 45, 172
    second draft 44–45
Miller, Daniel 35
Miller, Jon 116–117, 119
mirrors
    in photography 136, 150,
        151, 152, 192

Mulvey, Laura 142
My Favourite Things exhibition 37

National Film Board of Canada
    10, 72, 177, 178, *see also
    Challenge for Change*
    programme
No Editing Required (N-E-R)
    approach *see* community
    video-making
Nuttall, Sarah 36

Obama, Malia 155, 156–157
    see also girls–and photovoice
objects
    objects-in-inquiry 38–43, 43–49
    social texts 37
    things 5, 6, 11, 35, 36, 37, 39,
        49, 54
    see also socio-semiotics
orphans 42, 69, 102–103, 122,
    126, 185
    child-headed households
        101, 103, 196
*Our Photos, Our Videos, Our
    Stories* 32, 87, 167–168,
    170, 175, 199–200

Paley, Nicholas 38
participatory archiving *see*
    archiving
participatory video 10, 52, 53,
    71, 72, 86, 87, 90, 92, 93,
    116, 120, 135, 138, 148,
    161, 162, 164, 165, 167,
    170, 179, 192–193, *see also*
    community video-making;
    composite video
Pauwels, Luc 12, 160–161, 163
performance 7, 8, 9, 12, 35, 37,
    48, 67–68, 89, 91, 110
photo elicitation 50, 51, 65
photographs
    domestic snapshots 4, 115,
        135–136
    environmental portraits 109
    family photographs 4, 16, 28,
        44, 98, 100, 112–113,
        113–114, 116, 135–136,
        139, 144, 167, 185,
        192, 199–200, *see also*
        albums
    fictional photographs 32
    lost photographs 100–101,
        112–113
    photo documentary and
        social realism 66, 68–69,
        see also albums–album
        project
    school photographs 3,
        100–101, 108–109

photographs *cont.*
  see also mirrors; shadow
    effect in photography;
    'shooting back'
photo-story/novella 4, 9, 87, 89
photovoice
  captions 4, 56, 58, 62, 67,
    113, 180, 182, 187–188,
    see also display–posters
  curatorial statement 5, 32,
    63, 64, 138, 189
  environmental issues 17, 57,
    98, 184, 185, 191
  Feeling Safe/Feeling Not so Safe
    project 28, 52, 143, 145,
    180–181, 183, 198
  Friday Absenteeism project 68,
    168, 181–183
  group work 57, 59
  photo-narratives 59, 66, 120
  photo documentary 16, 66,
    136, 193
  photovoice projects, *see*
    Feeling Safe/Feeling Not
    so Safe project; *Friday*
    Absenteeism project; *TIG*
    Xpress project
  poster-narratives 59–60, 65
  PowerPoint 10, 32, 62, 133,
    181, 191
  printing 58, 61, 133, 141
  prompts 4, 55–56, 109, 122,
    136, 166, 194
  reflexivity 136–137, 150
  staging 32, 57, 64, 67, 108,
    109–112, 193
  storytelling 67, 110
  'through our eyes' approach
    64, 70
  see also girls–and photovoice;
    Wang, Caroline
Pink, Sarah xii, 11, 37, 85, 90,
  160, 163, 164
policy-making 51, 175,
  Chapter 10
poverty 20, 24, 28, 36, 52, 56,
  57, 59–60, 61, 66, 68, 80,
  84, 122, 126, 148, 178,
  181, 182, 183, 195, 196
Prosser, Jon 11, 15, 22, 100
Putting People in the Picture 53

Rape 31, 85, 87–89, 90–91, 92, 199
reflexivity 5, 8, 11, 16, 90,
  137, 158, 163, 172, 193,
  198, *see also* community
  video-making–reflexivity;
  composite video–
  reflexivity; *Listening Guide*;
  photovoice–reflexivity;
  photovoice–staging

Reinventing Ourselves as Teachers:
  Beyond Nostalgia 112
Researching Children's Popular
  Culture 45
Riggins, Stephen 21, 35, 36,
  41–42, 43
Rist, Ray 180
Rohde, Rick 98
Rose, Gillian xii, 11, 25, 65–66,
  98, 109, 119
Ruby, Jay 7, 16, 85, 90, 99, 124,
  159–160, 163
rural schools
  teachers and photography 27,
    89, 106–107, 195–196
  video-making 143
  see also The School Teacher
Rwanda xvi, 7, 16, 39, 41, 43,
  51, 52, 60, 61, 69, 75, 84,
  87, 118, 125, 126, 131,
  148, 185, 194

safety and security 10, 22, 31,
  51, 52, 57, 61, 67, 68, 126,
  131, 145, 181, 182, 193,
  see also photovoice–*Feeling*
  Safe/Feeling Not so Safe
  project
Scared at School study 7
School Teacher, The
schools, *see* rural schools
Schratz, Michael
  with Walker, Rob 13,
    91, 153
Sekula, Allan 118, 142
shadow effect in photography
  113–114, 136, 150, 152,
  192
'shooting back' 51, 150, 152
SHOWED model 60–61
Smith, Linda Tuhiwai 13
socio-semiotics 35, 37, 41
  connotative meaning 41,
    43, 44
  denotative meaning 41, 42,
    43, 44, 45
  mapping 41
  referencing 41
Soft Cover project 79, 154
Sontag, Susan 11, 99, 115, 198
South Africa 6, 10, 13, 21, 22,
  24, 37, 52, 53, 54, 56, 57,
  64, 72, 84, 87, 89, 97,
  117, 118, 123, 125, 131,
  134, 143, 145, 148,
  152, 167–168, 170, 185,
  189, 194, 195, *see also*
  gender-based violence;
  photovoice–*Friday*
  Absenteeism project; HIV
  and AIDS

South Africa *cont.*
  Khayelitsha (Western Cape)
    13, 29–30, 51, 92
  KwaZulu-Natal 13, 14, 55,
    57, 64, 68, 78, 101, 104,
    105, 120, 140, 148, 154,
    168, 189
Spence, Jo 67, 99–100, 110
  with Solomon, Joan 142, 176
Squiers, Carol 97–98
staging, *see* photovoice–staging
Steinberg, Jonny 101, 125
stigma 12, 26–27, 31–32, 52, 53,
  55, 56, 57, 64, 67, 68, 98,
  108, 110, 118, 120, 122,
  124, 125, 152, 185
studying up 28–30, 92
Swaziland 51, 52, 57, 66, 72,
  185, *see also* HIV and AIDS;
  photovoice–*Feeling Safe/*
  Feeling Not so Safe project;
  The School Teacher

Taking Action project 78–79,
  87
Taylor, Lou 43
textuality 154
  textual approaches to
    research 50, 142, 173
  see also Fiske, John
TIG Xpress project 55–56, 57,
  68, 148, 154
Tobin, Joseph 80
toilets 66, 98, 130, 191, 199 *see*
  also photovoice–*Feeling*
  Safe/Feeling Not so Safe
  project

vernacular photography 192
vernacular visuality 136
visual/video ethnography xii,
  30, 41, 119, 155, 159, 160,
  163, 164
visually verifiable data
  153–155

Wagner, John 51, 159
Wang, Caroline 51, 52, 69–70,
  98, 142, 195
Waugh, Thomas 179
Web 2.0 71
White, Shirley 72, 167,
  178, 179

youth
  youth as knowledge
    producers 132, 139
  see also activism; *Fire+Hope*;
    participatory video;
    photovoice
YouTube 14, 17, 71, 197